Understanding World Christianity:
India

Global Christian History
_____

18 | 9

③

Understanding World Christianity: India

Dyron B. Daughrity & Jesudas M. Athyal

Fortress Press
Minneapolis

UNDERSTANDING WORLD CHRISTIANITY: INDIA

Cover design: Laurie Ingram

Library of Congress Cataloging-in-Publication Data
Print ISBN: 978-1-4514-7666-8
eBook ISBN: 978-1-5064-1689-2

The paper used in this publication meets the minimum requirements of
American National Standard for Information Sciences—Permanence of
Paper for Printed Library Materials, ANSI Z329.48-1984.

Manufactured in the U.S.A.

This book was produced using Pressbooks.com, and PDF rendering was
done by PrinceXML.

In loving memory of
Thelma D. Ross (1912–1997) and Geraldine Daughrity
(1919–2006)

and

dedicated to
May Dell Daughrity
Sunde Gayle Daughrity
Clare Soleil Daughrity
Amanda Mae Daughrity
Holly Joy Daughrity

With gratitude and deep respect, the authors of this volume would like to pay tribute to the life and legacy of Dr. M. M. Thomas (1916–1996), on his 100 year birth centenary. Dr. Thomas was a theologian, Christian statesman, committed ecumenist, Governor, and prolific scholar. His impact on Indian Christianity during the twentieth century was profound, and his legacy is greatly appreciated.

Contents

Introducing the Fortress Press Series
Understanding World Christianity

The idea of a major project on world Christianity is timely. According to research from Pew, approximately two-thirds of the world's nations and territories are Christian majority.[1] Christianity continues to widen its global net, claiming the allegiance of well over two billion people. Of the ten largest national Christian populations—the United States, Brazil, Mexico, Russia, Philippines, Nigeria, China, D. R. Congo, Germany, Ethiopia—only two are from the Western world. Around one-sixth of the *human* population holds membership in the Roman Catholic Church. The modern Pentecostal/ Charismatic movement—only a century old—claims roughly 600 million people today. As Pew reports, "Christians are also geographically widespread—so far-flung, in fact, that no single continent or region can indisputably claim to be the center of global Christianity. A century ago this was not the case."

Of the eight cultural blocs of the world, Christianity is the

---

1. See Pew Forum's study "Global Christianity—A Report on the Size and Distribution of the World's Christian Population," December 19, 2011. Located at www.pewforum.org/ 2011/12/19/global-christianity-exec/.

largest religion in six of them: Latin America and the Caribbean, North America, Western Europe, Eastern Europe, Africa, and Oceania. Only in Asia and the Middle East is Christianity not the religion most people adhere to. However, some of the most important developments in world Christianity are happening in Asia, and the Middle East will forever be the land of Jesus—where the gospel was unleashed. Furthermore, Islam—by far the most dominant Middle Eastern faith—can scarcely be understood apart from the history it shares with Judaism and Christianity. Christianity's influence in the world is profound, and there is little reason to think it is abating.

In the 1960s, esteemed church historian Stephen Neill began noticing that—for the first time in human history—there existed a truly *world* religion: Christianity. Neill was ahead of his time. Due to his globe-trotting on behalf of the World Council of Churches, he was able to observe rather intimately how deeply Christianity was taking root in Africa and Asia, seemingly against all the odds. While the leviathan structure of European colonialism was collapsing, Christianity defied all predictions by indigenizing. Many thought that when the colonial administrators and missionaries left, Christianity would wither. But the opposite happened. When the Europeans and North Americans got out of the way, these people integrated the gospel into their cultures, into their own lands, on their own terms. And today, we are front-row observers to these events, many of which are still unfolding. Christianity is changing civilizations as civilizations change Christianity. These stories are fascinating, they are important, and they need to be told.

The Understanding World Christianity project addresses head-on the fact that many churches, colleges, and seminaries are struggling to come to terms with the reality that Christianity is now a worldwide faith, not just a Western one. There is a popular and hardened conception that Christianity is dependent upon the nations of Western Europe and North America. Some variants of the story prolong the worn-out narrative that Asia and Africa are being, somehow, held hostage by the white man's religion, and that Christianity has everything to do with colonialism and imperialism, and nothing to do with indigenization, freedom, and self-assertion. Thus many students even take degrees in Christianity under a long-outdated curriculum: Christianity is born in the Middle East, Constantine makes it a Western faith, the Enlightenment ushers in a modern era, Christianity fades, and now we inhabit a *postmodern* world.

This Eurocentric paradigm is obsolete, for many reasons. First of all, Christianity has expanded terrifically. No longer is it centered in the West. It is now broadly spread out across the world, especially in Africa and Latin America. Second, the important modern European thinkers—Bonhoeffer, Tillich, Barth—who are typically required reading in Western seminaries do not adequately represent the world's Christians. Christianity is so much more diversified now. We are in great need of hearing the southern voices such as John Mbiti, Kwame Bediako, Oscar Romero, and M. M. Thomas. The Western academy needs to think more globally, given the striking changes the Christian faith has undergone in the last century. Third, in what some call an era of globalization, we are much more exposed to the non-Western world. Media, immigration, and increased international travel have made cultures intersect and cross-pollinate, creating a hybridity that was not so obvious a generation or two ago. This is especially the case for people who live in cities. Los Angeles, Dallas, Chicago, New

York, and Miami are excellent examples of this diversification process, which has a trickle-down effect throughout America's smaller cities, towns, and villages. A woman in small-town New Mexico could very well have an Indian physician, a Vietnamese priest, and a Guatemalan housekeeper. These situations are increasingly common for the average American.

Thankfully, a corpus of research on Christianity's *global* history is proliferating, and there is a growing awareness that Christianity never was the exclusive possession of the Western world, and certainly is not today. In spite of the gains that have been made, there are fundamental questions that remain unaddressed or underaddressed. For example, what is the *meaning* of global Christianity? How will the drastic changes to Christianity's geography impact theology, mission, and ministry? Indeed, what does this new body of research have to say to the church? What can Christians do with this information? How must missionary work be reconceived? These are practical questions begging further investigation. It is critical that Christians respond to global Christianity in sensitive and thoughtful ways. The Understanding World Christianity series will equip specialists, leaders, and students with up-to-date, on-the-ground information that will help them get their heads around the stories and the data.

In the parable of the Sower, Jesus described a scene where seed was scattered on various types of soil. Some seed was unproductive, but some produced bountifully. Similarly, at the beginning of the twenty-first century, Christianity flourishes in surprising places. The continent of Africa is half Christian. China and the former Soviet Union are opening up to Christianity after decades of oppression. The 266th pope is from Buenos Aires. Korea is home to some of the largest Christian congregations in the world. Meanwhile, in

Christianity's old heartland—Western Europe—it appears faith is receding. Who could have foreseen these astonishing developments a century ago?

In the early years of the faith, when Christian gentiles began to outnumber believing Jews, the faith began to take on a decidedly different identity. Led by the apostles' ambitious missionary work, the early church adapted capably, and grew exponentially. Peter and Paul profoundly shaped "the Way" by fashioning it into an institution open to all people, all nationalities and ethnicities alike. It was a blended family par excellence, albeit with considerable growth pains. Today we stand at a similar crossroads. The Global South has become the new heartland of a faith that was anchored in the West for centuries. The composition of Christianity—easily the world's largest religion—is changing, right before our eyes.

An important question remains, however. Is it a *fait accompli* that Christianity will continue to move south, with little for the Western churches to do but watch?

Scholars such as Robert Wuthnow contend there is much that the churches in the Western world can do, and in fact are doing. In *Boundless Faith: The Global Outreach of American Churches*, he shows that American churches now spend $4 billion annually on overseas ministry, more than ever, and "full-time missionaries serving abroad has increased steadily." In contrast to paternalistic models of the past, where the sending church was the clear authority, mission work today follows a collaborative paradigm, "through direct partnerships with overseas congregations, engaging in faster and more efficient transcultural communication, interacting with a sizable population of refugees and immigrants, and contributing to large-scale international humanitarian and relief organizations."[2] Our mental maps of missionaries flowing from the West to the rest must be updated, as Brazil, Korea, and Nigeria are now sending nations with robust missionary programs. India, Vietnam, and the Philippines provide hundreds of Roman Catholic priests to serve in the United States. Indeed, Christians from the Global South are globally engaged, and North American churches are wise to partner with them.

The Understanding World Christianity series will contribute to this robust conversation in key ways. It will interpret these monumental changes for a larger audience. It will engage critical questions arising from a global, interconnected Christian faith. And it will draw upon some of today's best specialists—familiar with Christianity on the ground in their respective geographies—in order to create authoritative and readable composites of what is happening. Authors for the series come from a range of ecclesial backgrounds, including Orthodox, Roman Catholic, mainline Protestant, Evangelical, and Pentecostal.

The new era of world Christianity is impacting global politics, higher education, Christian ministry paradigms, and countless charitable organizations. This project will help professors, pastors, students, and professionals understand that with the global spread of Christianity comes a new opportunity for sharing the ongoing story, informed by sensitivity to local and contextual differences. As our world flattens and as Christians globally become more interdependent, a rich complexity is developing. Worldviews are shifting, societies are transforming, and theologies are being rewritten. This project will help Christians to navigate through the differences more carefully and more thoughtfully.

2. Robert Wuthnow, *Boundless Faith: The Global Outreach of American Churches* (Los Angeles: University of California Press, 2010), 1–2.

Read more about the Understanding World Christianity series online at: http://fortresspress.com/uwc.

Dyron Daughrity, General Editor
The Understanding World Christianity Series

Preface

The superlatives about India are many. It is expected to surpass China as the world's most populated nation in the year 2022. It is the world's largest democracy. It is a top ten nation according to area size. It has the second most English speakers in the world after the USA, and is probably the most ethnically diverse country. It is a top ten nation in its Gross Domestic Product and in Purchasing Power Parity. It is among the fastest-growing economies with a steadily increasing population. Its biodiversity is one of the richest on the planet. Its northern border views the largest mountains in the world. It contains the rainiest, most fertile land on earth. It can easily feed hundreds of millions of people, perhaps even billions. Its huge film industry rivals Hollywood. Its business culture is robust and increasingly powerful. It is one of only a handful of nations with nuclear capabilities.

So why do people often think of religion when they think of India? There are many reasons, but an obvious one is that India treasures its religious heritage. Hinduism, Zoroastrianism, Jainism, Buddhism, Judaism, Christianity, Islam, Sikhism, Bahai Faith . . . they all have substantive histories in India. India is the birthplace of numerous religions, and its religious culture is truly impressive, arguably more so than any other nation. Religiosity in India is palpable and complex, both practical and extremely philosophical. Attached to nearly every landmark is a religious idea, whether a monument, a story, an explanation, or a gathering of pilgrims. Religion exudes out of India, out of its temples, mountains, waters, and people.

One of the lesser-known stories is India's long and ancient relationship with Christianity. It is a fascinating history that begins far earlier than most Christians would think. Indians hold that the gospel entered their nation through the missionary work of the Apostle Thomas in the year AD 52. Thomas is revered by Indians for his missionary work. "Thomas Christians" take their name from him, and have done so for many centuries.

India's Christian population is as diverse as Christianity itself. Orthodox Christians, Catholics, and Protestants of all stripes are anchored deeply in the nation. The Thomas Christians (Orthodox) of Malabar are among the world's oldest Christian communities. The largest national Jesuit population is in India, where they have had a presence since 1541. Indeed Francis Xavier himself—the Jesuit co-founder—worked in India and still rests there. Protestantism has deep roots in India, as missionaries arrived to its shores in 1706. William Carey, one of the most famous Protestant missionaries of all time, landed at Kolkata in 1793. A burgeoning Pentecostal culture has been alive and active there at least since Pandita Ramabai's Mukti revival in 1905. The Church of South India—one of the world's first officially ecumenical churches—was inaugurated in 1947, just a month after Indian independence from Britain was achieved.

Indian Christianity, like India itself, is vast, vibrant, and fascinating. No one knows for sure how many Christians are in India. Educated guesses range anywhere between 30–80 million, depending on who is counting. Whatever the case, one thing is clear: Indian Christianity is worth studying. Tens of millions of Christians call this land home. Indeed Christianity is India's third largest religion after Hinduism and Islam. There are more Christians in India than there are Sikhs, Buddhists, or Jains. When university courses offer courses on the "Religions of India" they should have no excuse for excluding Christianity. But alas, that mistake is often made.

This book is a journey into Christian India. We invite you to join our exploration of the Indianness of Christianity. And while we travel, let us not forget that Christianity is a profoundly Indian religion.

Acknowledgments

From Jesudas Athyal:

Athyal wishes to thank the following persons who helped greatly in collecting the information needed for this book: Dr. Geevarghese Mar Coorilose (Metropolitan, Malankara Jacobite Syrian Christian Church), Ms. Premanjali Rao and Mr. Prem Chandran (both staff members of the Centre for Research on New International Economic Order, Chennai), Dr. Aruna Gnanadason (Former Programme Executive, Women in Church and Society, World Council of Churches), Dr. Roger Gaikwad (General Secretary, National Council of Churches in India), Dr. Saphir Athyal (Former Principal, Union Biblical Seminary, Pune), Dr. George Kovoor (Neuro Surgeon, Thrissur, Kerala), Dr. Jacob Cherian (Vice President and Dean of Faculty at Southern Asia Bible College, Bangalore), Rev. Abraham Alfred (Research Fellow, Southern Asia Bible College, Bangalore), Ms. Rachel J. Komanapalli and Rev. Sudarshan Jyoti Komanapalli (both leaders of the Manna Group of Ministries).

Athyal would also like to thank his wife Ms. Dinah Oommen and son Mr. Jacob Athyal for patiently putting up with him as he plunged himself, at short notice, into the work of this book.

No scholar can work effectively without such a supportive family.

*   *   *   *   *

From Dyron Daughrity:

I would like to thank the many people who have helped to bring this book to light.

First, at Fortress Press, I am deeply grateful to Will Bergkamp. His leadership and support has been vital in getting the Understanding World Christianity project up and running. Many thanks also go to Alicia Ehlers and all of the other editors—including anonymous readers—who helped make this book better.

Many thanks go to my colleagues at Pepperdine University. The Religion Division is a wonderful place to research and teach, and I salute the men and women who serve faithfully. I make special mention of Tim Willis, Rick Marrs, and Lee Kats. They have provided unfailing support and encouragement conducive for scholarship.

I thank my many students who continually inspire me in so many ways. They are so competent and gracious. Yet they manage to find time to come to my office, gather in my home, send occasional updates, and show kindness in countless ways. I have sheer joy watching them flourish as students and thrive after graduation. It is an honor and a privilege to serve them at Pepperdine.

I make special mention of my former student Daniel Spencer. He was gracious to read over drafts of this book and offer valuable insights. He also created the maps and tables in the Geographical chapter. I wish him the very best as he heads off to graduate school. His great competence will guide him to new heights of success.

I thank my colleagues in various scholarly societies such as the American Academy of Religion, American Society of Church History, the Yale-Edinburgh Group, the World Council of Churches, and the Center for Studies on New Religions. Thanks also to the many friends and colleagues all over the world who are working together to expose more people to the fascinating field of World Christianity. I make special mention of Philip Jenkins and Lamin Sanneh for inspiring us to think of Christianity as a global movement rather than a Western institution.

I extend my heartfelt thanks to my co-author, Dr. Jesudas Athyal, for a job well done. When my original co-author, Dr. V. V. Thomas, had to withdraw from the project, it was clear that Athyal was the person we should approach. And he did a very fine job while meeting a quickly looming deadline. Thank you very much, colleague, for making this book a priority. And my best wishes go out to Dr. V. V. as he ministers to his family so faithfully and admirably during a difficult time. I will probably never be able to repay the debt I owe to Dr. V. V. for recruiting Dr. Athyal, and for introducing me to the faculty and staff of several theological institutions in India.

I also extend my deepest thanks to the friends, students, colleagues, and professionals in India who helped to make this book possible. My deepest thanks go out to the following institutions for their valuable support during the researching of this book:

Aizawl Theological College (Aizawl, Mizoram)
All India Mission Seminary (Pilar, Goa)
Eastern Theological College (Jorhat, Assam)

Focus India Theological College (Nilambur, Kerala)
Indian Pentecostal Church Seminary (Kottayam, Kerala)
Mar Thoma Syrian Theological Seminary (Kottayam, Kerala)
Orthodox Theological Seminary (Kottayam, Kerala)
Serampore College (Serampore, West Bengal)
Union Biblical Seminary (Pune, Maharashtra)

The cheerful hospitality I experienced at these institutions was exemplary and humbling. I offer to them the words of Jesus: "Truly I tell you, whatever you did for one of the least of these . . . you did for me" (Matt 25:40).

Most of all I thank my immediate family: parents Jerald and May Dell, brother Varen, and children Clare, Ross, Mande Mae, and Holly Joy. As always, my greatest debt is to my wife, Sunde, a rock of stability.

Now unto him that is able to do exceeding abundantly above all that we ask or think, according to the power that worketh in us, Unto him be glory in the church by Christ Jesus throughout all ages, world without end. Amen. (Eph 3:20–21, KJV)

Dyron B. Daughrity
Malibu, California
23 April 2016 (Passover)

1

Chronological

A Very Brief History of Christianity in India

Introduction

This book aspires to help people understand the variety and complexity of Indian Christianity. We incorporate several perspectives throughout: sociological, political, theological, geographical, and anthropological. However, without a basic understanding of the *history*, our task will be fruitless. This first chapter is, therefore, critical.

What follows is a concise narrative of the pivotal, defining moments in Indian church history. The choices we have made are strategic and illustrative, and will help the reader to make sense of the rest of the chapters. Without the facts, the context, and the stories discussed below, understanding Indian Christianity would be hardly possible.

We take a fairly standard approach to this narrative. The

first section discusses the origins of the St. Thomas tradition, considering what portions of it could be true. We will look at the sometimes hazy history of the Thomas Christians up to the time of European contact. The second section looks at the arrival of Vasco da Gama and explores the profound changes that came alongside a rather militant Roman Catholicism. The third section deals with Protestant Christianity in India: its origins, connections to empire, and a discussion of how India came to be so closely associated with the English world. In the fourth section, we consider the meteoric rise of Pentecostalism in India and how it has made a tremendous impact on Indian Christianity in such a short period of time.

Orthodox Indians trace their origins to AD 52. Roman Catholic Indians take special notice of the year 1498. Protestant Indians uphold the year 1706 as particularly significant. Pentecostal Indians attach importance to the year 1905. We must point out, however, that when a new form of Christianity took root in India, *by no means did it supplant the previous forms.* Indian Christianity is a tapestry with four major, vibrant strands interlaced throughout: Orthodox, Roman Catholic, Protestant, and Pentecostal. And, generally, all four styles of Christianity intersect and interlace. Over time, they have impacted each other. Indeed, this reciprocity goes on not only within Christian traditions, but also between Christianity and India's vast, colorful, and multilayered religious tapestry.

Christian Origins and the Saint Thomas Traditions (from AD 52)

Any Christian who has traveled in India is aware of the Thomas Christians, based in the southern state of Kerala. Their remarkable story brings Indians—both Christian and non-

Christian—great pride. If true, the Indian church could lay claim to being the oldest Asian church outside the Roman Empire. The tradition is not seriously questioned by Indians. Indians claim the evidence for St. Thomas in India is as strong as St. Peter in Rome.[1]

Could "doubting Thomas" possibly have made the journey all the way to India to spread the gospel in AD 52, as Indians claim? Many expert historians are open to the possibility. Very few of them outright reject it.

There are many variations of the story. The best place to start is by looking at the *Acts of Thomas*, a text from at least the early-third century, which survives complete in Syriac and in Greek.[2] The book consists of about 170 good-sized paragraphs, is quite detailed, is full of miracles, and represents a strongly ascetic perspective. It assumes that Thomas is Jesus's identical twin brother—a tradition in some early Christianities that was based on Thomas's name. Toma is Aramaic/Syriac for "twin" and Didymus is Greek for "twin."[3]

The *Acts of Thomas* begins with the apostles gathered in Jerusalem, ready to fulfill Jesus's Great Commission that they go out into the world to preach, baptize, and create disciples. They cast lots to determine who should go where, and India gets assigned to Thomas. He is very reluctant, but Jesus appears to him during the night and encourages him.

Shortly thereafter, an Indian merchant named Abban arrives onto the scene. Abban is a representative of King Gundaphorus, from the northwest part of India (the Punjab, Pakistan, and Afghanistan). Abban is shopping for a carpenter who can build

---

1. See Robert Frykenberg, *Christianity in India* (Oxford: Oxford University Press, 2008), viii.
2. See Günther Bornkamm, "The Acts of Thomas," in *New Testament Apocrypha*, vol. 2, eds. Wilhelm Schneemelcher, Edgar Hennecke, and Robert McL. Wilson (Philadelphia: Westminster Press, 1964).
3. Ibid., 448 (section 11).

a nice palace for the king. Jesus appears and volunteers Thomas for the job.

During the sea voyage, they stop at a city called Andrapolis to rest and replenish supplies. While there, the king of Andrapolis invites the entire city to the wedding of his daughter. Thomas attracts the attention of the people due to his being foreign as well as his singing ability. A Hebrew flute-girl is present and translates for him. The king takes notice and asks Thomas to pray for his daughter and the man she will soon marry. Thomas complies, but right then Jesus appears to the couple and persuades them to abandon "filthy intercourse" and commit themselves fully to him and to chastity.[4] The king is incensed, but Thomas has already set sail. Later, the chaste couple and the Hebrew flute-girl convince the king to become a Christian, along with many of his subjects. Eventually, many of these converts sail to India to join Thomas.

When Thomas reaches Gundaphorus, he is given ample funds for the building project. However, Thomas notices the people are poor and in need, so he distributes the funds to them. The people are amazed at Thomas's piety, simplicity, and kindness. The king, however, puts both Thomas and Abban into prison and vows to execute them.

That very night, the king's brother, named Gad, falls ill and dies. His soul travels to heaven, where the angels show him that there is a palace being built for the king in heaven, rather than on earth. The brother's soul returns to his body and he tells the king what he saw; immediately, Thomas and Abban are freed. Gundaphorus and his brother promptly confess their belief in Christ. Then, Thomas baptizes them in a bath, anoints their heads with oil, and celebrates the Eucharist with them. Many of the king's subjects also convert to Christianity.

4. Ibid., 449 (section 12).

4

In chapter 6 of the *Acts of Thomas*, there is a young couple in love, but the young man decides to follow Christ. He tries to persuade his girlfriend to do the same, but she refuses. He kills her, so he will not have to bear watching her fall in love with another. The apostle Thomas, however, raises her from the dead and asks her what she experienced during death. She describes vivid scenes, quite similar to Dante's inferno, with people being tortured in horrible ways. Thomas then preaches to the people that they should forsake their families, their consorts, and their earthly pleasures in order to follow Christ, avoid the torments of hell, and enjoy the "true fruits" that cannot be taken away.[5]

About halfway through the *Acts of Thomas*, the apostle begins traveling to other parts of India, preaching and teaching. He ends up in the land of King Misdaeus (also known as Mazdai), in the southeast of India, known today as the state of Tamil Nadu. He conducts his ministry in the city of Mylapore (Mailapur: now a suburb of Chennai). Thomas preaches his ascetic form of Christianity, emphasizing chastity. Many of the prominent women of the kingdom accept his teachings, including the queen, and their husbands become outraged to the point that they plan his execution. He is then led to a mountain outside the city—today that place is revered as "St. Thomas Mount." After giving him a chance to pray, four soldiers "smote him and slew him."[6] That next day, however, Thomas appears to the people who were mourning him, and he encourages them, much like the appearances of Jesus after his death in the gospels.

Sometime later, one of King Misdaeus's sons becomes possessed by a demon. The king goes to the tomb of Thomas

---

5. Ibid., 476 (section 61).
6. Ibid., 530 (section 168).

for help. He thinks the bones of Thomas might have healing properties. On the way, Thomas appears to the king and mockingly asks him why he believes in the dead rather than in the living. He then tells the king that Jesus Christ is about to show him mercy. When he arrives at the tomb, the body of Thomas is not there; it had been taken over to the Western regions of India by some disciples. The king takes some dust from the tomb, however, and places it on his son while confessing his belief in the Lord Jesus Christ. The son is healed and King Misdaeus becomes a follower of Christ. The *Acts of Thomas* ends there, finally pointing out that Thomas was faithful to the Lord Jesus's commission—he had planted the gospel in India.

What is to be made of such a story? Can it be believed at all? It should be pointed out that coin evidence establishes the existence of a Parthian-Indian king named Gundaphorus. There is also a stone tablet from Peshawar, Pakistan, that helped scholars accurately date his reign to the first half of the first century AD.[7] He ruled over a large swath of territory in northwest India.[8]

Was the trip from Jerusalem to India even possible? Definitely. We know that monsoon winds carried Romans and others to the southwest of India, known as the Malabar Coast—the modern state of Kerala. Traders who made the journey were rewarded with bountiful supplies of pearls and spices that could be sold for huge profits in their homelands. India was well-known to the Romans; they had settlements

---

7. Samuel Hugh Moffett, *A History of Christianity in Asia*, vol. 1 (Maryknoll, NY: Orbis, 1998), 29.
8. See Frykenberg, *Christianity in India*, 98. See also Stephen Neill, *A History of Christianity in India: The Beginnings to AD 1707* (Cambridge: Cambridge University Press, 1984), 27. Neill provides a helpful discussion of Charles Masson, "The wizard who performed the remarkable feat of bringing Gondopharnes [Gundaphar] back to life" through his coin discoveries in the 1830s.

there in the first century AD.[9] The trip took about three months with a ship carrying 200–300 tons of cargo.[10] It would be surprising had Christians *not* made their way to India at that time, considering they fanned out in all directions as missionaries. The Jewish presence in India is ancient, and no doubt Christians would have connected with them upon arrival.

For centuries, Indian Christians have preserved the Thomas story through song, poetry, and ritual. They do not mention Gundaphorus, but they record much interesting information, such as Thomas establishing seven churches and converting thousands from the upper castes. They place his death at St. Thomas Mount, outside of Mylapore, just as in the *Acts of Thomas*. Tradition says he died in the year AD 72.

There can be little doubt that someone significant was buried at Mylapore since so many writers mentioned the tomb throughout the ages. Gregory of Tours discussed it in the sixth century and Marco Polo actually visited the site in the thirteenth century. It is possible the tomb belonged to another Christian who became conflated with Thomas over time. For example, the historian Eusebius, friend to Emperor Constantine, wrote of Pantaenus's mission to India in the second century. Pantaenus was a Jewish convert to Christianity who led the famed Alexandrian academy, where Origen and Clement were his students. When he traveled to India, he understood the Indians as saying that the apostle Bartholomew had visited there and left them a Hebrew version of the gospel of Matthew.[11] Some Indians claim he misunderstood "Mar

9. See Robert Louis Wilken, *The First Thousand Years: A Global History of Christianity* (New Haven: Yale University Press, 2012), 245.
10. See E. H. Warmington, *The Commerce Between the Roman Empire and India*, 2nd ed. (London: Curzon, 1974), 6ff, cited in Moffett, 32.
11. Paul Maier, trans., *Eusebius: The Church History* (Grand Rapids: Kregel, 2007), 166 [book 5, section 9].

Thoma" (Bishop Thomas) as "Bar Tolmai," which explains why the usually reliable Eusebius could make such a mistake.[12] But no Indian looks to Bartholomew as the founder of the Christian faith in India. That honor is reserved exclusively for Thomas.

How did the Christians of Kerala become so connected to the Syrian form of Christianity? After all, today, the Thomas Christians are regularly referred to as "Syrians" or "Nasranis"—a word referring to Jesus the Nazarene, but which is also connected specifically to the Syrian Christians of Kerala.[13]

The easiest explanation is that, historically, India was more connected to the Syrian forms of Christianity than either the Greek East or Latin West. Syria was a province of the Roman Empire, located on the eastern side of the Mediterranean. The Romans created the province of Syria Palestine in the 130s AD, a region that today includes portions of Syria, Palestine, Israel, Lebanon, and southeastern Turkey. As Christianity spread in the early centuries of the faith, three vague forms began to emerge along linguistic lines: Latin, Greek, and Syrian. The successors to these early developments are alive today: the Roman Catholic Church, the Eastern Orthodox Churches, and the Oriental Orthodox Churches. While the Oriental Orthodox Churches are very small today in comparison with the Eastern and Western European traditions, suffice it to say that there was a time when the Oriental Churches were strong, vibrant, and prolific in mission work.[14] In church history, they are known as the group that recognized only the first three ecumenical councils rather than all seven of them.

---

12. Moffett, 38.
13. See Leonard Fernando and G. Gispert-Sauch, *Christianity in India* (New York: Penguin, 2004), 55.
14. See Philip Jenkins's excellent work *The Lost History of Christianity: The Thousand-Year Golden Age of the Church in the Middle East, Africa, and Asia—and How it Died* (New York: HarperOne, 2008).

India became connected with the Oriental Orthodox family of churches due to geography more than anything else. The Oriental Orthodox Churches have always been closely connected to what is known today as the Middle East. Today, Oriental Orthodoxy is associated chiefly with the churches of Armenia, Ethiopia, Egypt, Syria, and South India. Their diaspora is now widespread due to global migration. South India has a vibrant Oriental Orthodox community although they have split into various factions throughout the centuries.

We should also mention here the Assyrian Church of the East, known historically as the Nestorian Church—named after a Patriarch in Constantinople named Nestorius, who lived from 386 to 450. In the West, Nestorius is sometimes referred to as a heretic for his belief that Mary should not be called "the mother of God." In reality, he was an early proponent of what many Protestants in the world believe today—that Mary was not divine, and it is dangerous theologically to elevate her to a position on par with the members of the Trinity. Nevertheless, Nestorius was condemned and removed from his see, which was, at that time, the most powerful position in Christendom.

The Nestorian Church is part of the Syrian family of churches. These churches produced some of the greatest missionaries of all time, especially in Asia. They were closely connected to the various Persian empires throughout history, which explains why they grew further away from the Greco-Roman traditions. When the Persian empires became dominated by Islam in the seventh century, Persian Christians became further isolated from Greek and Roman Christians. Muslim rule spelled disaster for them, but they managed to survive in various places. They survived in India because Muslim rulers never dominated the south as profoundly as they did the northern and central parts.

We should point out a very important fact about the Nestorian Church and its relation to India. Throughout history, Western Christians tended to label Christians east of the Byzantine Empire as being Nestorian, even if they did not share Nestorius's views about Mary—that she was the mother of the Messiah, but not the mother of God. Because the Saint Thomas Christians were in the Far East, they were considered Nestorian.[15]

The problem with carefully understanding the chronology of Indian Christianity before the arrival of the Portuguese in 1498 is the paucity of literary and archaeological evidence. We get hints here and there, but our first piece of "fully convincing" evidence does not occur until the mid-sixth century in a work entitled *Christian Topography*.[16] The author was Cosmas Indicopleustes, a Nestorian Christian from Alexandria, Egypt. He was a traveling merchant, but carefully recorded his travels and created wonderfully helpful maps. He wrote two very informative passages about India's Christians. He places them in Male, or the Malabar Coast (Kerala), and in Ceylon (Sri Lanka). He refers to them as Persian Christians, and he specifically mentions that their bishop had been appointed and consecrated in Persia. Scholars disagree about whether or not he actually visited India, but his references evince a clear awareness of Christians living there.

The Christians that Cosmas Indicopleustes wrote about did not assimilate their church into the fabric of India very well. They remained dependent on Babylon (also known as Chaldea, in modern-day Iraq) and later Antioch for their leadership.

---

15. See Frykenberg, *Christianity in India*, 105.
16. See Stephen Neill, *A History of Christianity in India*, vol. 1, 36. For a fairly comprehensive list of the earliest historical references to Christians in India, see M. K. Kuriakose, *History of Christianity in India: Source Materials*, 1–8. He includes excerpts from eleven different writers prior to Cosmas Indicopleustes, including Origen, Eusebius, Jerome, Gregory Nazianzen, Ambrose, Rufinus, and Gregory of Tours.

Syriac was their liturgical language and they never translated their liturgies or the Bible into Malayalam, the language of Kerala.

According to Indian tradition, there were various waves of Christians who came before the Portuguese, and they were almost always from Persia. Some were missionaries, some merchants, and some explorers. But by far the most significant numbers of Christians who came to India from Persia were refugees trying to escape persecution. In the fourth century, Shapur II (309–379)—a powerful Zoroastrian king of the Sasanian (Persian) Empire—became suspicious of his Christian subjects when Roman Emperor Constantine converted to Christianity. A terrible persecution ensued, sending many to seek refuge in South India, with like-minded Christians.

Thomas Christians believe one large group of Christian refugees arrived at the Malabar Coast in AD 345 under the leadership of a merchant named Thomas of Cana (possibly another name for Canaan, or, Jerusalem). He brought with him 336 Syrian Christian families, including some clergy, and made a significant impact upon Christianity in the region. Tradition holds that this wave of immigration led to the establishment of 72 churches.[17] Division within these Syrian Christians occurred early on as some of them chose to intermarry with Indians and some did not. Those who did were called Northists and those who did not were called Southists—referring to where they settled on the coast. The numerically smaller Southists claim a lineage of Syrian purity, refusing to intermarry with anyone else, even Northists. This division persists even today.[18]

---

17. See Cyril Bruce Firth, *An Introduction to Indian Church History* (Delhi: ISPCK, 2005), 28–29.
18. See Firth, 29–30. There are other theories as to the origins of the Northists and Southists.

In future chapters, it will be seen that Thomas Christians are rather famous for their propensity to divide and sub-divide.

A second group of Christian refugees from Persia arrived in AD 823. They were led by two Syrian bishops who were brothers, Mar Sapor and Mar Parut. The local ruler issued them land grants on five copper plates, which still survive in Kerala. They are written in four languages: Tamil and Malayalam (two languages of South India), Pahlavi (ancient Persian), and Arabic.[19] The plates show that, indeed, there was a thriving Christian community when this party of Persian refugees arrived, and that the Christian community was refreshed and encouraged by them.

With the advances of Islam in the seventh century came the alienation of the Oriental Orthodox Churches from the rest of Christendom. Islam's meteoric rise began in 632 and continued at a seemingly unstoppable pace for centuries. Syrian Christianity, and Middle Eastern Christianity, in general, began a long decline that led to the demise of Christianity in many parts of Asia. When Turkish civilizations began to accept Islam in the eleventh century, it disrupted the geographically united front that Christians—Latin, Greek, and Syrian—had enjoyed since apostolic times. The Christian world began to fray, recede, and vanish in places. The Mongols began converting to Islam in the late thirteenth century. They established the largest contiguous empire in human history, and the Christians of Asia and the Middle East were their casualties. One of their rulers, Tamerlane (ruled 1370–1405), carried out one of the most devastating persecutions in Christian history, leaving "a small and insignificant community in Mesopotamia with some outlying sections in a few places such as Malabar."[20]

---

19. For the Sapor-Parut arrival, see Firth, 31–32. The traditional date is 823, but Frykenberg (p. 111) puts the date at 825.

The Indian church was effectively cut off from the Syrian hierarchy during this time, which helps to explain their survival. Living outside the reaches of Islamic aggression, the Thomas Christians experienced a level of security that most Asian and Middle Eastern Christians did not enjoy. In fact, the Malabar Christians were quite prosperous throughout the centuries before the coming of the Europeans. They were given autonomy by Hindu princes. They were landowners. They were in charge of the extremely lucrative pepper trade that continues to be a defining feature of that part of India.[21] They were seen as high-caste, privileged aristocrats, second only to the Brahmins. They followed caste regulations, including untouchability. They traveled on elephants—a hallmark for high status in Indian society.[22] They were spared from large-scale massacres and genocidal campaigns inflicted by Mongols in northern India.

The major point here is that from the death of Islam's beloved prophet Muhammad in 632, until the arrival of the Portuguese in 1498, there was "a curtain of darkness and incomprehension" that separated Western civilization from India.[23] We do not have many sources that survive. These two parts of the world were almost completely cut off from each other. Islam had control of the seas. Westerners had almost no way to get to India without wading into Muslim-controlled waters. A quick look at a contemporary map illustrates the point: India is the sole land on the Arabian Sea that is not underneath the authority of a Muslim government today.

---

20. Firth, 35.
21. See Frykenberg, 118. This was the observation of John de Marignolli in 1349.
22. For this list of the social privileges of the Thomas Christians, see Woba James, *Major Issues in the History of Christianity in India: A Postcolonial Reading* (Jorhat: TDCC Publications, 2013), 69.
23. Frykenberg, 117.

Somalia, Yemen, Oman, Iran, and Pakistan are the others. India was close to becoming a Muslim land, however.

After powerful Islamic empires began to conquer and colonialize northern India, Christians were rarely allowed access to each other. First was the Delhi Sultanate, which lasted from 1206 to 1526. Next was the Mughal dynasty, which lasted from 1526 to 1857. Perhaps the salient question is not why so few Westerners reached India during these years. Rather, what should be asked is how Hinduism managed to survive during these centuries. Equally perplexing is how the Thomas Christians evaded the attention of so many Muslim rulers, given Islam and Christianity's titanic clashes going on in other parts of the world.

It is no wonder the Christians of India failed to expand throughout a politically tense context like this. The only place for them to look was inward. Perhaps this situation may also shed light on the tendency of Malabar Christians to divide. Rather than looking outward and witnessing for Christ, their only option was to cling to the few gains they already had made. Essentially, the only people who came to the Malabar Coast were refugees escaping the frequent Islamic advances that occurred throughout the centuries. But when these immigrants did manage to make it to the safety of the Thomas Christians, they essentially lost contact with the rest of the world. When foreigners relocated to Malabar, they left everything behind. This was the pattern for a thousand years.

Contact with Roman Catholics (from 1498)

The traditional date for Roman Catholic contact with India is Vasco Da Gama's arrival in 1498, but the date is misleading.

It neglects to account for several encounters that occurred before that year.[24]

- Around the year 883, two Catholic clerics from England, named Sigehelm and Aethelstan, were sent by the Anglo-Saxon King Alfred the Great (ruled 871–899). They brought alms with them and visited the tomb of St. Thomas at Mylapore.

- In 1293, John of Montecorvino—a Franciscan missionary and papal emissary from Italy—traveled to visit the Great Khan in Beijing (known then as Khanbaliq). He stopped in India for 13 months. He baptized around 100 people before moving on to China, where he became the first Roman Catholic Archbishop in 1307.

- Between 1292 and 1295, the famous Italian explorer Marco Polo visited Mylapore and sailed round Cape Comorin to visit the Malabar Coast. He wrote extensively about miracles associated with St. Thomas's tomb.

- In 1321, a French Dominican monk named Jordanus Cataline visited Mumbai, Quilon, and Gujarat. He met many Christians, and claimed to have baptized 300 Muslims and Hindus. He wrote an important chronicle of his travels, entitled *Mirabilia Descripta: The Wonders of the East*. He seems to have had a low view of the Indian Christians as a whole, likely because of his anti-Nestorian bias:

> In this India there is a scattered people, one here, one there, who call themselves Christians but are not so, nor have they baptism nor do they know anything about the faith. Nay, they believe St Thomas the great to be the Christ. There, in the India I speak of, I baptized and brought into

24. These visits are outlined in Frykenberg, 117–18. For a fuller account see Stephen Neill, vol. 1, 71ff.

the faith about three hundred souls, of whom many were idolators [Hindus] and Saracens [Muslims].[25]

- In 1325, a monk named Odoric recorded traveling in South India visiting Christians. He was present at a Palm Sunday service. He discussed the martyrdom of four priests in the town of Thana. His visit to Mylapore to see the tomb of St. Thomas was offensive to him, as he felt the church was filled with idols and was under the control of the Nestorians, whom he considered "vile and pestilent heretics."[26]

- In 1349, a Franciscan named John de Marignolli stopped in Malabar on his way back from visiting the Great Khan. He stayed fourteen months. He reported that Christians controlled the pepper trade. Importantly, he commented on "a church of St. George there, of the Latin communion, at which I dwelt."[27] It is not known what exactly he meant by referring to a Latin church, for we have no evidence of one existing before the arrival of the Portuguese. Either Jordanus Cataline had erected one in the 1320s, or else Marignolli was given permission to celebrate the mass in the Latin way.[28]

- Around 1440, a Venetian nobleman traveler named Nicolo de Conti visited South India and commented on the Nestorians surrounding the tomb of St. Thomas. He also commented that "These Nestorians are scattered over all India, in like manner as are the Jews among us."[29]

While these visits do not reveal a tremendous amount of information, at least we learn that Christians were in India,

---

25. Cited in Neill, vol. 1, 73.
26. Cited in Kuriakose, 18.
27. Cited in Kuriakose, 19.
28. See Neill, vol. 1, 80.
29. Cited in Neill, vol. 1, 81.

mainly in Malabar, and their practices and beliefs were Nestorian and Syrian. Whether it was "an apparent stagnancy" over the centuries, or simply a political reality due to the advances of Islam, we only know that the church remained somewhat insular, like a separate Christian caste on the coast of Malabar.[30] For the most part, they seemed to get on well with the Hindu and Muslim populations. When the Portuguese arrived, there may have been 200,000 Thomas Christians in Malabar, residing in some 60 towns.[31] The Christian population must have been quite small outside of Malabar.

It would not be hyperbolic to say that Vasco da Gama's discovery of a sea route from Lisbon to India—by sailing around the "Cape of Good Hope" at the extreme end of South Africa—changed the world. The year was 1498. Only ten years earlier, explorer Bartolomeu Dias proved that a ship could sail round southern Africa successfully.

Portugal suddenly became king of the seas, and would soon experience commercial profits unlike anything ever known in Europe. No one at that time could have understood the significance of the moment. Stephen Neill wrote, "One of the great revolutions of history was taking place before their eyes."[32] Portugal—and in due course, the major powers of Europe—now had access to trade with India. No longer would European merchants have to trek meekly through Muslim-held lands, paying exorbitant duty fees, and fearing molest from potentially hostile empires. They could effectively bypass Muslim civilization. Robert Frykenberg wrote:

> This event set in motion a process that would soon make all the oceans of the world into highways to fame, fortune, and power.

30. Frykenberg, 116.
31. For 200,000, see Fernando and Gispert-Sauch, 72. For 60 towns, see Frykenberg, 124.
32. Neill, vol. 1, 108.

At a blow, Europeans had leap-frogged over and bypassed the older civilizations of the ancient Near East. Thereafter, just as Arabs and Turks had used deserts and steppes for their caravans, traveling from oasis to oasis, so now Europeans would use the seas and oceans of the world for their convoys, setting up trading stations at strategic towns along the coastlines of every continent.[33]

There was a changing of the guard, and Europe's ascent was clear.

Crucial to the story is the fact that Spain and Portugal were conquered by Muslim forces in 711. For nearly eight hundred years, the Iberian Peninsula was home to a series of powerful Muslim dynasties. In the thirteenth century, it was clear that Muslim power was receding, and in 1492—the exact year Columbus set sail for the Americas—the last Muslim powers were defeated in Granada by Ferdinand and Isabella, the great Catholic monarchs. The Reconquista was complete. Spain and Portugal were under Christian rule once again. But it was no small accomplishment. It took the collective effort of untold generations of soldiers, and 781 years of resistance, to throw off the yoke of Islam. However, the titanic Christian–Muslim clash was far from over. In 1453, the great Eastern Christian capital of Constantinople had been toppled and its inhabitants slaughtered or enslaved. In northern India, Muslim rule had been firmly in place as early as 1192 under the Delhi Sultanate. In 1526, the powerful and expansive Mughal Empire began consolidating nearly the entire Indian subcontinent under the banner of Islam. At the same time, Catholic powers were in the process of subduing the Americas, and beginning in 1517, they would have to contend with a massive schism—the Protestant Reformation—back home in Europe.

33. Frykenberg, 121.

Understanding this background is critical to understanding the rather militant mentality of those southern Europeans who came in waves to India. They needed money as their empire was expanding exponentially. They had built up within them a crusading mentality, known in the Americas as *conquistadors*. They knew the power of Islam, and they were determined to fight it, continuing the great gains they had made recently on a global scale: in the Americas, in Africa, and in many parts of Asia. It seemed as if God was on their side, and finally, after many centuries, Christianity's long recession was beginning to turn the other way. This is the mentality behind the Crusades (1095-1204) and the Inquisitions, which began in 1478. And perhaps nowhere was the Inquisition more punishing than in Goa, where the otherwise heroic missionary Francis Xavier (1506-52) requested its installation in 1545. It was put into place in 1560, but Xavier did not live to see its horrors in India firsthand.

Vasco da Gama was in his prime, and he guided a successful journey across the Arabian Sea, reaching the land of spice on May 20, 1498. As the Europeans disembarked in the city of Calicut (today known as Kozhikode), there was an immediate sizing up on both sides. Fortuitously, the Portuguese discovered several people scattered about the coast having knowledge of European languages: "slaves, runaways, deserters, pirates, and respectable merchants."[34] These individuals were their interpreters, as the sailors knew nothing of Indian language or culture. In fact, some of them, including Vasco da Gama, thought the Hindu temples were Christian churches.[35] When locals asked what they were up to so far

---

34. Neill, vol. 1, 91.
35. Fernando and Gispert-Sauch write, "Vasco da Gama returned to Portugal (where he received great honors), wrongly convinced that the majority in the land he had finally reached were Christians." See p. 75.

from home, they responded that they were seeking Christians and spices. But clearly, these newcomers were different from others who had arrived to their shores through the ages. There was a confidence, an emanating power, a sense that more of them would be coming soon.

The second batch of ships, much larger, reached Calicut in September 1500. There were a thousand men, including nineteen missionaries, on thirteen vessels. Muslim fears were stoked, and several violent episodes broke out, leading to "heavy bombardment" of the city of Calicut. The Portuguese slaughtered six hundred locals in the maelstrom.[36] Calm was finally attained by force under Alfonso de Albuquerque, the Portuguese "Governor of India," who conquered the valuable and strategic region of Goa—"where the Muslim North and the Hindu South met"—in 1510.[37] Even today, Albuquerque's conquests are condemned by Muslims in the region. On a plaque at the important Miskhal Mosque in Kuttichira, Kozhikode [Calicut], it reads:

> This mosque was partly destroyed by the Portuguese Commander Alburkar [Albuquerque] on Jan 3rd 1510 AD (22nd day of Ramadan AH 915). The remnants of their misdeeds can be seen in the south west portion of the roof of 3rd floor as partly burned.[38]

This was the beginning of a new chapter as the Europeans now had a port where they were in firm control. They tenaciously and vigorously defended their little slice of India all the way until 1961—fourteen years after Indian independence from the British. The glory years of the Portuguese Empire, however,

---

36. Neill, vol. 1, 93.
37. Fernando and Gispert-Sauch, 76.
38. Recorded on site by Dyron Daughrity. The authors visited this site in 2014.

was during the sixteenth century. For a century, they utterly dominated the realm of the Indian Ocean.

The Portuguese seemed to make enemies and cause offense from early on in their stay. Their feud with Islam was deep and historic. An alliance with Muslims was impossible. So, they turned to Hindu rulers for political relations. This approach also was doomed to failure. Upper-caste Hindus had a highly complex system of social pollution that the European sailors could never hope to understand well. Initially, the Thomas Christians, scattered up and down the Malabar Coast, were thought to be an obvious ally. But the Portuguese considered Nestorians little better than the Hindus. Similarly, the Thomas Christians found these "Paranghi" ("despised foreigner") Christians to be uncivilized and uncouth.[39] But it was obvious that the foreigners were very powerful; dealing with them effectively would require diplomatic skill.

Much to the satisfaction of the Portuguese, the Thomas Christians controlled the spice trade. And spice was the main reason the Portuguese were in India. If the Thomas Christians could secure protection from expanding Muslim armies, then they were willing to allow the Portuguese a share of the spice trade. There was potential for it to be a win-win relationship.

The Portuguese Empire was legitimized by the Roman Pope in a series of treaties and agreements known as the *Padroado Real*, or, "royal patronage." In 1494, at the Treaty of Tordesillas, the Borgian Pope Alexander VI drew an arbitrary line down the Atlantic Ocean and gave the East to Portugal and the West to Spain. Portugal and Spain were granted the right to conquer and evangelize the world. And they did so, if at times

---

39. See Woba James, 81. Paranghi (or Farangi, Pfarangi, or Farang) probably comes from the word for "Frank," as in the Frankish kingdom of Europe. It is a word commonly used (both historically and today) in South and Southeast Asia for whites, or European-stock people. See also Frykenberg, 119.

ruthlessly. All the more impressive was how the Portuguese were able to dominate such vast lands—in Asia, Africa, and Latin America—with so few people. According to Stephen Neill,

> At no time in the sixteenth century were there in Asia more than six or seven thousand Portuguese males of military age and capable of bearing arms. This implies a total population of about four times that number, but these were scattered in all the Portuguese settlements from Mozambique (Africa) to Macao (China).[40]

Had Hindus and Muslims worked together, they probably could have resisted. Even after the conquest of Goa and the subsequent expulsion of all Muslims from the region, these "Western immigrants found themselves little more than a drop in an ocean of Hinduism."[41] Nevertheless, they transformed Goa into an "Eastern Rome."[42]

When the Portuguese first started arriving in South India, the environment was tense; at times, hostile. They discovered a highly political game of chess, involving two major groups: long-established Hindus and a large but powerful Muslim minority that was expanding further south, asserting itself. Due to deep-seated Muslim–Christian acrimony, it seemed natural to assume the Portuguese would be a welcome resource for the Thomas Christians. However, it was much more complex than that.

It did not take long for Europeans to realize the Thomas Christians were Nestorian, and, in the perspective of Roman Catholics of the time, heretical. Their liturgy and holy texts were in Syriac instead of in Latin. Their ecclesial authority was

---

40. Neill, vol. 1, 96.
41. Ibid., 98.
42. Frykenberg (p. 130) credits A. Mathias Mundadan with coining this expression. See Mundadan, *History of Christianity in India: From the Beginning up to the Middle of the Sixteenth Century* (Bangalore: CHAI, 1982).

the patriarch of Babylon rather than the bishop of Rome. They did not esteem Mary as the Mother of God, but only as the Mother of Christ; this was highly offensive to Catholics. The Indian Christians did not venerate images or statues because it was too similar to the idolatry of the Hindus. It was entirely normal for Indian priests to marry, while Catholics had, by this time, made clerical marriage unlawful.

Likewise, the Thomas Christians were shocked by these sailors from the West. The Portuguese killed and consumed beef—acts considered highly offensive to upper-class Hindus and Thomas Christians.[43] They viewed the Portuguese sailors as uncouth men, unrestrained in their appetites. Of course, Europeans were not aware of the intricate issues surrounding caste purity. In a very short time, it was clear that Portuguese men were having sexual relations with Indian women, often of low caste, and children of these unions were being born. Thomas Christians were caste-conscious, and looked askance on the habits of these foreigners, these *Paranghis* who honored neither their long-held customs nor their sacred religion.

In their attempt to civilize and Christianize the Indians as well as the European sailors, the Portuguese brought monks and priests and missionaries of all stripes: Franciscans, Dominicans, Augustinians, Carmelites, Capuchins, Oratorians, Theatines, and more. However, no Roman Catholic order was more important than the Jesuits, known formally as the Society of Jesus. Their distinguished leader, Francis Xavier—perhaps the greatest Christian missionary of all time—is deeply revered there, lying in state in Goa since 1553.

---

43. It is important to keep in mind that in the early years of Portuguese–Indian contact, virtually all Indian Christians were considered upper caste, and, therefore, refused to consume beef. Only later did Christianity begin to make gains in lower-caste peoples and Dalit communities. See Frykenberg, *Christianity in India*, 131.

Xavier arrived to India in 1542 and immediately began working among the Indian Christians and evangelizing the Hindus.

In India, the ministry of Xavier is closely linked to the Paravars, a South Indian caste known for its skill in fishing. In particular they are known for their deep diving in order to fetch pearl oysters. The Coromandel Coast is rich with pearl oysters, particularly in the Gulf of Mannar—the southernmost body of water that separates India from Sri Lanka. While the Hindu Paravars had fished these seas for centuries; for some time they had been losing control of the pearl industry to Muslim Arabs. Indian historian Woba James writes, "The Paravas had been reduced to slaves and day-laborers under the Muslim lease-holders."[44]

In the 1520s, the Portuguese were trying to consolidate control on the southern part of the Indian subcontinent—on the Malabar Coast of the west side and the Coromandel Coast of the east side. In the 1530s, a major conflict broke out, which originated with a Paravar woman being insulted by a Muslim man. The situation escalated rapidly and many were killed on both sides. Into this situation came the Portuguese, who made an agreement with the Paravars to protect them for a price. The Paravars were so enthusiastic about the hope of being liberated from Muslim aggression that, in 1535, they began to convert, en masse, to Roman Catholic Christianity. In just a couple of years, virtually the entire caste of 20,000 souls was baptized, although without much Christian instruction.[45]

When Francis Xavier arrived in 1542, he worked in Goa and was shocked by the rampant immorality he witnessed. He worked intensely with the children of the area, particularly the Indo-Portuguese offspring, instructing them on Catholic faith

---

44. Woba James, 71. Note: the "Paravars" are often called "Paravas."
45. Firth, 52.

and morals. After five months, he and a few helpers from the Goa Seminary sailed around Cape Comorin [Kanyakumari] to work with the Paravars, who were Christian in name only. He took a similar approach—catechizing the children and trying to establish local leadership. He was pioneering in his teaching. He and his helpers translated curriculum into Tamil, the local language. Later, he made his way to the Travancore Coast, in the deep southwest of India, where he baptized thousands from the Mukkuvar fisher caste.

Xavier and his helpers made a significant impact on the people they worked with, particularly the children. They trained them rigorously in Catholic doctrine. Xavier thundered against idolatry and took harsh measures to suppress it, even ordering houses with idols to be burned.[46] He argued for the establishment of an Inquisition in India, which was launched after his death. Described as "controlling," and having an "authoritarian will," Xavier employed "the principle of obedience," applying it "strictly to the letter."[47] His primary method of instruction was memorization, and in a short time masses of children were reciting the Catholic creeds and prayers. Xavier had ample funds from the Portuguese government for hiring local teachers who would continue the work once he moved on to other mission points, which he did with regularity. From India, his peripatetic missionary career took him to Malaysia, various stations in Indonesia, and all the way up to Japan—where he worked for two years.

After Xavier, probably the second most important Roman Catholic missionary in history is Robert de Nobili (lived 1577-1656), known to Indians as "Tattuva Podgar Swami"—the

---

46. Woba James, 77.
47. Ines Zupanov, *Missionary Tropics: The Catholic Frontier in India (16th-17th Centuries)* (Ann Arbor: The University of Michigan Press, 2005), 75-76.

teacher of reality.[48] Nobili was an Italian Jesuit who worked in India for over 50 years, mainly in the city of Madurai, in modern-day Tamil Nadu. His approach to missions was entirely different from Xavier's. Rather than starting initiatives and swiftly moving on to new ones, he longed to put his anchor down in one place and acquire a sophisticated understanding of the local culture. In Nobili's case, the culture changed him profoundly, to the point that some Europeans thought he had "gone native," or, had become a Hindu.

Nobili became a master of several Indian languages, including Tamil, Telugu, and Sanskrit. He is purported to have written over 50 books in Indian languages. He became something of a Christian Brahmin. Unlike Xavier—who was a champion of the low caste—Nobili's goal was to reach the highest castes by conforming to their standards. Since Europeans were considered outcastes, he had the following manifesto nailed to a tree in front of his house:

> I am not a *parangi*. I was not born in the land of the *parangis*, nor was I ever connected with their race. . . . I came from Rome, where my family hold the same rank as respectable *rajas* hold in this country. . . . The law which I preach is the law of the true God. . . . Whoever says that it is the law of the *parangis*, fit only for low castes, commits a very great sin, for the true God is not the God of one race, but the God of all.[49]

If the high castes accepted Christ, he reasoned, then the lower castes would probably follow suit since Brahmins are the religious teachers in Hindu society. By behaving like a highly disciplined guru, he would gain a fair hearing among Brahmins. He gave up all meat, eggs, and alcohol and took only one meal per day. He dressed like an Indian *sannyasin*

---

48. See Woba James, 79.
49. Cited in Neill, vol. 1, 288.

[renunciate] rather than like a Jesuit. He wore sandal paste on his forehead, like Hindu teachers did. He lived according to the Indian practice of caste purity—completely avoiding those of low caste status. Within the first year and a half, he had 50 converts.[50]

Nobili's career was full of complications and controversies. On the Indian side, he was plagued by high-caste accusations that his ministry was leading to the conversion of people from lower castes, even outcastes. And as Christianity expanded prolifically among the lower castes, the Christian faith became associated with them. Thus, throughout Nobili's career, it became increasingly difficult for him to attract Brahmins and other high-caste people. On the European side, Nobili was constantly plagued by charges that he had slipped into heresy by becoming too Indian. One of these controversies—over whether high-caste converts could remain Hindu in culture, but Christian in faith—required intervention from the Pope in Rome, and Pope Gregory XV ruled in Nobili's favor.

All in all, Nobili's mission was not a huge success numerically. At first, it appeared that he might attract major interest from the high castes, but it never materialized. Of the few Brahmins who became Christians, "some went back to their original faith."[51] Nobili's major contribution, however, was that he strove to create an *Indian* form of Christianity at a time when Europeans equated Christianity with Europe.

Nobili leaves us with a dilemma: to what extent must people change their cultural assumptions when they follow Christ? Indians struggle profoundly with this issue still today. Dalit [untouchable] Christians are extremely critical of Nobili's conclusion. His solution—to create two types of Christianity:

50. Woba James, 84.
51. Fernando and Gispert-Sauch, 101.

high caste and low caste, with two sets of clergy—was objectionable to them. Did Jesus preach a two-tiered faith—one for the honorable and one for social rejects? Or did Jesus challenge class distinctions? The gospels and apostolic teachings certainly indicate that the kingdom of God is a place of radical egalitarianism, equality among all people, whether Jew, gentile, slave, free, male, or female. But Nobili desperately sought to reach the upper castes by embodying the Apostle Paul's assessment that one must "become all things to all people so that by all possible means I might save some" (1 Cor 9:22).

During Nobili's life, two incidents irreversibly shaped the story of Indian Christianity: the Synod of Diamper in 1599 and the Coonan Cross Oath in 1653. The Synod of Diamper has been called "the most famous episode in Indian Church History."[52] However, from a Thomasite perspective, the more appropriate word to describe it would be "infamous."

The background of the 1599 Synod of Diamper is important.[53] These were the most punishing years of the Goa Inquisition, which began in 1560 and "had become an engine of domination and enforcement."[54] This was also a time when Catholics were reeling from the effects of a divided Europe. The Protestant Reformation went off like a continental bombshell. The Bartholomew's Day Massacre occurred in 1572 and sent a message that the Catholic Church would go to great lengths to hold onto its own. Under no circumstances would heresy be tolerated. As pointed out earlier, Spain and Portugal had worked for hundreds of years to reclaim their peninsula, and they were not about to show any signs of weakness. This

---

52. See Firth, 89.
53. See George Nedungatt, *The Synod of Diamper Revisited* (Rome: Pontificio Istituto Orientale, 2001).
54. Frykenberg, 134.

position required a militaristic defense of the faith, and several European wars of religion occurred during both the sixteenth and seventeenth centuries. The Inquisitions were a part of this militaristic, defensive stance.

Throughout the sixteenth century, the Roman Catholic Church initiated a process of Latinization in the churches. Nestorianism was being stamped out by the Goa Inquisition, but the Thomas Christians were not as pliable as some thought. One major problem had to do with venerating images; this practice was crucial for Catholics, but in the minds of Thomas Christians, it was tantamount to idolatry. Eventually, the Catholic and Syrian hierarchies refused ordination to one another's ministerial candidates. But the Catholic Church had much more power, and by 1515, thousands of Syrian Christians were aligning themselves with Rome. The ancient Thomas Christian community was dividing.

In 1595, Pope Clement VIII authorized Alexis de Menezes, the Archbishop of Goa, to sever the link that existed between Persia and South India. This was the only way to stop the influence of the Eastern Churches, and, finally, to gather the Thomas Christians into the Roman fold. With the supply chain from the East disrupted, the Thomas Christians became confused as to whether a bishop would be appointed for them or not. When one of their bishops arrived, he was taken into custody and Latinized.[55]

Archbishop Menezes called a synod at the town of Diamper (Udayamperoor) in 1599. He pressured the Syrian bishop, George, to resign. He also visited the Thomasite parishes and homes in order to build his argument that they should put themselves under Rome's authority. He ordained many priests into the Roman way, although many of these priests did not

55. Woba James, 104.

understand the larger issues at play. In a short time, Menezes had won over many, beginning with the communities of Kaduthuruthy, Mulanthuruthy, and Diamper.[56] The fact that Diamper was becoming a center of Roman Christianity was a key reason for why the synod was held there.

The synod began on June 20, 1599. There were over eight hundred Syrians present as well as key figures from the Portuguese community. On the second day of the synod, Menezes professed the Roman faith and asked the Syrians to do likewise. A group of about seventy resisted. In the following days, Menezes repeatedly denounced Nestorius and Nestorianism. He repudiated the Churches of the East and asserted that the only true authority was the Pope. He formalized that the Thomas Christians would now take on a more Roman approach to faith, including the Roman sacraments, feasts, fasts, administration, leadership, life and manners, and approach to non-Christians. The Syrians would now be cut off from the East and would be firmly under the control of Portuguese bishops. The context of the Synod of Diamper is important. It took place in the years of the Counter-Reformation, just after the Council of Trent (1545–63), which was Rome's formal repudiation of virtually all Protestant ideas.

It seemed that Archbishop Menezes had completely triumphed, as the Syrian Church capitulated and the synod was ended on June 26. In one week, he managed to accomplish an endeavor that had frustrated Roman Catholic authorities in India for a century. Menezes did not stop there, however. He worked to stamp out any residual Nestorianism by all means, including book burnings, which is "why we now have so little written evidence of the history of the Syrian Church in India before the sixteenth century."[57]

56. Ibid., 109.

Some years later, in 1652, a Syrian bishop named Ahatalla arrived to India with the intention to reconnect the East with the Indian church. He resurrected hopes among the Thomas Christians that perhaps their Syrian connection was not dead. After some time, he was apprehended by the Portuguese, tried by the Inquisition, declared guilty of heresy, and put on a boat headed to Europe. There were different versions of what happened to him, however. Some claimed he was killed by the Portuguese, but the true story remained a mystery. What was clear, however, was that many Syrian Christians were offended by the treatment of one of their bishops from the East, and they revolted.

On January 3, 1653, at the town of Mattancherry (in Cochin), many Syrian Christians declared a solemn oath. They swore that they would never again submit to the Roman Catholic authorities. This incident has become known as the Coonan (crooked) Cross Oath. The large crowd tied a rope to a cross and declared an oath: that Rome was no longer in control of their church. A few months later, some Syrian Christians gathered at Alengad (near Cochin) to ordain one of their archdeacons as bishop. He took the name "Mar Thoma I." Within weeks, however, sincere questions about the validity of his consecration arose, and most of those involved in the incident returned to the Roman fold. By 1663—a decade after the Coonan Cross Oath—eighty four churches had returned to Rome and thirty two churches stood firm with Mar Thoma.[58] This incident is the origin of the Syrian Catholic and Syrian Orthodox division that persists to the present day.[59]

It was around this time that the Dutch began to defeat the

---

57. Firth, 96.
58. Firth, 104.
59. Further ecclesial divisions followed in the wake of the Coonan Cross Oath. We will explore these divisions in greater detail in the next chapter.

Portuguese in battle after battle, taking their ports, turning them into Dutch possessions. The Dutch captured Ceylon in 1658 and began to capture various ports on the Malabar Coast in the 1660s. Cochin fell to the Dutch in 1663. Goa, however, was left in Portuguese hands. The Dutch were religiously tolerant. They had no problem with the Syrian Christians, and allowed them to renew their connections with the East.

When the Thomas Christians sent a request for a Metran (metropolitan bishop), they received a response from the Jacobite Patriarch of Antioch. While Jacobites share much with Nestorians, they are different in key ways. Their Christology is different from the Nestorians, but it also differs from the Western Church. Jacobites are monophysites—meaning, they believe Christ had only one nature. They reject the Council of Chalcedon, which in 451, concluded that Christ had two natures. Thus, the Jacobites are part of the Oriental Orthodox family of churches, which includes Syrians, Armenians, Coptics, and Ethiopians. Their great champion in the sixth century was Jacob Baradaeus (died 578). Today, they still wear his name: Jacobites.

Historians do not know how the Jacobite Patriarch—rather than the Nestorian Babylonian Patriarch—ended up receiving the invitation from South India. The Thomas Christians seemed rather uninterested in the Chalcedonian quarrels; thus, they received him. They knew the histories of the Syrian Christians—both Jacobites and Nestorians—were tangled. What was important to them was having a bishop who was well-versed in the ancient Syrian liturgies. Besides, their main goal was to escape the ecclesial clutches of Rome. Thus, in 1665, a bishop arrived in India with the title of "Mar Gregorios," the Jacobite Metropolitan of Jerusalem. To the present day, multiple "Jacobite" denominations exist in South India, as they have experienced several church splits.

Important Protestant Missions (from 1706)

Aurangzeb (1658–1707) was the Mughal emperor who expanded Islamic rule on the Indian subcontinent farther than anyone before or after him. He deposed the previous emperor—his own father, Shah Jahan—and instituted a strict form of sharia law. His big plans for a consolidated Muslim empire began to collapse shortly after his death, largely because numerous rebellions began to spring up in opposition to his strict interpretations of Islam. Both Shah Jahan and Aurangzeb had abandoned the rather secular leadership style of Akbar the Great and the earliest emperors. After the death of Aurangzeb, the overstretched Mughal Empire began its rapid decline as revolts and wars of succession badly weakened it. At the same time, European presence grew in India, making steady gains at the expense of Islamic control. The long decline of Mughal power culminated in 1857, when the British exiled Bahadur Shah II, the last of the Mughals.

In 1600, the British East India Company was formed, and in 1602, the Dutch founded a company as well. Both of them traded for spices and textiles at the Ganges Delta, in the Bengal region of India, but only after having to battle the Portuguese on several occasions. In the early 1700s, the French also got involved in the fight for control of the seas as well as the lucrative business of trading with India. It was a free-for-all. Mughal decline resulted in a scramble for the subcontinent, which only ended in the mid-nineteenth century, with the British emerging as the victors. For a century and a half, however, from about 1700 to 1858, European powers clamored for supremacy through warfare with each other and with local princely states, and through the establishment of treaties with local Indian rulers. The British emerged victorious in 1858 after crushing the famous Indian Rebellion of 1857. In 1858, the British monarchy dissolved the East India Company and assumed direct control of India in the form of the British Raj.

As Portuguese power declined, northern European powers ascended. Even Denmark was in on the action, establishing two trading ports that would become famous in the history of Indian Christianity: one at Tranquebar (in Tamil Nadu) in 1620 and another at Serampore (in West Bengal) in 1676. The trading companies from Protestant nations were wary of, even hostile toward, the idea of missions. They thought mission work destabilized culture and threatened trade. This is why Protestant trading ports functioned for decades, even a century, before the arrival of missionaries. Thus, while the Danes had been in India since 1620, overt evangelism did not begin until 1706, when Bartholomaus Ziegenbalg and Heinrich Plütschau landed at Tranquebar. This was the big difference between Catholics and Protestants: Catholics strongly encouraged propagation of faith from the moment of their arrival to India. However, Protestants were generally suspicious of converting Indians to Christianity until well into the nineteenth century. In other words, Catholic missionaries had about a 200-year head start over their Protestant counterparts.

Ziegenbalg and Plütschau were true pioneers. Indeed, Ziegenbalg is considered "the father of modern Protestant mission."[60] These two young men were evangelical Lutherans from Germany, and had studied at the cutting-edge University

---

60. See Daniel Jeyaraj, *Bartholomaus Ziegenbalg: The Father of Modern Protestant Mission: An Indian Assessment* (New Delhi: ISPCK, 2006).

of Halle under the brilliant and pious professor August Hermann Francke. Professor Francke's mentor was Phillip Jacob Spener, the famous father of modern Pietism—a Protestant movement that emphasized true inner piety, evangelical fervor, and social activism.[61] It is a very spiritual form of Christianity including deeply personal prayer, confession of sin, and righteous living. Pietism is also socially robust. Francke taught that universal literacy should be a goal that Christians should work toward. Indeed, education should be required of all Christians. Literacy was critical to Christian growth, so people could read the scriptures themselves. Francke did not simply have in mind religious literacy, however. He believed deeply that literacy and modern science would combine to aid the advance of the Christian gospel to the ends of the earth.

The King of Denmark, Frederick IV, dreamed up a plan to send these two young German missionaries to India. Arriving in 1706, Ziegenbalg and Plütschau encountered many obstacles—foremost was that they were not wanted at Tranquebar; in fact, they were completely ostracized by the traders there. They were determined to succeed, however, and they had the backing of their king, so they pressed forward learning Tamil and Portuguese. They secured the invaluable help of Aleppa, a Tamil man in his 40s who spoke Portuguese, Danish, German, Dutch, in addition to the multiple Indian languages of the region.[62] Ziegenbalg was a quick study, and with Aleppa's help, he completed a Tamil translation of the New Testament in 1711.[63] One of Ziegenbalg's most lasting

---

61. See Douglas Shantz, *An Introduction to German Pietism: Protestant Renewal at the Dawn of Modern Europe* (Baltimore: The Johns Hopkins University Press, 2013).

62. Brijraj Singh, *Bartholomaeus Ziegenbalg 1683-1719* (Oxford: Oxford University Press, 1999), 18.

63. Plütschau returned to Europe in 1711 in order to promote the mission and enter into

contributions to South India was the establishment of a printing press in 1712. Donated by Francke, his mentor at the University of Halle, it continues to serve the region to the present. Some Indian printers recognize Ziegenbalg as the father of their craft.[64]

Their first Lutheran baptism was in 1707, and the Tranquebar missionaries quickly established "The Jerusalem Church," comprising mainly low-caste Sudras. Later, Ziegenbalg and his helpers were able to convert many Portuguese Catholics, leading to great Protestant–Catholic animosity in the region. One Indian helper named Rajanaikan, a former Roman Catholic, converted over 300 people to the Lutheran faith.[65]

It is difficult to describe how Ziegenbalg was able to accomplish so much in so little time. He lived only until the age of 37 and spent only a decade in India.[66] In addition to his prolific translation work and publishing enterprises, he became an expert on Indian culture and religion, producing high-quality research. His pietistic background equipped him with a desire to serve the people, and he established five schools, including a school for girls, "the first of its kind in India."[67] He trained preachers, established an orphanage for boys, and developed curriculum. These accomplishments are all the more remarkable when we realize that Europeans had earned a terrible reputation in the area as offensive, aggressive, shameless, and profoundly immoral.[68]

parish ministry. See Stephen Neill, *A History of Christianity in India 1707-1858* (Cambridge: Cambridge University Press, 1985), 37.

64. See Christopher Gilbert's documentary film *Beyond Empires: Why India Celebrates Bartholomaeus Ziegenbalg* (Lamp Post Media, 2013).

65. Stephen Neill, vol. 2, 42–43.

66. Ziegenbalg was on furlough from 1714 to 1716. He married Maria Dorothea Saltzmann, his former student, in 1715. See Jeyaraj, 95–106.

67. Woba James, 152.

68. Years later, in 1780, C. F. Schwartz wrote, "The behavior of the Europeans in this

After Ziegenbalg's death in 1719, the mission carried on due to the continued support of Francke and his successors at the University of Halle. But it was not until the arrival of Christian Friedrich Schwarz in 1750 that Tranquebar had its next magnificent leader. Schwarz served in India faithfully for 48 years at Tranquebar, Trichinopoly, and Tanjore. Schwarz's time at Tranquebar was a real high point, but after his death in 1798, it suffered neglect. The British presence in the region was expanding during that time, and the German influence that had made it such a successful mission point was drastically reduced. Nevertheless, both Anglicans and Lutherans served the churches faithfully after Schwarz, but by that time the epicenter for Protestant missions in India had shifted north to Serampore, near Calcutta.

The Serampore Mission represents a new era in the history of Protestant missions. Its celebrated leader, William Carey (1761–1834), is considered "the father of modern missions" in the eyes of the Anglo-Saxon world.[69] Carey was a working-class shoemaker before he became an evangelical preacher. He was inspired by the German missionaries in India to the point that he made the cause his own, producing writings and helping to form the Baptist Missionary Society in 1792. His booklet, entitled *An Enquiry into the Obligations of Christians to Use Means for the Conversions of Heathens* (1792) was a huge success that set in motion the era of British, and, later, American missionary work. One of the core themes of this book was that the Calvinist doctrine of predestination did not mean Christians should refrain from doing missionary work. Carey and others

country is truly lamentable." See Christian Frederick Swartz, *Memoirs of the Life and Correspondence of the Reverend Christian Frederick Swartz* (London: J. Hatchard and Son, 1835), 375.
69. Robert Frykenberg, "Christians in India: An Historical Overview of Their Complex Origins," in *Christians and Missionaries in India: Cross-Cultural Communication since 1500*, ed. Frykenberg (Grand Rapids: Eerdmans, 2003), 56.

had to fight hard to overcome this long-held bias, which they did rather effectively. Ultimately, his work inspired two of the most important missionary societies in history: the London Missionary Society in 1795 and the Church Missionary Society in 1799. These two organizations made an immeasurable impact on the propagation of Christianity all over the world. Many, many Christian communities in the world today trace their faith origins to the work of the LMS and CMS.

The British government did not allow missionaries to work in India until the Charter Act of 1813.[70] Thus, when Carey arrived in British Calcutta in 1793, he had to work in a secular occupation, managing an indigo plant. He quickly set himself to learning Indian languages, which proved to be his great genius.

In 1800, Carey moved to nearby Serampore, a tiny Danish settlement, in order to function more freely, as Denmark was far more open to Christian missions. Carey was joined by Joshua Marshman and William Ward, "each of whom was almost as remarkable as Carey himself."[71] The "Serampore Trio" and their mission became famous not so much for converting Indians, but for establishing a printing press and producing the Christian scriptures in forty seven Indian languages between the years 1800 and 1834.[72] They also translated important Hindu texts into English, sparking the Bengali Renaissance that later fed Indian nationalism. They established a Baptist church, numerous schools with native teachers, and a botanical garden which became well-known.

---

70. Frykenberg, "Christians in India," 58.

71. Stephen Neill, "William Carey," in the *Concise Dictionary of the Christian World Mission*, eds. Stephen Neill, Gerald Anderson, and John Goodwin (London: Lutterworth Press, 1970).

72. Timothy George, "Let It Go: Lessons from the Life of William Carey," in *Expect Great Things, Attempt Great Things*, eds. Allen Yeh and Chris Chun (Eugene, OR: Wipf and Stock, 2013), 4.

Perhaps their most lasting contribution was the founding of Serampore College in 1818. To the present day, Serampore is the official accrediting institution for theological degrees in India.

William Carey's motto was "Expect great things from God; attempt great things for God." This mindset of expectation and hard work combined to inspire generations of missionaries, not just in India but around the world. The era of the Serampore Trio—Carey, Marshman, and Ward—is fixed in the history of English Protestant missions as iconic, well worth emulating. They accomplished much and they showed profound respect toward the people they ministered to. Emphasizing cross-cultural understanding and empowering the local context with education, they created opportunities for countless Indians who came through their classrooms. While England was taking millions of pounds from India, the missionaries of Serampore were, rather, giving all they had to the people of India. They understood the principle of cultural reciprocity, and for that Westerners and Indians alike can be grateful. William Carey's model for missions—to educate, to inspire, and to serve—continues to receive affirmation from Indian Christians and Hindus alike.

The nineteenth century could be called the century of Protestant mass movements. As the British Empire gave increasing attention to their relationship with India, they slowly but surely realized that missionaries were not the threat to stability they believed them to be in earlier decades. Over time, as Britain consolidated control of the subcontinent, Protestant missionaries functioned more freely, without fear of Muslim Mughals or Portuguese Catholics. In 1813, Britain formally allowed missionaries into their lands. In 1858, Britain assumed political control of the subcontinent in what is known as the "British Raj," allowing missionaries even greater latitude in their work.

In earlier years, the prolific Protestant missionaries, such as Ziegenbalg, Schwarz, and Carey, had planted the gospel on Indian soil, and it began to indigenize very quickly. Missionaries excelled most when they engaged the culture and allowed the gospel to indigenize. Schwartz was particularly effective in this regard. He trained many preachers, his most illustrious being Sathiyanathan Pillai, Vedanayakam Sastri, and David Sundaranandan.[73] Vedanayakam's adage, "it takes an elephant to catch an elephant and a quail to catch a quail," proved true as thousands of people—usually from the lower castes—began to turn to Christ.[74]

The early generations of Protestant Indian missionaries recruited Tamils to the Christian faith like none before or since. Their preaching and incessant travels sparked numerous mass movements in India, in spite of widespread persecution. In the intricate social fiber of India, it was scandalous for a person or a family to change religions. It disrupted caste, imperiled social standing, and threatened age-old family vocations. It also shook Hinduism to the core. Mass movements were a major threat to Indian cultural norms and social arrangements, and the fallout continues apace in Indian politics and culture to the present day.

In response to Christian persecution, various "Villages of Refuge" were established, especially in the region of Tirunelveli, in Tamil Nadu. Often, these villages were given biblical names such as Bethlehem, Nazareth, Jerusalem,

---

73. See Robert Frykenberg, "Historical Introduction," in *Tirunelveli's Evangelical Christians*, eds. David Packiamuthu and Sarojini Packiamuthu (Bangalore: SAIACS Press, 2003), xxii–xxvii.
74. For the saying from Vedanayakam, see Frykenberg, "India," in *A World History of Christianity*, ed. Adrian Hastings (Grand Rapids: Eerdmans, 1999), 185.

Samaria, and Galilee. Others, such as Megnanapuram, Sawyerpuram, Suviseshapuram, and Dohnavur, have become well-known due to their being strongly Christian towns, often with major connections to Western missionaries. Such was the case with Dohnavur, a Christian village of refuge that was closely associated with the British missionary Amy Carmichael (1867–1951). Invariably, missionaries—both Indian and Western—came to the aid of these villages in order to offer education and health care.

In nineteenth-century India, notable Protestant mass movements broke out among the Telugu-speaking people of Andhra Pradesh and among many tribes such as the Badagas, Bhils, Khonds, Mundas, and Santhals. However, the most spectacular and thorough mass movements occurred in Northeast India, where entire people groups—often with no historic connection to Hinduism—converted to Christianity en masse. Some of these tribes, such as the Khasis in Meghalaya, the Mizos in Mizoram, and the Nagas of Nagaland, are almost entirely Christian today. It is important to point out that while missionaries were almost always involved in planting Christianity among Indian people groups, the great preachers of the mass movements—those who actually went out and converted thousands—were Indians. For example, the American Baptists supported the major mass movements among the Telugu peoples, but the great evangelist of the era was Mr. Periah, an illiterate Indian man with an unparalleled ability to persuade people to follow Jesus Christ.[75]

Generally, the mass movements were initiated by a connection between a Western Protestant denomination and a certain people-group in a particular geographical area. Here are a few examples:

75. See Woba James, 199.

- American Presbyterians had great success in the Punjab—in the north of India-Pakistan.

- In Uttar Pradesh, which borders Nepal and the Himalayas, evangelical Anglicans from the Church Mission Society converted many Sikhs and lower-caste Hindus.

- On the Chota Nagpur Plateau—in the east of India—it was German Lutheran missionaries who had success. To get a sense of the scale of conversions, in 1891, there were around 100,000 Christians in Chota Nagpur. By 1931, that number had grown to around 400,000.

- If we look at the Northeast of India, we find a region with the highest percentage of Christians in all of India. It was the American Baptists, British Baptists, and Welsh Calvinist Methodists who reached out to these extremely remote, tribal communities.[76]

While the nineteenth century witnessed many Indians coming to Christ, it began to become clear to many Indian Christian leaders that their faith was terribly divided. The glaring problem was that Jesus and his apostles emphasized repeatedly the need for Christian unity.

In the twentieth century, a movement known as Christian ecumenism rose up as an attempt to repair the deep divisions within Christianity. Christianity in India was becoming known all around the Christian world as a particularly fractious context due to so many different forms of the faith. It was scandalous that new sects and denominations were breaking away from each other with great frequency, and tensions between Christians of all stripes were obvious.

With unflinching leadership from Gandhi, in 1947, India gained its independence from Britain. He had managed to lead a relatively peaceful revolution to push out the Westerners from their land. It was largely successful. British

---

76. These examples are from Woba James, 199ff. His primary source is J. Waskom Pickett, *Christian Mass Movements in India* (New York: Abingdon Press, 1933).

administrators, various classes of workers, businessmen, their families, and most of the missionaries returned home. That same year, 1947, Indian Christians created the Church of South India (CSI), a united church movement that brought together Anglicans, Methodists, Congregationalists, and Presbyterians.[77] In 1970, the Church of North India (CNI) was established, bringing together Anglicans, Disciples of Christ, Methodists, some Brethren, British Baptists, Congregationalists, and Presbyterians. The CSI has around 3.5 million members today while the CNI has around 1.5 million members, according to the World Council of Churches.

The Pentecostal Awakening (from 1905)

The most dynamic Protestant movement in Indian church history has been the Pentecostal revival that began in the early twentieth century. Pentecostalism emphasizes the gifts of the Holy Spirit given to the apostles during the feast of Pentecost in the book of Acts: tongue speaking, healing, miracles, visions, great enthusiasm, prophecy, talk of end times, and mass evangelism. Pentecostalism is often described as an American Holy Spirit movement radiating out of the Azusa Street Revival in Los Angeles in 1906 under the leadership of William Seymour, an African American Holiness preacher. There were many precedents, however. Seymour studied under a preacher-healer named Charles Fox Parham. The Holiness movement itself was an offshoot of the Methodist movement, rooted in the teachings of John Wesley in eighteenth-century England. Even in India, there were several revivals that predate Azusa Street, such as John Christian Aroolappan's revivals in

---

77. See Dyron Daughrity, "South India: Ecumenism's One Solid Achievement?," in *International Review of Mission* 99:1 (April 2010): 56–68.

Tamil Nadu (1860) and Travancore (1874), and (former Brahmin) Justus Joseph's Revival Church, founded in 1875.[78]

Just before the famous Azusa Street Revival, there was a spiritual awakening that occurred in Wales from 1904 to 1906; it had a direct impact on the Indian context because of the links between Welsh Presbyterian missionaries and their mission stations in the Khasi Hills, in modern day Meghalaya.[79] One historian wrote, "By far, the most significant overseas event influencing the life of the Indian Church in the early twentieth century was the Welsh Revival of 1904."[80] It is estimated that over 100,000 people converted to Christianity in about six months during that revival.[81] The Pentecostal message traveled almost immediately to the remote tribes of Northeast India, and during 1905, news of a Khasi Hills revival spread far and wide. The Pentecostal preacher and writer Frank Bartleman described the genealogy aptly in 1925:

> The present world-wide revival was rocked in the cradle of little Wales, it was "brought up" in India, following; becoming full grown in Los Angeles later.[82]

A high-caste, influential Indian woman named Pandita Ramabai heard of the revivals in Wales and the Khasi Hills, and was determined to bring some of that spiritual fervor to her Mukti Mission, in the Indian state of Maharashtra.[83] Ramabai was a Christian convert who had become known all over the English-speaking world for her work rescuing and educating

---

78. Woba James, 334–36.
79. The best treatment of the origins of Pentecostalism in India is Michael Bergunder, *The South Indian Pentecostal Movement in the Twentieth Century* (Grand Rapids: Eerdmans, 2008). For the Khasi Hills Revival, see p. 7. See also Frykenberg, *Christianity in India*, 408.
80. J. Edwin Orr, *Evangelical Awakenings in India* (New Delhi: Masihi Sahitya Sanstha, 1970), 50.
81. Ibid., 55.
82. Frank Bartleman, *How Pentecost Came to Los Angeles* (Los Angeles: self-published, 1925), 21.
83. See Orr, 63.

rejected women and girls. In 1889, she established a thriving mission that grew to employ a staff of 85.[84]

In 1898, Ramabai's influence spread remarkably as she attended a Keswick "higher life" convention in England, requesting participants to pray that such spiritual renewal might take place in India.[85] The annual Keswick conventions shared much in common with the later Pentecostal movement with their focus on deep personal piety, complete surrender to Christ, emphasis on the Holy Spirit, and global evangelism. People attended these conventions from far and wide, and the Keswick network throughout the vast British Empire became fertile ground for the Azusa Street missionaries who went out after having their life-changing experience in Los Angeles.

In 1905, "a glorious Holy Ghost revival" broke out among Ramabai and her prayer circle at Mukti.[86] She claimed that this revival spread throughout India, and judging by the widespread, indigenous impact that Pentecostalism has had in India, she was right. She wrote that the Holy Spirit burned like a flame within her, and even caused her to speak in Hebrew involuntarily. The younger girls of the group, who had been rescued, experienced glossolalia and became joyful, loud, and exuberant over their feelings of liberation and salvation. The experience was much like that experienced on Azusa Street the following year in Los Angeles: ecstatic utterances, apocalyptic visions, expectant talk of the return of Christ, and healings.

Pentecostalism spread rapidly in India, especially after 1906, when the globally-minded missionaries from Azusa began to

---

84. Frykenberg, *Christianity in India*, 402. Today, Mukti is a huge, robust mission, ministry, healing, and education compound that serves hundreds of women, children, and others who have been rejected.

85. Bergunder, 23.

86. Frykenberg, *Christianity in India*, 408.

arrive. The Keswick network was influencing Christians all across the British Empire. Historian Michael Bergunder writes:

> Azusa Street went global from the very start and began to channel its message through the vast international evangelical and missionary network that was receptive to revivals.[87]

The small, local revivals became global almost immediately.

Another very important issue here is the English language. The Keswick participants spoke English, the Americans from Los Angeles spoke it, Pandita Ramabai spoke it, and, increasingly, Indians were speaking it as it was the language of the British Raj as well as the language of Western education. Furthermore, the work of Scottish missionary Alexander Duff (1806–78)—the legendary proponent of higher education in India—convinced many that "English was the best way to impart Christian truth." In Duff's view, teaching English went hand in hand with missions. He believed the English language prepared people's hearts for the gospel. However, in spite of all of his accolades for transforming education in India, "few of his students actually became Christians."[88] The task of evangelism was better accomplished by the Pentecostals.

It is difficult to emphasize how profound an effect the Azusa Street Revival had on the global spread of Pentecostalism. Imbued with African American spirituality, the revival immediately crossed racial lines and attracted people from all over the Western world. It was multiracial, cosmopolitan, socially progressive, and energetic. It lasted nearly a decade, impacting thousands of people with a newfound emphasis on holiness, revival, spiritual gifts, and exuberance in worship. Azusa pilgrims established newspapers in many languages and

---

87. Bergunder, 7.
88. Frykenberg, *Christianity in India*, 324.

went out into the world to evangelize, many of them led by the idea that the last days had dawned.

In 1906, Christians from all over the world heard about the Azusa Street Revival, and many of them made the journey there in order to catch some of its spiritual fire. Almost without fail, their experiences exceeded their expectations, and they set out to spread the message. Many of them felt called to visit India—that great and populous land with very few Christians.

Norwegian evangelist Thomas Ball Barratt visited Azusa in 1906 and became "the Pentecostal apostle to northern and western Europe."[89] What is lesser known is his work in India.[90] Barratt wrote about the miracles that he witnessed there—notably, the gift of tongue-speaking, and he rationalizes about how it may have happened:

> Of course physicians know that there are cases in which people have spoken in foreign tongues when delirious, or under some operation on the brain by the surgeon. Or when the speaker is under hypnotic influence. They therefore judge that this must be similar. Cells of the brain under high nervous pressure emit words or sentences, stored up there some time before. We do not deny the possibility of this at all. But it merely proves that there is a means, a channel, in the human being, whereby God, if He chose, may speak through us. . . .
>
> I could relate numerous cases. Take the case in India . . . which was related by several missionaries, and about which I obtained a written statement from the missionary on the station where it took place. Two native women, one deaf and dumb from childhood, often spoke in the Hindustani language perfectly, as the Spirit gave utterance, although they were perfectly unacquainted with that language, and had been taken from mission station to mission station to speak to the Mohammedans, whose language it was, in that way.[91]

89. Vinson Synan, *The Century of the Holy Spirit* (Nashville: Thomas Nelson, 2001), 6.
90. His base was at the hill station of Coonoor, in Tamil Nadu. See Bergunder, 24.
91. Thomas Ball Barratt, *In the Days of The Latter Rain* (Clapham London: Elim Pub. Co., 1928 rev. ed., 1909 1st ed.), 40. Located online at http://www.dealpentecostal.co.uk/Latter%20Rain%20TB%20Barratt.pdf (accessed October 16, 2014).

47

Amazing accounts such as these were common in the early days of Pentecostalism.

Azusa missionaries flooded into British India following their Pentecostal experience in Los Angeles: Frank Bartleman (Ceylon), Alfred and Lillian Garr (Calcutta), George E. Berg (Bangalore and Kerala), Robert F. Cook (Tamil Nadu and Kerala), and others. Some came to India working for non-Pentecostal denominations, but once they experienced the charismatic fervor—usually after visiting Ramabai's Mukti Mission—they took up the Pentecostal cause.[92] Many times, these Westerners arrived in India thinking that God would allow them to speak local languages upon arrival. It did not happen, and often they were disillusioned because they had placed so much emphasis on tongues. Missionaries struggled over the glossolalia issue, and they came to different conclusions about how to interpret it.[93] Some of these fractures caused reservations about the Pentecostal movement itself. Bergunder writes, "Ramabai and the Mukti Mission as an institution later definitely backed out of the Pentecostal movement."[94]

What had, for years, been the red-hot hub of Pentecostalism in India eventually cooled because there were so many different ways of understanding a free-wheeling, rapidly changing movement such as Pentecostalism. There was no primary authority, no systematic theology, and no creed. Rather, hundreds of leaders—both Indian and foreign—who felt they had experienced the Holy Spirit in some special way

---

92. For example, Christian Schoonmaker and Herbert Coxe were with the American denomination Christian and Missionary Alliance, but became Pentecostals due to the influence of the Mukti Mission. See Bergunder, 25.
93. Woba James (p. 333) discusses how missionaries conflicted over glossolalia. Some thought it was indispensable for proving they had been baptized by the Spirit, but others disagreed, such as Minnie F. Abrams, a close colleague to Pandita Ramabai.
94. Bergunder, 24.

were, thus, entitled to teach. This is the Achilles heel *as well as* the genius of Pentecostalism; it is based on experience. And experiences are extremely subjective. However, individuals are empowered to spread the faith without the clunky encumbrances of an overseeing denominational framework, freeing people to evangelize more efficiently.

Western missionaries could accomplish very little without Indian Christians, who interpreted for them, provided food and shelter, and introduced them to networks of Christians. In a very short time, Indians themselves became the protagonists of the story of how Pentecostalism spread across the subcontinent. And the Indian evangelists tended not to emphasize tongue-speaking to the degree that their American counterparts did.[95] They received the missionaries and learned from them, but when it came time to proclaim the Pentecostal gospel to people, they had to indigenize it appropriately, adapting it to make it more comprehensible and attractive. Western missionaries who had no idea of Indian languages and very little understanding of Indian culture had to trust their Indian colleagues. They could not do otherwise unless they were to plant themselves on the subcontinent for years, learning the languages. But very rarely did the Pentecostal missionaries stay in India. Typically, they preached, made connections with English speakers, and moved on after a short period of time. This is a key reason why Pentecostalism indigenized so rapidly in India, and partly explains why it has grown so successfully. The best estimates are that "Already 20 percent of south Indian Protestants are Pentecostals," or,

95. Woba James writes that Western Pentecostal preachers refused to fully recognize Indian Pentecostalism as legitimate because Indians downplayed glossolalia. Tongue speaking was crucial for Western missionaries, even though they were unsure of what it meant since they had failed at speaking Indian languages. They had to reinterpret the doctrine of glossolalia, which gave rise to several different theories.

about half the size of the Church of South India, the largest Protestant denomination.[96]

There are plenty of Indian Pentecostal evangelists throughout history who are virtually unknown in the Western world. Western historians often include footnotes that say, in effect, "Very little is known about this person." One reason so little is known is because, often, Indians preserved their history orally rather than in written form, although that is changing.

Many of the earlier leading Indian Pentecostal evangelists got their start while working with George Berg and Robert Cook, the Pentecostal apostles to south India. For instance, Robert Cumine was an Anglo-Indian who spoke Tamil, and, with Berg and an Indian pastor named Paruttupara Ummachan, established India's first Pentecostal congregation at Thuvayoor, Kerala, around 1911. It remained the only Pentecostal congregation in Kerala until the early 1920s. Berg also trained two young men who went on to become legendary for their work in Kerala: Umman Mammen and Pandalam Mattai.[97] T. M. Verghese, "the foremost Indian leader of the Church of God till his retirement in 1965," was connected with Cook.[98]

In the 1920s, the towering figure K. E. Abraham emerged onto the scene as an associate of Robert Cook and Mary Chapman. Together, they had success converting Brethren Christians to the Pentecostal cause. Abraham, however, became enamored with the Ceylon Pentecostal Mission (CPM, known today as The Pentecostal Mission) because of their strict refusal to allow Westerners any foothold in their churches.

96. Bergunder, 14–15.
97. Ibid., 26–27.
98. Ibid., 34.

They were a Pentecostal church that was Indian, through and through. Persuaded by this conviction, Abraham joined with them and turned away from his Western cohorts. He worked with the Ceylon Pentecostal Mission until 1924—which is when he decided to break off and form his own group, "fully controlled by him."[99] Later, in 1935, Abraham reorganized his group as the Indian Pentecostal Church (IPC), and it is one of the largest indigenous Pentecostal denominations today.

Splits were common in the early days of Pentecostalism. By the mid-1930s, there were four main Pentecostal denominations in India: the US-based Assemblies of God, the US-based Church of God, and the indigenous denominations CPM and IPC. There were also numerous independent churches and networks. The Assemblies of God took root in India largely because of the work of Mary Chapman, who had split earlier with Robert Cook and K. E. Abraham. Chapman's main colleague was an Indian named A. J. John. In 1926, they brought on board a young American missionary named John H. Burgess, who played a leading role in establishing the Bethel Bible School (now Bethel Bible College)—the first Pentecostal theological institution in India. Burgess's strategy was that Indians lead the churches while he oversaw the Bible School. Burgess brought much-needed stability to the Assemblies of God until his return to the United States in 1950.[100]

After the 1940s, Pentecostalism spread more intentionally beyond Kerala into neighboring states Karnataka and Tamil Nadu. In the second half of the twentieth century, the Pentecostal movement proliferated into different denominations and fellowships in India, just as it had done in

---

99. Ibid., 29.
100. See Bergunder, 30–31. See also Stanley M. Burgess, "Pentecostalism in India: An Overview," in *Asian Journal of Pentecostal Studies* 4:1 (2001): 91–92.

the US and elsewhere. Its impact spread far and wide, even into the Roman Catholic establishment of India.[101] Some of the more prominent Pentecostal groups are the Sharon Fellowship Church (est. 1975), the New India Church of God (est. 1976), New India Bible Church (est. 1975), and the Believers' Church, run by the Gospel for Asia ministry (est. 1978) under the leadership of K. P. Yohannan, from a St. Thomas Syrian Christian background. Raised in India and theologically educated in the United States' Southern Baptist realm of influence, his ministry claims 20,000 churches, 16,500 missionaries, and 67 Bible colleges with 9,000 students enrolled.[102]

Pentecostalism in India has indigenized. This is obvious on numerous levels, from small village ministries to megachurches. For instance, the Mark Buntain Memorial Assembly of God Church in Kolkata holds services in eight languages: English, Bengali, Hindi, Malayalam, Nepali, Oriya, Tamil, and Telugu. The Full Gospel Assembly of God Church in Bangalore, founded by Paul Thangiah, a theologically trained Indian, claims 17,000 attendees each Sunday and a television viewership of 300 million per week.[103] Another Bangalore megachurch, the Bethel Assembly of God Church, has an impressive media ministry—Twitter and all—that rivals its American counterparts. The pastor, Rev. Varughese, is a former air force scientist from an Orthodox background;

101. See Burgess's discussion of The Catholic charismatic movement in India, in "Pentecostalism in India," 94.
102. See Gospel for Asia website: http://www.gfa.org/about/the-missionaries (accessed October 17, 2014). See also Dan Wooding's interview with Yohannan, "Gospel for Asia's K. P. Yohannan a Quiet Revolutionary," November 23, 2007, located at http://www.christianheadlines.com/articles/gospel-for-asias-kp-yohannan-a-quiet-revolutionary-11560077.html (accessed October 17, 2014).
103. For the two previous churches, see Imchen K. Sungjemmeren, "Indian Megachurches' Centripetal Mission," Lausanne World Pulse (January/February 2011 issue). Article located at: http://www.lausanneworldpulse.com/perspectives.php/1360/01-2011 (accessed October 17, 2014).

however, today he is a highly successful Pentecostal entrepreneur who oversees 70 church-related meetings weekly.[104]

Conclusion

Indian Christianity continues to indigenize as "missionaries from abroad have almost disappeared."[105] However, facility with English has made India a fertile ground for globalization. Many Indian churches are still connected to the West, in a way unlike that of other Asian nations such as, say, China. India's Roman Catholics are still in full communion with Rome, whereas Chinese Catholics are split over relations with Rome. One problem that pervades India's Catholics is the long-fraught relationship between Latin Catholics and the Eastern Catholics (Syro-Malabar and Syro-Malankara). In spite of this, Indian Catholicism is thriving. The Catholic Church already claims half of India's Christian population, and now Indian priests are commonly found in the secularizing nations of the West due to shortages.

More than any other Indian Christian community, the Thomasite Orthodox Churches enjoy the favor of non-Christian locals. This is largely because they are so well-established, are thoroughly indigenized, and are not closely connected to the Western world. They are accepted as fully Indian by their compatriots. However, the Orthodox churches will likely decline since they have almost no evangelical ambitions. They are content to be admired as high-caste people, with a pedigree going back to the apostle Thomas. Their community cannot be described as thriving, but rather

---

104. See the church history section of their website: http://www.bethelagindia.org/brief_history.php (accessed October 17, 2014).
105. Frykenberg, "India" (in Hastings), 188.

as maintaining, like many other Orthodox churches around the world. Their insularity hampers their ability and desire to reach out to those around them.

The Pentecostal Christians of India are probably the fastest growing today. They are movers and shakers, establishing schools, churches, and benevolent institutions at every turn. Pentecostals are often critiqued for their unabashed determination to convert other Christians, such as those from the mainline Protestant traditions and the Orthodox community. Indeed, they have had major success in reaching other Christians. But the future of Pentecostal Christianity hinges on whether they are able to reach non-Christians.

No one knows for sure how many Christians are in India. The official number is around two and a half percent. But the estimates vary widely. There is a strong movement in India today, however, that perceives Christianity to be a much larger threat than the numbers attest. Hindu nationalists "continue to view Indian Christians as belonging to a foreign power."[106] Government policies, sporadic persecutions, and even occasional destruction of church property keep Christians guessing whether India operates by principles of religious freedom or not. Christians—on account of being identified as non-Hindu—are regularly shortchanged when it comes to government benefits and equal entitlement to good jobs. Equal recognition for Christians is a battle that continues to be fought.

---

106. Frykenberg, "India" (in Hastings), 189.

2

———

Denominational

The Christian Traditions of India

This chapter provides context for understanding some of the Christian movements and institutions of India. It also puts forth estimates of how many Christians are in India, even though this topic is fraught with tension in recent Indian history. We begin with a discussion of some of the more obvious problems in researching church membership in India, and Indian religion in general. A consideration of these problems will shed light on the questionable and at times perilous task of defining religion in India today. In order to illustrate the great diversity of Indian Christianity, the chapter also provides a basic typology of India's Christian denominations, highlighting several of the larger ones. Interspersed within the discussion of denominations are personal interviews conducted with students and faculty at several seminaries and various churches in different parts of

India. These interviews will provide readers with a sense of the more pressing issues taking place on the ground.

Religion in India: Some Challenges

It is notoriously difficult to find accurate statistics for Christianity in India. Scholars disagree on basic issues such as who can be counted as a Christian, which Christian groups are largest, whether census figures can be trusted, and whether Christianity is growing or retracting.

There is also the problem of inflated numbers. As with many religious movements, it is important that growth is emphasized for purposes of legitimization. The more recent Christian movements in India are prone to "preacher counts"—meaning they need supporters to believe they are growing, in spite of the fact that, historically, India has been a nation deeply resistant to foreign evangelism—whether by Christians, Muslims, or other groups.

Buddhism, for example, had astounding success in India in the first few centuries of its existence. Born in India around the fifth century BC, the religion was later endorsed personally and publicly by one of the great emperors of Indian history: Ashoka the Great, who ruled 269–232 BC. However, around a thousand years ago, Buddhism went into a seemingly irreversible decline. Perhaps it is not entirely accurate to say it declined. It might be more precise to say it was absorbed by the larger Hindu narratives. For example, many Hindus consider Buddha to have been an avatar of the god Vishnu.

Scholars regularly point out that Hinduism is not really a religion if we have in mind a singular, monolithic understanding of religion. Rather, Hinduism is a tapestry of *religions* that share tendencies such as a respect for vegetarianism, a devotion to an ultimate reality known as Brahman, and a deep veneration for the holy, whether in nature or even in other religions. In their own pantheon of gods, Hindus typically hold Siva and Vishnu in highest regard, but there is ample room for other major deities: Ganesh, Parvati, Hanuman, Lakshmi, Saraswati, and Kali.

There is also an enormous amount of space for other ideas to fit underneath the Hindu umbrella. Hinduism is far more diverse than the three monotheistic religions of Judaism, Christianity, and Islam. At least, in those religions, there is a general sense of the nature of God, the esteemed prophets, and a rather coherent history of practice. Hinduism does not have this uniformity. Some try to emphasize its diversity by citing the rather shocking idea that Hinduism has millions of gods. While it would be a stretch to claim Hinduism has millions of gods, the point is that extreme variety and complexity is at the very heart of Hinduism.

Complicating the theology of Hinduism is the notion that its gods have many different avatars on earth. For example, Vishnu is deeply esteemed in his numerous avatars, notably in Rama—the key figure of the *Ramayana* text, and in Krishna—the chariot driver and great god of the *Bhagavad Gita*. Hinduism also has a rich goddess tradition known as Devi. The divine feminine incarnates in numerous feminine figures who are weaved throughout India's religious traditions and local histories. By no means are these stories meant to be scientific or even consistent across the various schools and traditions of Hinduism. Rather, the feminine stories are meant to inspire female followers to embody virtues in their own lives, to live the Indian way, to aspire to the noblest of traits in the culture's history.

This brief diversion into Hinduism might appear irrelevant

to Christianity in India, but it is intended to demonstrate that Hinduism has a way of allowing its followers tremendous breadth in their interpretation of religion. For example, a person might be a Hindu, yet respond to an evangelistic sermon by a Pentecostal preacher and get baptized—yet, without cutting ties with Hinduism at all. Some Hindus might gravitate toward Christianity if it promises an earthly benefit; these individuals have been disparagingly labeled "rice Christians" in the past. Some Hindu intellectuals such as Gandhi might even consider Jesus Christ as their primary guru while holding firmly to a "Hindu" identity.

Many smaller Hindu communities encountered Jesus Christ only in recent decades. They search for ways to make sense of Christianity, in an Indian way, without Western attachments. Can a person be a Hindu-Christian? Must one completely quit Hinduism or is one allowed to frequent Christian services while retaining a Hindu identity? May a Christian equate God with Brahman? Can Christ be considered an avatar among many other avatars? These are questions that spawn diverse responses.

Scholars of Indian Christianity discuss these matters routinely. Robert Frykenberg writes of the "astonishing recent developments" concerning "non-baptized believers in Christ." These individuals are absolutely loyal to Jesus as teacher and even savior, but "do not mingle with congregations or darken the door of a church sanctuary." Some of them have been turned off by corruption within Christian churches, or by the "ceaseless squabblings" that seem to plague many Indian Christian institutions. Two of the great heroes here are the famous Indian Christian converts, Pandita Ramabai and Sadhu Sundar Singh—two intensely devoted disciples of Jesus who refused to join specific churches.[1]

Other Christian movements that defy neat categorization are the Khrist Bhaktas (devotees of Christ) of Varanasi. They worship alongside Roman Catholics, but refuse to join the church in any official way. There are also Indians who seek some sort of healing, and thus turn to Christ for a miracle, albeit temporarily. Chad Bauman and Richard Fox Young write that in rural India, "healings and exorcisms account for the vast majority of Christian conversions." However, these conversions are by no means considered by devotees to be lifelong commitments. Rather, as is common in India, people are constantly in search for help, relief, power, or opportunity. Thus, "making the rounds from one saint or shrine to another . . . is nothing new."[2] John Allen Jr. writes of a crowd of thousands that gather every Wednesday at St. Michael's Church in Mumbai to receive priestly blessings. Not surprising for a nation that, according to Gallup, has the highest religious population on earth. But "what makes St. Michael's story most remarkable is that the vast majority of these pilgrims aren't Catholics, or even Christians. They are faithful Hindus."[3] Indeed, defining Christianity in India can be tricky.

There is no doubt that some Indian Christians are reluctant to join Christianity officially because of the extremely tense conversations around religious conversion in the nation, a precarious topic that can erupt into violence. While Muslim–Hindu tension is more acute, there continue to be horror stories for individuals and families that begin to

---

1. Robert Frykenberg, *Christianity in India: From Beginnings to the Present* (Oxford: Oxford University Press, 2008), 482.
2. Chad Bauman and Richard Fox Young, eds., *Constructing Indian Christianities: Culture, Conversion and Caste* (New Delhi: Routledge, 2014), xiii. During this discussion, they site the important work of Michael Bergunder, Susan Bayly, and Chandra Mallampalli.
3. John Allen Jr., "Nun's tale captures the paradoxes of India's love affair with religion," *Crux*, July 23, 2015, http://www.cruxnow.com/faith/2015/07/23/nuns-tale-captures-the-paradoxes-of-indias-love-affair-with-religion.

associate themselves more with Christianity than with Hinduism.

We must pause to point out, however, that this dual identity of Hindu-Christian is not altogether typical. It would be a mistake to think that all—or even most—Indian Christians easily weave into church on Sundays and into the Siva Temple on weekdays. Most Indian Christians know exactly what they are: faithful, even persecuted, devotees of a minority religion, living in a sea of Hinduism (or Islam, in certain areas of India). Most baptized members of the Catholic Church would have no problem identifying themselves on the national census as being Christian. Most Pentecostal Christians would be loath to attend a Hindu temple; they would shudder at the thought of prostrating before Lord Vishnu. Nay, only Jesus Christ is Lord.

Thus, while many scholars like to point out the Indianness of Christianity—and rightly so—they occasionally go too far in their arguments, giving the impression that Christianity in India is so totally different from Western Christianity as to be naturally closer to Hinduism. The vast majority of Christians in India are—from a Western perspective—recognizably Christian. Indeed, many Indian Christians are despised and even ostracized because of their faith in Christ. They know without any ambiguity—it is regularly reinforced—that they are Christians. Not Hindus.

The specific point here is that, in all likelihood, there are far more Indians connected to Christ or to the church than the Indian census indicates. These problems are not unique to India. Indeed, who is a Christian? It all depends on the perspective used to answer that question. In the absence of any objective definition, we must resign ourselves to our various and very human perspectives on the matter.

How Many Christians Are in India?

Indian Christians often bristle when discussing the national census figures on religion because religion is a sensitive, heavily politicized subject in India. Presumably, this is why the government withheld the data on religion from the 2011 census for so long. *The Wall Street Journal* expressed the frustration of many when, in 2015, it published an article entitled "Where are India's 2011 Census Figures on Religion?"[4]

In 2016 the figures from the 2011 census finally became available, and the percentage of Christians was at 2.3 percent once again, meaning there are around 28 million Christians in the nation. By virtually all accounts, that number is too low. Pew Research estimates the percentage of Christians in India at 2.5 percent while noting that some "identify as Hindu when completing official forms."[5]

The World Christian Database—considered by many academicians to be the most reliable source of world religion statistics—estimates the percentage of Christians to be 4.9 percent, meaning there are roughly 65 million Christians in India.[6] The respected Association of Religion Data Archives (ARDA)—headed by sociologist Roger Finke—estimates India's Christian population to be 4.68 percent.[7]

Is Christianity growing in India? Not according to the last six

---

4. Authored by Joanna Sugden and Shanoor Seervai, January 9, 2015. See http://blogs.wsj.com/indiarealtime/2015/01/09/where-are-indias-census-figures-on-religion.

5. Conrad Hackett, "By 2050, India to Have World's Largest Populations of Hindus and Muslims," Pew Research Center, April 21, 2015, http://www.pewresearch.org/fact-tank/2015/04/21/by-2050-india-to-have-worlds-largest-populations-of-hindus-and-muslims.

6. Center for the Study of Global Christianity, Gordon Conwell Theological Seminary, "Christianity in its Global Context, 1970–2020: Society, Religion, and Mission," June 2013, http://www.gordonconwell.edu/resources/documents/1ChristianityinitsGlobal Context.pdf, p. 38.

7. See the profile on India at http://www.thearda.com/internationalData/countries/Country_108_1.asp.

censuses. In 1961, Christians were at 2.44 percent. In 1971, that number increased to 2.6 percent. In 1981, it was back to 2.43 percent. In 1991, it went further down to 2.34 percent. In 2001, the number was unchanged at 2.34 percent.[8] In 2011 it was at 2.30.[9]

Furthermore, recent growth rates of the overall population (23.79 percent) have exceeded the growth rate of Christians (16.89 percent), leading Christian scholars to search for a silver lining:

> This [gradual percentage decline of Christianity in India] is not a source of discouragement. On the contrary. Many find inspiration in the fact that their situation is similar to that of the earliest and most dynamic foundational Christian communities around Palestine in the first century CE.[10]

Robert Frykenberg points out a silver lining of his own. He cites the World Christian Database figures, and points out that if these numbers are to be trusted, then India has more Christians than any Western European country, with the exception of Germany. He writes, "As such, India has the seventh largest Christian population in the world."[11]

Indeed, Christianity is the third largest religion in India. This has been the case for many decades, and will, no doubt, continue for decades to come. Only Hinduism (80 percent) and Islam (14 percent) are larger, whereas Sikhism (1.7 percent), Buddhism (.7 percent), and Jainism (.4 percent) are smaller. It would, therefore, seem appropriate that any university course

---

8. See Sugden and Seervai, cited above.
9. See the 2011 Census results for religion, located at: http://www.censusindia.gov.in/2011census/C-01.html.
10. Leonard Fernando and G. Gispert-Sauch, *Christianity in India: Two Thousand Years of Faith* (London: Penguin, 2004), xiv. The growth rates mentioned are from 1981 to 1991. See p. xiii.
11. Frykenberg, *Christianity in India*, vi–vii.

on Indian religions should offer at least a few lectures on Christianity.[12]

A General Typology for Understanding the Indian Church

As noted in the previous chapter, Christianity came to India in the early centuries after Christ, possibly even during apostolic times. From early on in Indian church history, those Christians identified with the apostle Thomas, and continue to do so. Indeed, it is common for many Indian Christians—Orthodox, Catholic, and Protestant—to take great pride in calling themselves Thomas Christians, descendants of the labors of the great apostle, and the missionaries who traveled to India in his wake. In India, the Thomas Christians are typically referred to as "Nasranis"—a term that probably stems from Jesus's hometown of Nazareth. While there are many different denominations that identify with St. Thomas, the different communities are united by this larger, umbrella term "Nasranis," which in India connotes, specifically, Syrian Christians.

The earliest missionaries to India established churches that became the seedbed for India's Orthodox family of churches. The Catholic Church arrived in the late-fifteenth century and grew by grafting Orthodox Christians into the Catholic fold, sometimes by choice, sometimes under coercion. The Protestant movements began in 1706, with the Lutheran missionaries Bartholomaus Ziegenbalg and Henrich Plütschau, who set up a mission at Tranquebar, in modern-day Tamil Nadu.

Thus, the most common typology for understanding

---

12. For statistics on Religion in India, see http://www.censusindia.gov.in/2011census/C-01.html.

Christianity—not just in India, but in church history generally—is this: Orthodox, Roman Catholic, and Protestant. Globally, the Roman Catholic Church is the largest denomination, representing about half of the world's Christians. Protestantism—a very general and messy umbrella term for thousands of denominations that are neither Catholic nor Orthodox—accounts for about 40 percent of the world's Christians. And Orthodoxy accounts for approximately 10 percent of global Christianity. Incidentally, Indian Christianity is probably not too far off of that measurement. Specialist Rowena Robinson estimates that Catholics comprise nearly half (47%) of India's Christians, Protestants account for about 40 percent, and Orthodox Christians comprise about 7 percent. She labels the remaining 6 percent as "indigenous sects"—groups that separated from their mother churches in the West, whether Orthodox or Protestant. It is not altogether clear, however, what Robinson means by "indigenous sects" since many Indian Protestant groups consider themselves fully indigenized, without any major connections to the West.[13]

It is very difficult to know with any certainty what percentage of India's Christians are Orthodox, Roman Catholic, or Protestant. The reasons for this are obvious: estimates of Christianity in India vary significantly, from 25 to 65 million. And while the more established and hierarchical Indian denominations keep relatively good membership statistics, there are many, many Christian denominations, movements, and house-church fellowships that do not. How does one count Pentecostals in India? It is an impossible task, as new Pentecostal fellowships are created and divided with regularity. Many of the Christian movements of India are freewheeling, spontaneous, disconnected from other groups,

---

13. Rowena Robinson, *Christians of India* (Thousand Oaks: Sage, 2003), 28.

comprising voiceless Dalits, and grassroots-oriented. This bottom-up type of Christianity (as opposed to hierarchically arranged groups) is common in India. These are groups that rarely, if ever, count their memberships. In fact, in their view, keeping tight statistics on church membership would put limitations on the unpredictable work of the Holy Spirit. Many of these groups are little more than local family-like fellowships, meeting faithfully with people they have known and loved for years. Some meet clandestinely. Many churches in India are fervent in their congregational autonomy, as with many Christians across the world. They are an independent group of Christians who have no need to connect with a larger denomination. They are isolated in principle.

Nevertheless, with all that being said, we could venture an estimate of how many Christians are in India, and from what general denominations:

Christians in India (approximately 45 million):

- Roman Catholic: 20–25 million
- Protestant: 16–25 million
- Orthodox: 4–6 million

The categories for Catholic and Orthodox are rather straightforward. The Roman Catholic Church functions according to three major rites in India: Latin, East Syrian, and West Syrian. The Orthodox Church in India has two major groupings: Malankara Orthodox Syrian and (Jacobite) Syrian Orthodox. There are several other small Orthodox groups, but these two are, by far, the largest. The Protestant churches are numerous and varied. In order to make sense of the complexity of Protestantism in India, we have tried to develop a sensible typology using the following schema:

- Historic Protestant (also known as Mainline or Oldline)
- Mar Thoma
- Evangelical Protestant
- Pentecostal

Naturally, there is some overlap, as is the case with Protestants all over the world. For example, Evangelicalism and Pentecostalism can appear virtually indistinguishable to the non-specialist.

The Roman Catholic Church in India

The Roman Catholic Church estimates its membership in India to be around 20 million, or, about 1.6 percent of the nation's population.[14] Projections for 2050 are that it will be 26 million strong, placing India in the top 20 Catholic nations in the world, above former Catholic stronghold, Germany.[15] This is likely a conservative estimate, given the widespread belief that statistics for Christianity in India are muted.

The Catholic Church is well-organized in India. While it "upholds the universal authority of the Pope of Rome over the Christian world," it is overseen by the Catholic Bishops' Conference of India (CBCI), based in New Delhi.[16] The CBCI is the umbrella for the church in all three of its distinct rites in India: the Latin Church, the Syro-Malabar Church, and the Syro-Malankara Church. Each of these three rites has its own respective episcopal body (or, synod). The three churches are in fellowship with one another in spite of having unique

---

14. Telesphore Placidus Cardinal Toppo, "Catholic Bishop's Conference of India," in *The Oxford Encyclopaedia of South Asian Christianity* (Oxford: Oxford University Press, 2012), 134. See also http://www.catholic-hierarchy.org/country/sc1.html.
15. John Allen Jr., *The Future Church: How Ten Trends are Revolutionizing the Catholic Church* (New York: Doubleday, 2009), 51.
16. Fernando and Gispert-Sauch, *Christianity in India*, 56.

histories. They are allowed significant leeway in the way they practice the faith, especially when it comes to liturgy. By far, the largest is the Latin rite, but the other two are robust and healthy, even if much smaller. The Syro-Malabar rite has four to five million members while the Syro-Malankara rite claims roughly half a million members.[17]

Syro-Malabar Catholic Church

With over four million members, the Syro-Malabar Catholic Church is either the largest or second largest (after the Ukrainian Greek Catholic Church) of the 22 Eastern Catholic Churches in full communion with the Roman Catholic Pope.[18] They consider themselves Saint Thomas Christians, or, Nasranis. The Syro-Malabar Christians are the ones "who either did not share in the Coonan Cross revolt of 1653 or afterwards returned to Roman obedience."[19] The official name of the church reinforces the three pillars of their identity: they are Syrian, from Malabar (modern Kerala), and are Roman Catholic. They follow the East Syrian rite (sometimes known as "Chaldean") liturgy, which has an illustrious past due to its being rooted in the important, ancient Christian city of Edessa—home to one of the earliest forms of Christianity in the world. This East Syrian rite liturgy comes from the liturgy of the Assyrian Church of the East, historically known as the Nestorian church. They hold on to some very ancient practices, such as facing east during worship, stopping for prayer seven times per day, and preserving the Aramaic term for holy

17. For church statistics, see http://www.syromalabarchurch.in/syro-malabar-church.php (for Syro-Malabar) and http://www.cnewa.org/source-images/Roberson-eastcath-statistics/eastcatholic-stat12.pdf (for Syro-Malankara).
18. See http://www.cnewa.org/source-images/Roberson-eastcath-statistics/eastcatholic-stat12.pdf.
19. C. B. Firth, *An Introduction to Indian Church History* (Delhi: ISPCK, 2005), 227–28.

Eucharist: *Qurbana.* Like other early Christian traditions, there are echoes of a Jewish background, such as the liturgical day beginning in the evening (at six), and a style of music that sounds more like chanting than singing.[20]

One of the most important Syro-Malabar scholars of recent memory, Father Placid Podipara (1899–1985), is said to be the originator of the oft-repeated description of the Syro-Malabar Catholic Church as being "Catholic in faith, Indian in culture, and Oriental [meaning East Syrian] in liturgy."[21] With nearly 40,000 members of religious orders, 8,000 educational and charitable institutions, and 55,000 baptisms a year, this impressive church is poised for future growth.[22] Along with the other Thomas Christians, they will, undoubtedly, continue the disproportionately high level of influence on the Indian subcontinent that they have enjoyed for centuries.

Syro-Malankara Catholic Church

At half a million members, the Syro-Malankara Catholic Church is the smallest of the three Indian Catholic churches. It follows the Western Syrian rite liturgy, which has roots in the Antiochian tradition, historically known as a monophysitic church.[23] It is a more recent church, established only in 1930, after a series of disagreements culminated in their breaking from one of the many Indian Orthodox churches. Some of their clergy turned towards Rome and were warmly accepted. The church is flourishing today. In 2005, Pope John Paul II raised

---

20. For recordings of Syro-Malabar prayers, see http://www.nasranifoundation.org/liturgyofhours/malayalam.
21. See a biography of Father Placid at website for the Nasrani Foundation: http://www.nasranifoundation.org/articles/FrPlacidPodipara.html.
22. See church statistics at http://www.syromalabarchurch.in/syro-malabar-church-at-a-glance.php.
23. See Aidan Nichols, *Rome and the Eastern Churches* (San Francisco: Ignatius Press, 2010), 128–29.

the church to the rank of a Major Archiepiscopal, alongside the Ukrainian Greek Catholic, Syro-Malabar, and Romanian Greek Catholic churches. Although ultimately under the Roman pontiff, each of these churches is permitted a significant degree of autonomy.

The word *Malankara* (known today as *Maliankara*) is the name of the village in Kerala where it is thought Thomas the apostle first landed in AD 52. The Thomas Christians are believed to have been completely united until the arrival of the Portuguese in 1498. With the imposition of Latin practices in the church, a disastrous number of splits and offshoots occurred throughout the centuries. The Syro-Malankara Catholic Church is the result of one of those splits, although it is unique in that it was an Orthodox church that connected itself to Rome relatively recently. Based in Kerala's capital city, Trivandrum (officially Thiruvananthapuram), the church has seen dynamic growth in its short lifespan.

The current head of the Syro-Malankara Catholic Church is Archbishop Baselios Cleemis, a major figure in Indian Christianity today. In 2012, he was appointed cardinal by Pope Benedict, and in 2014, was elected as the President of the Catholic Bishops' Conference of India.[24] Another important figure associated with the church is the famous British Benedictine monk Bede Griffiths, who was a leading figure in the field of interreligious dialogue. Griffiths became well-known in the West for his work in establishing the Kurisumala Ashram in Kerala in 1958.[25]

---

24. See "Mar Baselios Cleemis is Cardinal," *The Hindu*, October 25, 2012, http://www.thehindu.com/news/international/mar-baselios-cleemis-is-cardinal/ article4027832.ece.
25. On Griffiths, see http://tinyurl.com/Griffiths-Kurisumala. See also Jessica Richard, "Kurisumala," *The Oxford Encyclopaedia of South Asian Christianity*, 385–86.

The Impact of India's Roman Catholic Church

The Catholic Church in India is currently organized into 168 dioceses containing roughly 10,000 parishes, and those numbers are growing steadily.[26] Of India's dioceses, 131 of them are Latin, 29 are Syro-Malabar, and 8 are Syro-Malankara. The church is divided into 30 Ecclesiastical Provinces with Metropolitan Archbishops serving as overseers. The church has five cardinals and around 250 bishops. Overall, the Catholic Church in India has about 125,000 "religious" men and women. That number includes about 25,000 priests (both diocesan and religious) as well as members of religious orders, both male (around 20,000) and female (around 80,000). Importantly, India is home to the largest national Jesuit order in the world, with around 4,000 active members.[27] The Indian Jesuits are a force to be reckoned with, both within India and in the Catholic Church.

One might be tempted to think the Indian church must be overstocked with priests, but the reality is that it needs many more, as they often move abroad for greater opportunities in the West. For example, in 2001, there were 39 priests from India working in one Italian diocese alone.[28] There are over 800 Indian priests serving in the United States.[29] India has become one of the world's top exporters of priests.

The Catholic Church in India is associated with education

---

26. For the most updated source for statistics and information related to the Roman Catholic Church in India, see the website for the Catholic Bishops' Conference of India: http://cbci.in. See also the website for the (Latin) Conference of Catholic Bishops in India: http://ccbi.in.

27. See Christopher Joseph, "Religious in South Asia adjust to demographic changes," *UCAnews.com*, July 24, 2015. See also http://www.catholic-hierarchy.org/country/sc1.html.

28. Allen Jr., *The Future Church*, 45.

29. Laurie Goodstein, "India, an Exporter of Priests, May Keep Them," *New York Times*, Dec. 29, 2008, www.nytimes.com/2008/12/30/us/30priest.html?pagewanted=all&_r=0.

and charity works. One immediately thinks of Mother Teresa's famous "Missionaries of Charity" in Calcutta. For millions of Indians, however, the Catholic Church is best known for its stellar academic institutions. The church operates roughly 10,000 primary schools and 5,000 secondary schools. Less than a quarter of these students are Catholic. Over half of them are Hindu and nearly 10 percent are Muslim.[30] Catholic colleges and universities are respected in India; gaining admission to the most prestigious ones is a coveted achievement. As in other places in the world, Catholic institutions of higher education are associated with excellence, especially the famed Jesuit institutions.

India's Catholic Church is young and vibrant. It is reaching out with surprising success in its evangelization efforts—in spite of a broad anti-conversion mood in India that has accelerated in recent years during the return to power of the ultra-nationalist BJP (Bharatiya Janata Party). It is not fair to state that anti-conversion is exclusively the domain of the BJP. Attempting to convert people from one faith to another is problematic in India, and became even more taboo after independence from Britain in 1947. When conversion does occur, there will likely be wretched consequences: social stigma, family turmoil, and even violence. Thus, the anti-conversion movements are at least as strong as the evangelistic movements in India, whether from Muslims or from Christians. Sometimes, the anti-conversion movements come across as

---

30. Judith Chapman, Sue McNamara, Michael Reiss, Yusef Waghid, *International Handbook of Learning, Teaching and Leading in Faith-Based Schools* (New York: Springer, 2014), 606. On August 1, 2015, I received an email from Father Joseph Manipadam at the Commission for Education and Culture, estimating the total number of Catholic educational institutions in India to be 15,168. This includes medical colleges, universities, professional colleges, degree colleges, junior colleges, high schools, middle schools, primary schools, pre-primary schools, schools for special children, and vocational/technical schools. He stated that seminaries are not in his department, and are therefore not included in the estimate.

paranoid, such as with the "love jihad" furor that has deepened tensions between Hindus and Muslims.[31]

News of reconversion campaigns is common in India today, stirring up charges similar to the old "rice Christians" accusations of a previous era.[32] This time around, however, the purportedly coerced conversions are happening to Christians rather than to Hindus, and they are being called "homecoming" ceremonies—celebrating the "return" of Christians to the Hindu fold. US President Obama weighed in on the brouhaha in a 2015 speech in India when he urged Indians to avoid splintering along religious lines. His speech was "widely interpreted as a message to Prime Minister Narendra Modi and his Hindu nationalist Bharatiya Janata Party."[33]

In spite of this rather well-documented pressure against Christian evangelization, the Catholic Church has seen impressive gains in northeast India. Today, there are over 1.5 million Catholics in the region only a century after the first Catholic missionaries began work there. In northeast India, fifty new Catholic priests are ordained each year, not nearly enough to keep pace with growth. In Arunachal Pradesh—the farthest northeast corner of India which shares a long and strategic border with China—the Catholic population has grown in only a few decades from nothing to 200,000.[34]

Collectively, the Catholic Church in India has made and is

31. Rupam Jain Nair and Frank Jack Daniel, "Love Jihad and Religious Conversion Polarise in Modi's India," *Reuters*, September 5, 2014, http://in.reuters.com/article/2014/09/04/india-religion-modi-idINKBN0GZ2OC20140904.

32. Jason Burke, "India investigates reports of mass 'reconversion' of Christians," *The Guardian*, January 29, 2015, http://www.theguardian.com/world/2015/jan/29/india-mass-reconversion-christians-hinduism.

33. Frank Jack Daniel and Roberta Rampton, "In parting shot, Obama prods India on religious freedom," *Reuters*, January 27, 2015, http://www.reuters.com/article/2015/01/27/us-india-obama-idUSKBN0L00FD20150127.

34. Allen Jr., *The Future Church*, 29, 351.

making a disproportionately high impact. One striking example is in the political realm, where Sonia Gandhi, a Roman Catholic from Italy, has led the Congress Party since 1998. She is the widow to Rajiv Gandhi—prime minister of India from 1984 to 1989. Rajiv's mother was Indira Gandhi, prime minister of India from 1966 to 1977, and again during 1980–1984. Indira Gandhi was the only child of India's beloved first prime minister, Jawaharlal Nehru. Sonia Gandhi is the unequivocal heiress to that unbroken line of influence of the Nehru-Gandhi dynasty. And her son, Rahul Gandhi, is clearly next in line for the mantle of leadership in the Congress Party. Sonia Gandhi is a very private person, but her time-tested power in Indian politics is without equal. It is unclear how big a role her Catholic faith plays in her life and decision-making, but when she first entered politics, there were suspicions that she would be susceptible to Vatican influence.[35] Those suspicions still raise their heads in the media.

In spite of all of her political clout, the greatest impact India's Catholic Church has made came not through the politics of Sonia Gandhi, but through a diminutive nun working in the slums of Calcutta. Mother Teresa (1910–97), India's most beloved Catholic, continues to inspire people all over the world through her amazing commitment to the poorest of the poor. While originally from the Balkans, in modern-day Macedonia, she moved to India at the age of 19 and served there nearly 70 years, until her death in 1997. She was only the second private citizen to receive a state funeral in India's history, the first being Mahatma Gandhi. Indeed, the same carriage that transported Gandhi's remains carried hers.[36]

---

35. Ibid., 352.
36. Barbara Crossette, "In Great Pomp, Calcutta Buries A Modest Nun," *New York Times*, September 13, 1997, http://www.nytimes.com/1997/09/13/world/in-great-pomp-calcutta-buries-a-modest-nun.html.

While Sonia Gandhi and Mother Teresa were foreign-born, India itself has produced numerous noteworthy Catholics in recent memory. Cardinal Ivan Dias has been a prominent figure in the Roman Catholic Church for decades, and between 2006 and 2011, he headed the Congregation for the Evangelization of Peoples. According to Vatican insider John Allen Jr., his name was "mentioned prominently" alongside Ratzinger (Pope Benedict) and Bergoglio (Pope Francis) in 2005.[37]

While Cardinal Dias is known for his staunchly conservative views, there are other leading Indian Catholics who lean left of center, especially when it comes to interreligious issues. In 2014, Indian Jesuit Michael Amaladoss was investigated by the Vatican for charges of religious pluralism. Jacques Dupuis, a Belgian Jesuit who spent most of his career in India, was censured in 1998 over his writings on Christianity's relationship to other faiths. After hearing he was under investigation by the Congregation for the Doctrine of the Faith, he became severely distressed, having to recover in hospital. His health never rebounded and the investigation effectively ended his teaching and publishing career.[38]

Indian Catholics are also naturally attuned to the plight of the poor. They are strong advocates for the lower classes, as Dalits make up somewhere between 60 and 75 percent of India's Catholic population.[39] The church in India understands injustice and what it means to be desperately in need. And because of a fluency in English, Indian Catholics are well-positioned to reach the ears and pluck the consciences of Western Catholics. Distinguished Indian professor of religion

37. Allen Jr., The Future Church, 47.
38. See obituary by John Hooper, "Father Jacques Dupuis," The Guardian, January 12, 2005, http://www.theguardian.com/news/2005/jan/13/guardianobituaries.religion.
39. John Allen Jr., "India Is a Rising Catholic Power Too," National Catholic Reporter, November 25, 2009, http://ncronline.org/blogs/ncr-today/india-rising-catholic-power-too.

Felix Wilfred—a prolific scholar who is highly respected in the West—has opposed globalization in the staunchest of terms, arguing it punishes the poor and marginalized. Globalization and the free market "seem to be charged with the spirit of eugenics and the philosophy of the survival of the fittest."[40]

And while the Catholic Church is in a position to make an impact here, the fact is that they have room for improvement. India's first Dalit Catholic archbishop, Marampudi Joji of Hyderabad, has lamented that discrimination against Dalits is "very much practiced" in the Church. Joji has been described by John Allen Jr., as being an Indian Desmond Tutu. His leadership will be desperately needed as the church tries to overcome its innate tendency to marginalize the Dalit. The Indian Catholic Church has a less than stellar record on incorporating Dalit leadership. Only a very small percentage of the church's clergy are Dalits. In 2000, only six of 156 Catholic bishops in India were Dalits. Out of 12,500 priests, only 600 were Dalits. In the 1970s, some Catholic bishops complained to Prime Minister Indira Gandhi about the treatment of Dalits, and she chastised them, telling them to manage the problem in their own churches before complaining to her.[41]

Another issue that India's Catholics are well-positioned to lead is coping with the rise of radical Islam, and Christian–Muslim relations in general. Pew Research shows India's Muslim population to be third in the world, behind only behemoths Indonesia and Pakistan. In 2010, India's Muslim population was 177 million; by 2030, it will be 236 million. South Asian Islam is growing extremely rapidly. Of the four top Muslim nations of the world, South Asia claims three: India,

---

40. Felix Wilfred, "Church's Commitment to the Poor in the Age of Globalization," address delivered at the General Body Meeting of the Catholic Council of India in Bangalore, December 14–16, 1997, http://sedosmission.org/old/eng/wilfred1.html.

41. Allen Jr., *The Future Church*, 352, 373.

Pakistan, and Bangladesh.[42] As with Hindu–Muslim relations in India, however, there is also longstanding bad blood between India's Catholics and Muslims. It should be remembered that when the Catholics arrived to India in the late fifteenth century, they clashed violently with Muslims on the Malabar Coast. That episode is still remembered among Kerala's Muslim population. Nevertheless, no nation is better positioned than India to deal with radical Islam in the future. And, undoubtedly, India's Catholics will be a key part of that conversation.

On the issue of Christian ecumenism, India's Catholics are in for a challenge, as the Orthodox Christians have a grudge for all the sheep stealing that has taken place through the years, while the Evangelicals and Pentecostals often fail to see the Catholics as fully Christian. On a 2015 trip to Mumbai, journalist John Allen Jr. met with some Indian Pentecostals from a tribal background. Zealously evangelistic, yet routinely subjected to persecution by the culture around them, they spoke disparagingly of Catholics: "They're idol worshippers. There's really no difference between Catholics and Hindus, since both pray to idols, both drink, and both quarrel."[43]

In my own research, I have come across similar views from other Protestants. One of my interviewees, Manoj George, is a well-educated, 40-year-old Pentecostal who teaches at Focus India Theological College in Nilambur, Kerala. He is from a Roman Catholic background, but was dissatisfied with Catholicism because the church allowed his father to drink alcohol. Eventually, his father became an alcoholic, and the

---

42. Pew Research, "Table: Muslim Population Growth by Country," www.pewforum.org/2011/01/27/table-muslim-population-growth-by-country.
43. John Allen Jr., "India showcases the maddening complexity of religious persecution," *Crux*, July 25, 2015, http://www.cruxnow.com/faith/2015/07/25/india-showcases-the-maddening-complexity-of-religious-persecution.

church did little to discourage his alcohol consumption. Indeed, it was because of Pentecostalism's teetotalism stance that Manoj's mother encouraged him to start attending church services with three elderly ladies who reached out to him. She was afraid Manoj might turn out like her alcoholic husband. The rest of the family opposed his conversion; however, he became very involved to the point of becoming a pastor. When I asked Manoj about his conversion, he described the Catholicism of his youth thus:

> Mary was the hero. Jesus was secondary. Jesus was an infant. Ninety percent of their prayers go to Mary. Studying the Bible was the turning point. In Sunday School I came to know I'm a sinner. I did not know this stuff. When we began to study the Bible, we began to see a big problem. These other practices had no biblical precedent, this worshiping of idols. The Catholic people say it is not worship, but they do it. Catholics are encouraging a loose life: alcohol, smoking, drinking, all kinds of things. They don't encourage, but they don't take a strict line. Alcohol leads to loose living.[44]

Manoj George is typical of some of the more radical Protestants in India, who see Catholics and Hindus as two sides of the same coin. Catholics are perceived as being nearer to Hinduism than to Christianity.

The Orthodox Churches of India

The story of how the Orthodox churches came to be so fragmented is a very complicated one that very few non-Orthodox Christians can claim to fully understand. The story of how Orthodoxy came to India, however, is fairly straightforward. Orthodoxy came to India from Edessa (modern day Sanliurfa, Turkey)—one of the most important

---

44. Manoj George, interview with Dyron Daughrity, June 26, 2014, Nilambur, Kerala.

centers of Christianity in the early centuries of the faith. Edessa was in ancient Syria, which explains the strong connection between Syria and Indian Orthodoxy.

Tradition holds that an important Nestorian Christian merchant by the name of Thomas of Cana (or, Kanai Thoman) arrived in Kodungallur (or, Cranganore) in the year AD 345. He brought with him several hundred people, including priests and deacons and even a bishop. They were fleeing Persian persecution under Sasanian king Shapur II. They received protection from the king of Malabar, Cheraman Perumal. These Syrian refugees were granted a high caste status by the king. They quickly ran into some of the Thomas Christians who had lived in the region since the first century. Indian tradition holds that some of these Syrian Christians intermarried with the people around them—these are known as Northists. A smaller faction—known today as Southists—practiced endogamy. While the history is very patchy, it is generally assumed that the Syrian liturgy became standard among all south Indian Christians, thereby establishing Syrian Orthodox Christianity as normative on the subcontinent.[45]

Shortly after the arrival of the Portuguese in 1498, the Syrian Christians of South India began to fragment. The Catholic Church was at the height of its powers and was able to exert enough pressure to cause many Syrian Christians to join with them. There were strongholds of people that refused; those who stood firmly within Syrian Orthodoxy are the ancestors of the Indian Orthodox groups that still exist today.

Earlier in this chapter, we put forth an estimate for the number of Orthodox Christians living in India to be somewhere between four and six million souls, scattered among several

---

45. See Paul Joshua Bhakiaraj, "Thomas of Cana," in *The Oxford Encyclopaedia of South Asian Christianity*, 688.

denominations. By far, the largest of the Orthodox groups in India are the Syriac Orthodox Churches, which are today split into two distinct-but-related institutions: the Malankara Orthodox Syrian Church and the (Jacobite) Malankara Syrian Orthodox Church. The Jacobite faction received their name from a sixth-century Syrian leader named Jacobus Baradaeus.[46] This split is the source of much confusion, as some of the churches are "Syrian Orthodox" and some are "Orthodox Syrian."

In the grand scheme of Christianity, the Indian Orthodox churches are categorized as "Oriental Orthodox," which means they are in fellowship with the Coptic (Egypt), Ethiopian, Eritrean, Syriac, and Armenian Orthodox churches. And while these churches are each autocephalous, they regard the head of Egypt's Coptic Church—known to them as the Pope—as being "first among equals." There are between 80 and 100 million Oriental Orthodox Christians in the world. By far, the largest is the Ethiopian church, which has around 50 million members. The Oriental Orthodox churches split with mainline Orthodox Christianity in 451 at the Council of Chalcedon over christological issues. The Oriental Orthodox family is sometimes referred to as the Monophysite (one nature) or non-Chalcedonian churches. They are not in communion with the much larger Eastern Orthodox Churches (such as Greek and Russian), but ecumenical efforts are ongoing.

The two major Orthodox churches of India share the same theology and liturgy. They are both properly considered Oriental Orthodox churches. Where they disagree is on authority. Their division dates back to a major quarrel over leadership that took place in 1912. They repaired this division briefly in 1958, only to break apart again in 1975, after the

46. See Philip Jenkins, *The Lost History of Christianity* (New York: HarperOne, 2008), x.

Indian Supreme Court made a decision having to do with the control of church property. Reunification is hoped for by some, but is not expected any time soon.

It is important to note that both churches ascribe great spiritual authority to the Syriac Orthodox Patriarch of Antioch. However, only one, the Jacobites, recognize the *supreme* authority of the Antiochian Patriarch. In fact, the Jacobites excommunicated the Malankara Orthodox Syrian leader, known as Catholicos, in 1975, which is where the situation still stands.[47]

The 1912 split led to two separate hierarchies. One, the Malankara Orthodox Syrian Church, is based in Kottayam, Kerala. The other—the (Jacobite) Syrian Orthodox Church—has a Catholicos of its own, but he is subordinate to the traditional patriarchate of Antioch. This Antioch (modern-day Antakya) is the famous biblical city now located in Turkey. Due to frequent persecution from various empires and theological squabbles with other Christians, this Antiochian Patriarchate's headquarters was moved to Damascus, Syria. Recent instability in Syria has caused the church headquarters to move again—albeit temporarily—to Beirut, Lebanon.[48]

There are three other small Indian denominations that could be described as Syrian Orthodox in some ways, but in other ways are considered outside the fold. First is the Malabar Independent Syrian church, based in Kerala. This small, one-diocese church is connected to the Syrian churches, but broke

---

47. For more on the 1912 and 1975 splits, see John Fenwick, "India, Syrian Christianity in South," in *The Blackwell Dictionary of Eastern Christianity,* ed. Ken Parry et al. (Oxford: Blackwell, 2001), 254.

48. See Lucas Van Rompay, "With Wisdom and Courage, New Syriac Orthodox Patriarch Reaffirms the Church's Commitment to Syria," *ISLAMiCommentary,* May 20, 2014, http://islamicommentary.org/2014/05/with-wisdom-and-courage-new-syriac-orthodox-patriarch-reaffirms-the-churchs-commitment-to-syria.

away in 1772 over issues of authority. Estimates for membership range between 10,000 and 35,000.[49]

East Syriac (Chaldean)		West Syriac (Antiochian)				
Assyrian Church	Catholic Communion		Independent (Reformed)	Independent	Oriental Orthodox Communion	
Chaldean Syrian Church (1814)	Syro-Malabar Catholic Church (1665)	Syro-Malankara Catholic Church (1930)	Malankara Mar Thoma Syrian Church (Mar Thoma Church) (1876)	Malabar Independent Syrian Church (Thozhiyoor Church) (1771)	Malankara Orthodox Syrian Church (Indian Orthodox Church)	Malankara Jacobite Syrian Church (Syriac Orthodox Church)

St. Thomas Christian groups chart (Created by Daniel Spencer)

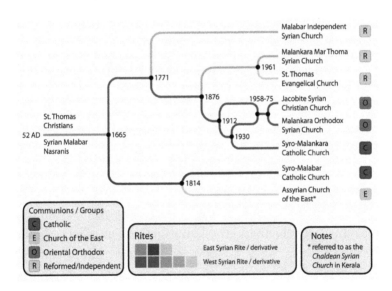

Public domain: https://upload.wikimedia.org/wikipedia/commons/thumb/d/de/St_Thomas_Christians_divisions.svg/2000px-St_Thomas_Christians_divisions.svg.png.

---

49. Fenwick, "India, Syrian Christianity in South," 255.

Second, there are the Nestorians. What most Westerners call the Nestorian Church is, rather, known in India as the Chaldean Syrian Church. It is an archbishopric in the larger Christian denomination known formally as the Assyrian Church of the East, or Church of the East. Chaldea is an historical, geographic term roughly equivalent to the modern-day nation of Iraq. Throughout history, this region was known variously as Mesopotamia, Assyria, and Babylonia. The church claims 30,000 members and is based in the city of Thrissur, Kerala.[50]

The third church that is occasionally grouped within Syrian Orthodoxy in India is the Mar Thoma church. It will be discussed below in the section on Protestantism because it is in communion with the global Anglican family of churches. Its liturgy is (West) Syrian, but its theology has been impacted quite heavily by European Protestant ideals.[51]

Indian Orthodoxy, An Indigenous Religion?

In India, the Christian religion is often associated with the Western world. However, a good argument can be made that Orthodox Christianity is every bit as Indian as Hinduism—a faith which probably came from Persia. Granted, the Persians beat St. Thomas to the subcontinent. But with Christianity's heritage in India going back at least 1700 years, and quite possibly two millennia, it makes little sense to refer to Syrian Orthodoxy as being a "Western" religion, as "Western" Christianity did not take root in India until the arrival of the Portuguese in 1498. And since Hinduism most likely originates with the Aryans in Persia, must it be considered a "Western"

---

50. See Mar Aprem, "Chaldean Church/Church of the East in India," *The Oxford Encyclopaedia of South Asian Christianity*, 147.
51. There are very small numbers of Armenian, Greek, and Russian Orthodox Christians in India, but numbers are not significant enough to elicit a discussion here. They are not directly connected to Syrian Christianity and are not considered mission churches.

faith? It would be beside the point to mention that Christianity has a much older presence in India than Islam, which arrived to India in the seventh century—again, from the West.

Ironically, when the Westerners first arrived in India, they considered the Syrian Christians to be too Indian, due partly to their caste practices. Nasranis believe that when Thomas came to their land, he converted 32 Brahmin families. While these families initially may have lost their caste status due to their conversion, they gained it back through the centuries. Over time, the Nasranis became quite respectable, occupying a mid-level in the overall caste structure. By no means did the Syrian Christians discard their Indian culture when they converted.

Rather, the Portuguese—and later, the British—routinely noticed just how similar the Nasranis were to caste-conscious Hindus: in food preparation, dietary and dining restrictions, alcohol taboos, occupations, belief in horoscopes, marriage and purification rituals, rites of passage, and distance pollution (from low castes). One scholar writes, "Nowhere else in India did such a complex and refined system of ritual pollution exist: a person from the lowest caste was not only untouchable but unapproachable in Kerala."[52] Indeed, the Thomas Christians still have the reputation of being highly conscious of caste, especially when it comes to marriage and personal contact. Syrian Christians rarely evangelize those outside their community, especially if those others are from low castes. In an interview I conducted with a Western-educated Dalit woman from Pondicherry, she stated boldly, "Syrians are Brahmanical in their thinking."[53]

---

52. George Joseph, "India, Syrian Christian Community," *The Blackwell Dictionary of Eastern Christianity*, eds. Ken Parry et al. (Oxford: Blackwell, 2001), 249.
53. Pearly Walter, interview with Dyron Daughrity, November 7, 2013, Busan, South Korea. Walter did point out that there are exceptions to this generalization, such as Bishop Coorilos of Kerala.

Orthodox Theological Seminary, Kottayam

In 2014, I (Daughrity) conducted some very helpful interviews with students and faculty at the Orthodox Theological Seminary (OTS) in Kottayam. These interviews provided contextual, on-the-ground insight into Indian Orthodoxy, particularly through the eyes of its 170 students; most of them were working on a BD, Bachelor of Divinity.

Known locally as the Old Seminary, OTS was established in 1815. This seminary is the official ministry training center for the Malankara Orthodox Syrian Church. Before the seminary was created, ministry training was done informally, "centered around certain revered senior priests (Malpans) who were scholars of Syriac language and liturgy."[54]

I sat with Dr. Jacob Kurian, who served as principal from 2012 to 2015. The first matter he brought up was that St. Thomas probably evangelized Jews first when he arrived in India. Repeatedly, he emphasized the Jewish background of the Nasranis. He disagreed with the idea that Thomas evangelized Brahmins, for, in his view, "There were probably not Brahmins until the fourth century." Thus, St. Thomas converts must have been Jews and Dravidians. South India had very few Aryans, or, "Sanskrit people," in those days. Dr. Kurian was touching on a very sensitive topic in India: to whom does South India belong—the Aryans or the Dravidians? In his mind, it was important to understand the context of South India throughout history in order to properly understand how Christianity took root.

After a brief visit, Dr. Kurian gave us access to a few faculty members and a group of students, who were happy to share

---

54. See Joseph Zachariah, "Orthodox Theological Seminary, Kottayam, Kerala," *The Oxford Encyclopaedia of South Asian Christianity*, 513.

their perspectives on life in the seminary and on Indian Christianity.

My interviewees were eager to point out that Kottayam is the cultural heart of Kerala culture—which is seen by everyone in India as being advanced, developed, and generally ahead of the curve in virtually everything. The Malayalam script is from Kottayam. The British missionaries from the Church Mission Society (CMS) immediately took notice of Kottayam's importance and began teaching English and undertook translation work there. These English missionaries were responsible for erecting the seminary building, which in 2015, celebrated 200 years.

Early in the interview, the topic of division in the church came up: Orthodox Syrian versus Jacobite Syrian Orthodox. "We will respect the Patriarch [of Antioch], but we don't have to put ourselves under his rule." In their view, the split happened largely because of problems arising from British interference. However, they pointed out, ecclesial fragmentation seems to be in the fiber of Christian India. Rampant division is not unique to Orthodoxy; indeed, the Lutherans have at least eleven different denominations in India while the Mennonites have nine.

My interview seemed to confirm the notion that the Nasranis are not keen on evangelism much at all. One said, "Our basic idea is not conversion, rather to give people some aid. We have to share the love of Christ." The goal is to "go to those people who are in need," such as HIV patients and those with leprosy. In their minds, the Protestants tend to think in terms of soap, soup, and salvation. The Pentecostals are focused on converting people. The Nasranis do not share this desire to convert others.

When asked about the Great Commission—to go out into

the world and baptize others—they conceded that if someone wants to join, they can. But overt evangelism "has led to so much persecution and misunderstanding." One faculty member, who had taught there for 37 years, put it pointedly: "We do not condemn other religions." Our Orthodox interviewees described themselves as being "Christian in faith, Hindu in culture, and Oriental in worship." They respect religious pluralism. The Orthodox Christians are known to have remained rather insular for hundreds of years in India. They take a "live and let live" approach, surrounded by non-Christians, and having virtually no conflict with them.

The interview was well under way before I realized that most of the students at the table were not from an Orthodox background. In fact, only 10 of the 170 students are Orthodox. This was astonishing, and illustrated the radically ecumenical outlook of the Nasranis. When I asked why there were only 10 Orthodox students, the response was that the Orthodox do not engage the youth very well. They said the younger generations are not attracted to a form of Christianity where they just "have to sit there for an hour." They contrasted this lackluster response with the Nasrani churches in the United States, especially in Florida, where their churches are thriving because the youth are "allowed to worship according to younger methods."

The Orthodox students brought up the need for revival in their churches, which is beginning to happen—at least among the youth. They claim it is something of a chore to sit through an entire Syrian liturgy. This is why the Pentecostal movement is making such a big impact among virtually all churches in India. Its revivalist services are precisely what the youth are craving. One of the interviewees is Mennonite, and freely admitted worshiping at the Pentecostal churches. Indeed,

"Many of the youth are migrating to other churches, especially charismatic ones." However, they have reservations about some of the more illustrious Pentecostal pastors, such as Paul Thangiah, an Assembly of God pastor in Bangalore. "Three people carry his Bible to the pulpit. People polish his shoes. It is all money. He is the one who came to be served."

The topic of the charismatic movement stirred great interest. They claimed the mainline churches are hemorrhaging due to the great gains made by the charismatic movement. One Baptist interviewee from Nagaland said even the Baptists are taking a hit from the growth of Pentecostal churches. Now, the Baptists are even discussing the possibility of speaking in tongues. Another stated, "The charismatic movement is really finding its way into Manipur."

I asked them why not simply resign oneself to the Pentecostal movement and join them. One retorted, "My church would be very offended. They believe themselves to be a strict Presbyterian church. It has to do with culture. It is not really a doctrinal problem. We dance around the fire and all those things. This form of worship is in our blood, but we would be offended to be called a Pentecostal." The Baptist students agreed heartily with this assessment.

When the sensitive issue of gender came up, the general consensus was that women and girls are still second-class citizens, even though progress has been made in some quarters. In Orthodoxy, women are raising their voices. Equality is being discussed. The greater problem has to do with caste, however, especially in the Orthodox churches: "Syrians do not want to identify with the low castes in marriage, and many other things." They claimed the Syrians focus little on the culture around them. They do not study the other religions at all. They remain aloof from non-Orthodox people. Seemingly unfazed by me being an American, near the end of the interview, we got on the topic of globalization, and they had few good words for the pernicious influence of Western ideas, which are "destroying some of the cherished traditions of the past." The youth are fixated on how to be more like the West, and it is taking a toll on the identity of the church. I sensed ambivalence in the students, Orthodox and Protestant alike. They are drawn to Western currents, but they do not know how to resist the advance of Westernization. The youth, and apparently seminary students as well, respond very favorably to Western-style Pentecostalism. But there is an inner turmoil going on. In my view, the deeper questions have to do with identity. By embracing charismatic worship—clearly rooted in the West—it is feared they may leave their community's traditions in the past. This is a conflict that Orthodox Christians all over the world are facing in an era of globalization. It was fascinating to hear how this tension is playing out among Indian Protestants as well.

The Protestants of India

Protestantism in India is estimated to be around 40 percent of the Christian population. As discussed earlier in the chapter, the number of Protestants is probably in the ballpark of 16 to 25 million. It is a great challenge to make sense of the varieties of Protestantism, whether in India or anywhere else, for that matter. Nevertheless, the typology we have created for this book is the following, with estimates as to how many members each major grouping might have:

- Historic Protestant (also known as Mainline or Oldline): 8 million
- Mar Thoma: 1 million[55]

- Evangelical Protestant: 7 million
- Pentecostal: 5 million

Historic Protestantism in India

As discussed in chapter 1, Protestantism in India began with the impressive work of Lutheran missionaries Bartholomaus Ziegenbalg and Henrich Plütschau, at the beginning of the eighteenth century. The Lutherans have maintained a presence in India ever since. Today, in India, the Lutheran church is organized into eleven denominational bodies, with a combined membership of around two million.[56] One Lutheran educational institution in India—Gurukul Lutheran Theological College—deserves mention. It is considered one of India's best Protestant seminaries.

The Methodist Church arrived in India in 1817, with the British Wesleyan Missionary Organization. The Methodist Church in India today claims 700,000 members.[57] They operate over 200 schools, 19 colleges, and 25 hospitals or health care centers.[58]

India's Presbyterian Church began in 1841 in the modern state of Meghalaya with two Welsh missionaries, Thomas Jones and his wife Anne.[59] The region was then known as the Khasi Hills. Today, the church claims around 1.3 million members, based mainly in the northeast states.[60]

---

55. The Mar Thoma Church website, http://marthoma.in/overview, claims 1.5 members. However, in an interview with the principal of Mar Thoma Syrian Theological Seminary, his estimate was 800,000 members.
56. For statistics for Lutheranism in India, see the Lutheran Forum, http://www.lutheranforum.org/extras/the-lutheran-churches-of-india.
57. See Global Ministries of the United Methodist Church, http://www.umcmission.org/Explore-Our-Work/Asia-and-Pacific/India.
58. See the World Council of Churches entry for the Methodist Church in India, https://www.oikoumene.org/en/member-churches/methodist-church-in-india.
59. Frykenberg, *Christianity in India*, 446.
60. See statistics for the Presbyterian Church of India at https://pcigenassembly 2012.wordpress.com / pci-assembly-2012.

The largest Protestant denomination in India is the Church of South India (CSI). The CSI is legendary in the Protestant world for being one of the most significant ecumenical church initiatives in history. What makes it important is that it was a union created out of episcopal and non-episcopal denominations. Today, it is basically considered the successor of the Anglican Church in India. However, when it was formed in 1947, it was not clear that it was destined to become so closely aligned with the Anglican way. The churches involved in the merger were from several different backgrounds: Congregationalists, Presbyterians, Reformed, Anglican, and Methodists. Today, the CSI has 21 dioceses and around four million members located in the South Indian states of Andhra Pradesh, Karnataka, Kerala, and Tamil Nadu. Central offices are in Chennai. It runs 2000 schools and 130 colleges.[61]

The Church of North India (CNI) is also a united church with a somewhat different history than the CSI. It came together in 1970 as a union of several traditions: Anglicans, Congregationalists, Presbyterians, Baptists, Methodists, Disciples of Christ, and Brethren churches, although some Brethren churches withdrew in 2006. Like the CSI, it is basically a successor to the Anglican Church in India. Although the geography of the denomination is huge—it covers all of India with the exception of the four CSI states—its membership is only about 1.5 million.[62] The CNI fully recognizes both infant baptism and believer's baptism, which is a slightly different policy from the CSI's recommendation of infant baptism for people born in Christian homes.

The CSI, CNI, and Mar Thoma churches are all in communion

---

61. See CSI International Resource Center at www.csimichigan.org/ChurchofSouth India.html.
62. See CNI church statistics at https://www.oikoumene.org/en/member-churches/church-of-north-india.

fellowship with one another, proving themselves to be among the most ecumenically-minded Christians in the world.

Aizawl Theological College, Mizoram

To get a sense of the conversations taking place in one of the historic Protestant seminaries, I visited Aizawl Theological College (ATC), located in Aizawl, Mizoram, in northeast India.[63] ATC is a Presbyterian college although it welcomes students from other denominational backgrounds. The college was founded in 1907 by Welsh missionaries in order to train Mizos for ministry. The college is affiliated to the Senate of Serampore College, meaning its degrees are widely recognized in India. A degree from a Serampore-affiliated college comes with a certain prestige in India. ATC trains around 160 students each year.[64]

Students at ATC are intensely interested in researching their own denominations. Virtually all of the students interviewed were studying aspects of their church, such as the history, ministry formation, theological education, and ecumenical initiatives. It is important to know that virtually all Christians in northeast India are from tribal backgrounds. They understand themselves as being from a particular tribe. Mizos, for example, are like a large family, making it impossible to be unknown in the community. They became Christians together.

In the interviews, the students were asked what their major challenges were in northeast India—as the vast majority of them are from there. They were united in their answer: corruption coming from Korea. "This phenomenon came up just four or five years ago and each night *every house* is

---

63. The visit took place in June 2014.
64. See H. Vanlalauva, "Aizawl Theological College, Aizawl, Mizoram," *The Oxford Encyclopaedia of South Asian Christianity*, 11.

watching the Korean shows. Teenagers are trying to make their faces white like South Koreans. Skin color is a big part of all of this." They repeatedly mentioned the affluence, dress, and style of Koreans. There was an obvious ambivalence. Korean culture is "intoxicating," but evidently, corrosive on their culture and values.

The story narrated to me was that the northeast is just now being exposed to globalization on a broad scale, due largely to an increasing prosperity that has allowed people to purchase televisions and access the internet. It is a new world for them, and there are no easy answers of how to respond. In my view, northeast India seems more Westernized than most other parts of India. This surely has to do with their strong connections to the British Isles and the United States. But as it was explained to me, the northeastern people are now admiring Korean culture more than Western culture. Koreans have all the enviable traits of the West, but they are also Asian, and northeast Indians can relate to them much more than to Western Caucasians.

Northeastern culture is breaking up. Drugs are rampant. Insurgencies keep people on edge. Media pulls people away from traditional ways. Suicide rates are rising. "People are getting so much access to outside ideas, leading to many problems." Skepticism of their own culture—and of Christianity—is growing. The church is a deeply revered institution in the northeast, but it can only do so much as traditional society shatters, new ideas are introduced daily, and the insular ways of the past evaporate.

I was struck by how little these students care about whether they are Baptist or Presbyterian—the two dominant denominations of the northeast. There is a genuinely ecumenical sense that people are far more associated with their tribe than with their tribe's denomination. And while each tribe is dealing with slightly different problems, in the northeast, there is a remarkable degree of unity in their realization that the past is fading. And they are struggling to maintain some sense of identity amidst profound cultural change. This is the issue that unifies all of the northeast tribal Christians. The church will, undoubtedly, play a key role in how these tribes adjust to a rapidly encroaching globalization. Indeed, at this point, the church may be the institution wherein their tribal cultures are best preserved.

Mar Thoma Syrian Church

The Mar Thoma Church emerged during the nineteenth century as a response to the teachings of several evangelical Anglican missionaries. Led by the clergyman Abraham Malpan, it was essentially a reform movement in India's Syrian church. Much like the Protestant Reformation three centuries before, it emphasized the following teachings: the liturgy should be translated into the local language—in this case, Malayalam, a stronger emphasis on Bible teaching, a downplaying of the role of saints, a more missional outlook, and a renewed commitment to purity in one's personal life and conduct. These reforms shook the Thomas churches to the core, resulting in schism.

The Mar Thoma Church is known for its massive gathering in Kerala each February, called the Maramon Convention. Begun in 1895, it is now one of the largest Christian gatherings in the world. Estimates for the number of attendees range from 150,000 to hundreds of thousands. It has attracted many distinguished speakers, such as the famous American

Methodist E. Stanley Jones and the Indian Christian mystic Sadhu Sunder Singh.[65]

While the Mar Thoma Church maintains a deep awareness of its St. Thomas heritage, today, it is known for its extremely ecumenical sensibility. The church has good relations with India's Orthodox Christians and is also a founding member of the World Council of Churches. The Mar Thoma Church is in fellowship with the worldwide Anglican Communion and even works with Pentecostal Christians at some levels.

Mar Thoma Syrian Theological Seminary, Kottayam

I interviewed the president of the seminary, Dr. Pothen, along with Dr. Mathew, a church history professor. Though unequivocally committed to their Mar Thoma denomination, they are extraordinarily charitable toward other churches. They offered the following perspective: "We are the right one, but we are all from the same root. But the other Orthodox churches would say the same thing."

The Mar Thoma Church has many members living in diaspora, such as in New York, Singapore, and Australia. Somehow, the church is able to hold this scattered flock together, in spite of big problems that have emerged in recent years: the lack of vitality among the youth, a crisis over how to keep the youth engaged, what to do about a liturgy that is viewed as irrelevant, and whether to bring technology and multimedia into the services.[66] These are familiar problems being faced by churches that esteem their history and

---

65. See Jesudas Athyal, "Maramon Convention," in *The Oxford Encyclopaedia of South Asian Christianity*, 430.

66. An excellent, scholarly article on how migration is impacting the Mar Thoma church is Prema Kurien, "The Impact of International Migration on Home Churches: The Mar Thoma Syrian Christian Church in India," in *Journal for the Scientific Study of Religion* 53:1 (March 2014): 109–29.

traditions. Upstart churches with little history do not have to deal with these issues. But in churches with a rich history—such as the Thomas Christian denominations of India—there has begun to emerge an enormous disconnect between generations. Older members esteem the liturgy and traditions primarily *because* they are ancient. Younger generations often do not share this high regard for the past. They look toward the future. The pace of change in India's old church traditions has accelerated so fast that the older and younger generations have little in common anymore.

The Syrian Christians are known to be high caste in India. However, Dalits and low caste people have joined the Mar Thoma church through the years. The interviewees explained, "Some Mar Thoma churches are Dalit churches. Mar Thoma does have some low caste clergy, members, and churches. We have more than 10,000 families in Karnataka from low caste backgrounds." In the Indian church, "caste issues are huge." And while the specific issues will vary from place to place, they can become "hostile," especially when it comes to marriage. And while the interviewees claimed "the pollution idea is completely wiped out" in the Mar Thoma churches, there is still discrimination. A very positive development is that Dalits are now getting educated, and they "can make good money." Some have been placed in high echelons of government. Nevertheless, as long as the caste system persists, there will be acrimony. Dr. Pothen made an interesting parallel:

> Dalits are proud of their identity. Just like American Blacks. Dalits are proud of their past; it was painful, but they are trying to come up. "Dalit" is not "crushed" anymore. Now the meaning has changed to "sons of the soil."[67]

67. The interviewees cited Bama Faustina Soosairaj as popularizing this understanding of Dalit. Bama, as she is known, is a contemporary Indian writer from a Roman Catholic

The interviewees provided very good insight into the Dalit situation, emphasizing that there is no monolithic Dalit experience. "The Dalit voices are disparate. For some the experience is not there at all. For some it is 'crushed.' And for others it is another type of voice altogether."

Evangelical Protestants in India

Evangelical Protestants in India include various Baptist groups, Brethren churches (such as Assemblies Jehovah Shammah and Indian Brethren), and the Seventh-day Adventists. According to the Baptist World Alliance statistics, there are 21 Baptist denominations in India, with a membership of nearly three million. Baptists have made great gains in the northeastern states of Mizoram, Meghalaya, Manipur, and especially Nagaland. They also have significant memberships in Odisha and Andhra Pradesh.[68] The Seventh-Day Adventists claim around 1.5 million members.[69] There are also many smaller evangelical fellowships in India, such as Evangelical Church of India, which has twelve dioceses and thirteen Bible schools or seminaries.[70]

Eastern Theological College, Assam

In order to understand an Indian Evangelical Protestant perspective, I conducted interviews at Eastern Theological College, a Baptist institution located in Jorhat, in the state of

background. Her novels and stories are written from a Dalit Christian subaltern perspective.

68. See global Baptist membership statistics at Baptist World Alliance, www.bwanet.org/about-us2/statistics.

69. For Seventh-Day Adventist statistics in India, see the "Office of Archives, Statistics, and Research," http://www.adventistdirectory.org/viewAdmField.aspx?AdmFieldID=SUD.

70. See the Evangelical Church of India website at www.ecionline.org/index.php?option=com_content&view=article&id=71&Itemid=517.

Assam. The college is affiliated to Serampore College and offers degrees as high as the Doctor of Ministry. There are around 20 faculty members. The college graduates around 80 students per year.

The first interview was with four faculty members.[71] I asked them to identify their challenges in Christian education. The issue of patriarchy came up immediately. "Women are not empowered. All the societies are patriarchal." Ordination for women has been permitted since 1992, though "women rarely serve as pastors."

Dr. Woba James, a very articulate historian on staff, pointed out what he thought to be "the chief challenge": the proliferation of theological schools. It brings down the value of theological education when inferior degrees from inferior schools are established constantly. These "unrecognized theological colleges . . . start today and close tomorrow. . . . There is no accountability." These so-called pastors receive a poor education and destroy ecumenicity through "sheep stealing." They start new churches and fledgling institutions at an alarming rate, with no regard to the local forms of Christianity already present.

I could not help but wonder whether these small theological colleges were, in fact, meeting a deep need in Christian India. These students need education, they need English skills, but they are not advanced enough in their education to gain admission to the Serampore-affiliated schools. Thus, they turn to these upstart independent theological colleges. Dr. James noted that "Kerala has over 1000 colleges."

Another problem identified is that Koreans are planting

---

71. Interview was conducted in June 2014. Faculty participants were: Rev. Dr. Akheto Semo (principal), Rev. Dr. Elungkiebe Zeilang, Rev. Dr. Woba James, and Rev. Dr. Narola Imchen.

churches all over India. They are "expert missionaries" with unlimited funds, but they are not known for their ecumenicity. (There are over 100 *Presbyterian* denominations in South Korea alone.) South Indians also come up to the northeast to establish new churches and schools. As a result, the delicate fabric of Christianity in the northeast gets tugged in various directions.

Dr. Elungkiebe claimed it was tribalism that presented the deepest challenge. This is an extremely poignant issue for the college because there are currently students from 44 different tribes studying there, out of the roughly 200 that inhabit northeast India. The problem with tribal affiliations is that they outshine the religious identity. For example, both the Nagas and the Kukis are Baptist, but violence ravaged their relationship in the 1990s. Hostility between tribes remains just underneath the surface. Although tensions may have cooled recently, "the next flashpoint is around the corner."

Another challenge confronting Eastern Theological College is that it is located in Assam, which is "a thoroughly Hinduized state." The Assamese are proudly Hindu—something the Western missionaries noticed, prompting the evangelization of the tribes in the surrounding regions. The Assamese people are leery of Christianity, including the seminary at Jorhat. They consider themselves to be truly Indian while the tribes are considered to be something different—more Chinese than Indian. Indeed, northeast missionaries are often sent to China because of their similar appearance. The northeastern tribes are fiercely protective of their land, thus, they are suspicious of the Indian government. Land protection is a crucial issue for the tribal peoples. For example, "Nagaland allows foreigners, but not Indians. Indians cannot buy land in parts of northeast India. They have to receive a special permit or a special visa to travel to Nagaland."

Many of the tribes of northeast India are strongly Christian today. They are missional, some of them even going overseas with the help of Korean or American funding. They are capable of producing excellent theologians as well, such as Dr. Wati Longchar, Dr. Taka Temjan, and Dr. Narola Imchen from Nagaland; Dr. K. Thanzauva, Dr. Hrangkuma, and Dr. R. L. Hnuni from Mizoram; Dr. O. L. Snaitang from Meghalaya; and Dr. Shimreingam Shimray from Manipur.

Dr. Woba James left me with an important insight. He pointed out that the very nature of identity is being shattered in northeast India today. Traditionally, the tribal peoples are very communitarian. They live, act, and believe together. However, with globalization has come individualism. Tribal people are not accustomed to living individualistically. This challenge, whether to be communitarian or individualistic, may be the most pressing one for tribals today and in the future.

My interview with 13 students at Eastern Theological College in Jorhat was equally fascinating. When asked about challenges they faced, the usual suspects were brought up: unhealthy competition between denominations, sheep stealing, women's role in the church, conflict between Serampore (too liberal) and non-Serampore (overly fundamentalistic) institutions, and the alarmingly rapid growth of charismatic Christianity. However, a few issues came up among the students that did not come up among faculty—among them Satanic worship and marriage.

I was surprised to hear about Satanic worship. Apparently it is a trend that began in Mizoram, but has spread to Nagaland and Meghalaya. These are Christian people, but for some reason they turn their attention toward Satan, thinking he will bless them. They are said to perform rituals such as bloodletting, and they hold worship gatherings in cemeteries. "This is one of the main issues going on right now. It is mainly a teenager issue. However, now even grandmothers are getting involved. It is growing very fast."

In northeast India in particular, and in India more generally, the centuries-old custom of arranged marriage is being challenged to the point that, according to one Naga student, "Very rarely does arranged marriage occur. There are still some parents who stick to arranged marriage. But parents are much more open now. Education has played a huge role. The northeast context is changing."

The female students emphasized how rapidly the culture and long-held social customs were changing. "Women are very much liberated now when it comes to marriage. Eloping is fairly common when there is a disagreement between children and parents. Elopement is also a cheaper alternative since the marriage simply occurs without a big show with invited guests."

The students also spoke up about other problems, such as drug addiction, prostitution, and the spread of AIDS. They regretfully acknowledged that secularization was arriving in northeast India. "Church attendance is declining. Activities are declining. Children are going against their parents. They are siding with their school teachers. And parents are washing their hands from their responsibility of training the children in Christian teaching."

On a more positive note, there are good things happening in the northeast of India. Tribes are realizing their unity as tribal peoples, rather than constantly fighting against each other. Christianity is actually uniting tribes under the banner of Christ. Christianity has made peaceful people out of headhunters. The old idea that India's northeast hill people are "savages" is completely gone now. And Christianity can take much credit for that transformation. There is a deep and abiding sense of gratitude toward those American and Scottish missionaries who came and gave their lives in the propagation of the gospel.

Pentecostalism in India

India's Pentecostal and charismatic churches have been going strong since the mid-to-late 1800s.[72] Today, there are many Pentecostal denominations in India, including the big ones such as the Assemblies of God, the Indian Pentecostal Church of God, and the Church of God. There are hundreds of smaller, independent denominations and groups, such as New Apostolic Church, New Life Fellowship, Manna Full Gospel, International Zion Assembly, Sharon Fellowship, New India Church of God, Philadelphia Fellowship, Soul Winning Church, Ceylon Pentecostal Mission, and many more.

Michael Bergunder, one of the foremost authorities on Indian Pentecostalism, estimates India's Pentecostal population in South India to be about 20 percent of the Protestant Christian population.[73] That number is in line with the estimates earlier in the chapter. According to Robert Frykenberg, the problem with counting Pentecostal memberships is that its churches are "inherently fissiparous" and have frenetic tendencies.[74]

Nevertheless, Pentecostals are boundlessly optimistic

---

72. For Indian Pentecostalism, see Michael Bergunder, *The South Indian Pentecostal Movement in the Twentieth Century* (Grand Rapids: Eerdmans, 2008); Allan Anderson and Edmond Tang, eds., *Asian and Pentecostal* (Oxford: Regnum, 2005); and Stanley Burgess, "Pentecostalism," in *The Oxford Encyclopaedia of South Asian Christianity*, 543–45.

73. Bergunder, *The South Indian Pentecostal Movement*, 15. Robert Frykenberg agrees with these numbers. See Frykenberg, *Christianity in India*, 465.

74. Frykenberg, *Christianity in India*, 466–67.

people, and their numbers reflect that optimism. Rarely do they speak of stagnation or decline. From their vantage point, the Lord is constantly adding to their numbers. And according to the church growth statistics, the worldwide expansion of Pentecostalism continues. The statistics are often deceiving, however, and church leaders are not unbiased statisticians.

Nevertheless, Pentecostalism in the twentieth century enjoyed marvelous growth. In the Indian context, it is extremely difficult to know what is happening on the ground. There are endless stories and anecdotes of growth, but it is not known how large the movement has actually become. What is known is that conversion to Christianity comes at a heavy price. It could result in a loss of government entitlements, social exclusion, and even bodily persecution. Indians who convert make difficult decisions, and punishing sacrifices.

In 2014, I was the guest of Rev. Abey Peter, principal of the IPC (Indian Pentecostal Church of God) Theological Seminary in Kottayam. Rev. Abey is a highly educated, articulate, and extraordinarily hospitable man, even for India, where hospitality is the great strength. He too believes the Pentecostal churches are still mushrooming, even after a century of growth. His seminary is well-funded. The facility is modern and smart. The IPC is "the largest indigenous Pentecostal movement in India," and has good connections with Pentecostal Christians in the United States.[75]

When asked about the growth of charismatic Christianity in India, Rev. Abey chose to focus more on the huge sacrifices these converts make. People often have to break ties with their families. "They sacrifice everything to become Christian, but they can move on with their lives by joining another social

---

75. John Alex, "Indian Pentecostal Church of God," *The Oxford Encyclopaedia of South Asian Christianity*, 334.

group. They throw themselves into the arms of the church because that is their new family. The church becomes their life."

Focus India Theological College, Kerala

In order to home in on a specific example of what is going on in the more grassroots Pentecostal movement, I spent time at a Bible college headed by V. V. Thomas.[76] He founded the college in 2008 in the state of Kerala, and oversees operations from his residence in Pune, Maharashtra, where he serves as a professor at Union Biblical Seminary, one of India's top evangelical seminaries.

The primary purpose of Focus India Theological College is to train future (male) Pentecostal ministers. Currently, the college accommodates around 24 young men, but eventually the goal is to have 60 students enrolled. It operates according to fundamental Christian convictions, including the virgin birth, immersion baptism, the gifts of the Holy Spirit, the establishment of Christ's millennial kingdom, an actual Satan, and the belief that eternal bliss or eternal punishment awaits all humans.[77] The college receives its funding mainly from benefactors in the United States. Students enroll for three years and are expected to live according to a stringently Christian code of conduct. Their lives are bathed in worship, prayer, fasting, Bible study, and Christian fellowship during the duration of their education there. Around 75 percent of the students become missionaries and the rest typically go into some form of education.

---

76. Focus India Theological college is located in Nilambur, Kerala. I visited in June–July, 2014.
77. See the section on the college website entitled "We Believe," http://www.focusindiaministries.com.

The medium of instruction is English and students come from all over India. Indeed, one important draw of the college is that they help students acquire English fluency. In India, the teaching of English is often very poor. Students may have studied English, but the language of instruction would have been their vernacular. At Focus India, they are surrounded by English for three years, and by the time they graduate, they are generally quite fluent. About half of the students are from Kerala—which has better English than most of India, and about half of the students come from other states, such as Odisha, Tamil Nadu, the northeast of India, Uttar Pradesh, Jharkand, and even Nepal. Some of them do not have much of an English background, therefore the college enacts a strict prohibition against the speaking of any other languages: "We will not allow any student to speak any language other than English in the campus."

College students in the Western world would be shocked by the austere ambiance of the school. White, long-sleeved shirts are worn for preaching and gospel meetings, no alcohol, no tobacco, no movies, and no involvement in secular politics (although they are permitted to vote). One student was dismissed for proving unable to stay away from his cell phone. They rise at 5:00 a.m. and proceed to prayer. Devotions are at 6:45. Chapel is at 8:15. Classes then dominate the day until 4:00 p.m., when they have to take up their assigned duties, such as cutting the grass, picking up, and cleaning bathrooms. At 5:30 p.m., they are given an hour of personal time to wash clothes, play sports and chess, and perhaps watch a soccer game on television—in India, half cheer for Argentina and half cheer for Brazil. Evening chapel occurs at 6:45 p.m. Library and study time occurs after dinner. Lights out at 10:00 p.m.

I interviewed four students. All came from Christian

families, but each story was unique: one's grandfather came to Pentecostalism from Syrian Orthodoxy, another had a grandfather who converted from Hinduism, two of the four came from formerly CSI (Church of South India) families. The students are proud of their education at Focus India, particularly their advancement in English. They claim the disciplined atmosphere has been very good for them, allowing them to learn effective time management skills. In their downtime, they all love playing cricket and carrom, a popular Eastern shuffleboard-like game. They tend not to struggle with homesickness; rather, they see themselves as being on a mission—to eventually lead Indians to Christ.

Is Pentecostalism the wave of the future in India? It is difficult to tell at this stage. What is very clear is that it has made a big impact in a relatively short period of time. Russian sociologist, Nikolai Mitrokhin, argues that Pentecostalism is "the ideal form of religion for the globalized world."[78] It challenges religious monopolies. It empowers individuals who have been marginalized by the mainstream. It provides community for the disenfranchised. It is intensely personal, allowing for more creative interpretations of the faith. It is not so tightly hierarchical, thereby creating opportunities for lay leaders to rise up to positions of leadership. It is "highly portable" because of its strongly congregational approaches to organizational structure. Make no mistake, Pentecostalism, once a rejected step-child of Protestantism, is now mainstream. And in plenty of places in the world, its numbers are surpassing the religious establishment.

78. Mitrokhin, quoted by Allen Jr., *The Future Church*, 398.

Conclusion

The Christian denominations of India are, at once, united and divided. They are united in the sense that they are Christians living in a majority Hindu culture. They worship Christ as Lord and celebrate their long history on the subcontinent.

Indian Christians are also divided, however. Their history is, in many ways, an unfortunate one: a united Thomasite church splinters upon meeting European Catholics, splinters again with the arrival of Protestants, and accelerates in its proliferation with the advent of Pentecostalism.

However, for all of its "fissiparous tendencies," it would be a mistake to isolate Indian Christians as somehow unique in this regard. After all, the Catholics and Protestants brought these tendencies. And, as the West has learned, once the church begins to fragment, there is no turning back.

The redeeming quality of the long catalogue of Indian denominations is that the church—at large—is able to make a difference in the lives of people in many different castes, conditions, and walks of life. Christianity has assimilated into India, with all of India's profound diversity. It is a fantasy to think India was at one time some halcyonic utopia where the people were all of one mind, language, caste, and creed. What makes India India is its diversity. This has always been the case. And Christianity's rampant diversity on the subcontinent points to its superb ability to reach out to all.

3

Sociocultural

Understanding the Indian Society

India is a land of stories, folklores, and anecdotes and one of them is of the five blind men who went to "see" the elephant. They touched different parts of the animal and later fought among themselves as to whether the elephant's body was like a wall, a spear, a snake, a tree, or a fan. The same is, more or less, the case with understanding the Indian society, or, for that matter, any society. In this chapter, our attempt is not to provide the readers with some new information or expert opinion on India, for such information will soon become outdated or challenged. Instead, this chapter will attempt a cursory glance at some of the prominent issues in Indian society. Few countries in the world are as complex as India when it comes to the sociocultural context, and we are unable to unpack here the deep history, or the thick description, of Indian social life. What is attempted here is a general overview of some of India's most obvious issues, which would be helpful to readers. And we do so from a Christian perspective. Second, we know that India is an ancient land, the heritage and civilization of which go back several thousand years, and in this chapter we will certainly consider that historical dimension. Our primary concern here, however, is to discern the changes in society in recent times, with a focus on the question of where these changes will take us, in a globalized and multipolar world.

In this chapter, we will look at several aspects of India's sociocultural life that figure in the complex social milieu that is India today. We will begin with an overview of India through different stages—from the ancient times to the current period. The next section will take a closer look at Hinduism and the various interpretations that center around it. The specific issue of caste is subsequently addressed, essentially from a Dalit perspective. The realities of poverty and inequality that linger on even in the midst of the giant strides made by India in science, technology, and industry are also discussed. There is subsequently a detailed discussion of secularism and religious fundamentalism in India, starting with the vision at the time of independence and coming up to the harsh realities of the current period. The next few sections discuss the response of Indian Christianity to various national situations in public life, such as the Emergency regime and discussions on the freedom of religion. A hotly discussed topic during the current period, whether Christianity has failed in India, is subsequently addressed. Finally, we turn our attention to the immigrant forms of Indian Christianity and the challenges they face. All in all, this chapter covers the major areas that concern Indian Christianity as a public religion, especially in the current period.

India through the Ages

The name "India" is derived from the Indus River (also called Sindhu River), which flows through the northwest of the country. India is the seventh largest and the second most populous country in the world. According to the Anthropological Survey of India, there are 325 languages and 700 dialects in the country.[1] The country is divided into twenty eight states and six union territories. While the origin of civilization in India is shrouded in mystery, the tribals are considered to be the indigenous people of the land (Tribals are also called "Adivasis," which literally means "the first inhabitants"). The Aryans are believed to have migrated to northwest India around 1500 BC. As the Aryans advanced into the heartland of the country, most of the indigenous people fled to the mountains and forests.

While around 80 percent of Indians follow Hinduism, practically all the religions of the world are present in India. The country, however, is a secular state and does not officially favor or discriminate against any religion. "Hinduism is the confluence of the Vedic religious and social tenets of the Aryans with the beliefs and practices of the natives."[2] Apart from Hinduism, India also gave birth to Buddhism, Sikhism, and Jainism. Even though Buddhism flourished in India during the period of Emperor Asoka, the revival of Hinduism and its spread all over the country meant that the growth of Buddhism was greatly curtailed. Sikhism was confined largely to the Punjab region though the successful Sikh community has now

1. Paula Banerjee, Sabyasachi Basu Ray Chaudhury, Samir Kumar Das, Bishnu Adhikari, *Internal Displacement in South Asia: The Relevance of the UN's Guiding Principles* (New Delhi: SAGE Publications, 2005), 145.
2. A. Mathias Mundadan, "India" in *Oxford Encyclopedia of South Asian Christianity* (New Delhi: Oxford University Press, 2012), 329.

spread out all over India and abroad. Christianity is one of the ancient religions of India though the followers of the faith always remained a small minority of the nation's population. Islam was brought to India in the eighth century by the Arab traders and remains the second biggest religious group in the country.

India experienced waves of colonial powers ruling over it during various stages. The Mughals controlled large parts of the Indian subcontinent from 1526 to 1707. The golden period of the Mughal rule began with the reign of Akbar the Great, who is considered the finest Mughal ruler. Akbar had an ecumenical worldview and he went beyond Islam and became the advocate of religious tolerance. He even attempted to float a new religion—"God-ism" (*Din-i-ilahi*)—which was a blend of Islam, Hinduism, Christianity, and Sikhism. He also maintained a harmonious relationship with the various religious communities. The economic progress and social harmony in Akbar's time continued during the reign of Jahangir as well.[3]

The Portuguese reached India as traders toward the end of the fifteenth century, though later, they developed colonial interests. Initially, Calicut was the base of the Portuguese, and later they moved to Goa, both places located on the Western coast. With Goa as the capital, the Portuguese extended their domain to large parts on the western and eastern coast of India. Pockets of Portuguese influence remained in India even after independence in 1947, though in 1961, the Indian Army took over the control of Goa, Daman, and Diu, which remained till the end as Portuguese territories. Even though the formal control of Portugal ceased, cultural footprints in terms of the architecture of houses and churches, food habits, and other

---

3. John Richards, *The Mughal Empire* (Cambridge: Cambridge University Press, 1996).

practices remain till today in the erstwhile territories, especially Goa.

The Portuguese laid the foundation of the Latin Catholic Christian community in the Indian subcontinent. According to historian Mathias Mundadan, it was the coming of the Portuguese and the first contact with them in the early sixteenth century which helped the ancient St. Thomas Christian community of India to break through their traditional pattern of life and enter into a meaningful communication with world Christianity. The initial encounter with Western Christianity set the pace for their history in succeeding decades and centuries.[4] The most significant change, perhaps, was that this encounter with the foreigners compelled the Indian church to redefine its cultural and religious identity as a caste-based community.

The Portuguese were followed by other Europeans—notably, the French, Dutch, and the British. All the colonial rulers had their areas of influence and control in the country. While the British too arrived initially for trade as the East India Company, gradually, most of India came under the direct control of the British government. As Indians groaned under the colonial yoke, the nationalist movement gained momentum and spread all over the country. M. K. Gandhi took over the leadership of the freedom struggle. His goal was swadeshi (self-rule) and his methodology was ahimsa (non-violence). Even as the struggle led by Gandhi gained momentum, Muhammad Ali Jinnah and the Muslim League demanded the creation of a separate Muslim state, Pakistan. On August 15, 1947, as the independence struggle was brought to a fruitful culmination

---

4. A. M. Mundadan, *History of Christianity in India*, vol. 1 (Bangalore: Church History Association of India, 1984), 1.

with India's independence, the separate nation of Pakistan too was created.

India's independence from British rule created history in several respects. One was the non-violent path to independence that India pursued. The early decades of the twentieth century saw independence movements against colonialism in several Asian and African nations. As a leader of these nations, India proved that independence can be achieved even when the might of the colonizer is met with pacifist resistance and prolonged struggles. The central role Mahatma Gandhi played in this process is most important. On the one hand, Gandhi affirmed the non-violent path, and, on the other, employed persistent and prolonged struggles to achieve the goal. The path Gandhi showed had long-lasting impact that went beyond independence movements. From Martin Luther King Jr. to Nelson Mandela, leaders around the world had acknowledged the impact his person and method had on their own struggles in different contexts.

Unfortunately, the Gandhian path to non-violent struggles against colonialism could not often be sustained in settling domestic problems. Immediately following independence, India witnessed unprecedented bloodshed and violence when the country was partitioned into two—India and Pakistan. In the genocide and violence that followed, the Hindus traveling from Pakistan to India and Muslims from India to Pakistan, around 200,000–500,000 people, are believed to have perished.[5] The animosity between India and Pakistan lingered on in the following decades and led to several wars between the two nations. Of particular relevance in this context is the genocide

---

5. Paul R. Brass, "The Partition of India and Retributive Genocide in the Punjab, 1946–47: Means, Methods, and Purposes," *Journal of Genocide Research* 5:1 (2003): 71–101 at 75.

in East Pakistan in 1971 that eventually led to the formation of the new nation of Bangladesh.

Undoubtedly, the two most important achievements of free India were democracy and secularism. With over 1.2 billion inhabitants, out of which, over 800 million can vote, India today is the largest democracy in the world. It was commonly believed till then that liberal democracy could survive only in contexts where the citizens were as educated and financially secure as in the West. India, with its large population of illiterate and poor people, obviously, did not fit in with that description. And yet, democracy survived and thrived in India even as the vast majority of erstwhile colonies in Asia and Africa either did not accept the democratic path, or, even where they did, soon succumbed to the temptations of authoritarian rule. While both India and Pakistan gained independence at the same time and held elections, on numerous occasions during the last few decades, the democratic institutions in Pakistan were taken over by the military. Even when a democratically elected government is in power there, the military interferes frequently with the affairs of the government. As Sumit Ganguly put it, the "differences between Pakistan and India could not be more striking, and, yet, both of these countries emerged from the same colonial experience."[6]

After six decades of independence, it is relevant to pose the question—how far have the fruits of independence been achieved? The country has certainly made great strides in the development of science and technology (especially, space science), industry, business, and education. However, poverty

---

6. Sumit Ganguly, "The Story of Indian Democracy" in *Foreign Policy Research Institute*, http://www.fpri.org/articles/2011/06/story-indian-democracy (Accessed September 6, 2015).

and malnutrition still exist on a large scale in the country, especially the rural areas. According to the figures available in 2015, the Socioeconomic and Caste Census (SECC) of the country paints a stark picture of widespread rural poverty and deprivation, with a large majority of the poor living in the villages.[7] There is also widespread malnutrition and poor hygienic surroundings in the country. It is obvious that the benefits of independence and self-rule have not yet reached large parts of the country.

Religion in the Making

"Despite the stereotypes of 'unchanging India' and her 'unhistorical' religions and peoples, the historical writing on ancient India goes back for more than two centuries and exhibits an instructive series of changes in interpretation,"[8] thus begins Romila Thapar's introduction to ancient Indian society. The first group of people to study the Indian society systematically were the Western scholars—who we now call Orientalists or Indologists—and their work go back to the eighteenth century CE. Their study reflected, largely, the ideological attitude that was dominant in Europe at that time, though it was considerably different from the context and traditions of the Indians at that period. The source materials that were available for the study of the European scholars were primarily in the Sanskrit language and were written by Brahmins (who were considered as the highest caste and the elite of the society). "The fact that these were texts emanating from and relating to a particular segment of society was often

---

7. Ritika Katyal, "India Census Expose Extent of Poverty," *CNN News*, www.cnn.com/2015/08/02/asia/india-poor-census-secc (Accessed September 13, 2015).
8. Romila Thapar, *Ancient Indian Social History: Some Interpretations* (New Delhi: Orient Longman Limited, 1978), 1.

overlooked."[9] As for the marginalized and oppressed people, including the untouchables, poverty, ignorance, and lack of education kept them "as superstitious as ever, given to the fear of evil spirits and addicted to rituals of propitiation."[10] Because of the ideas of purity and pollution built into the Brahminical literature, the European Orientalists also, by and large, ignored the richness of the non-Brahminical sources. It was much later, from the latter part of the twentieth century onwards, that subaltern scholars began academically studying the values, traditions, rituals, and religious beliefs of the marginalized and oppressed people.

Recent studies have revealed the serious fallacy in promoting one stream of Hinduism as representative of the religiosity of an entire nation. Sanskrit was the language of the Brahmins and in the eighteenth century, Sanskrit and the Vedas and the Upanishads were alien to the vast majority of Indians. As Wendy Doniger, in her book, *The Hindus: An Alternative History*[11] argues, the Western Indologists who tried to understand the Indian society and religion seemed to have a bias toward Sanskrit and Brahminical Hinduism. In his review of the book, Pankaj Mishra says,

> In "privileging" Sanskrit over local languages, she writes, they created what has proved to be an enduring impression of a "unified Hinduism." And they found keen collaborators among upper-caste Indian scholars and translators. This British-Brahmin version of Hinduism—one of the many invented traditions born around the world in the 18th and 19th centuries—has continued to find many takers among semi-Westernized Hindus suffering from an inferiority complex vis-

9. Ibid., 3.
10. A. M. Abraham Ayrookuzhiel, "The Dalits, Religions and Interfaith Dialogue," *Journal of Hindu-Christian Studies* 7 (1994): 18.
11. Wendy Doniger, *The Hindus: An Alternative History* (Penguin Books, 2010).

à-vis the apparently more successful and organized religions of Christianity, Judaism and Islam.[12]

By holding Sanskrit and Brahminical Hinduism as representative of all Hindus, the European Indologists and Orientalists played an important role in accelerating the process of the modernization and homogenization of Hinduism. B. R. Ambedkar, in his critique of Hinduism, sought to overturn the age old triumph of Brahminism over Buddhism. As Ajaz Ashraf noted, "For the RSS bosses wishing to reconfigure Ambedkar's thoughts through an undue emphasis on just an aspect of his prodigious writings, it might make tremendous sense to read his The Untouchables: Who Were They and Why They Became Untouchables?"[13] Ambedkar, along with his followers, ultimately rejected Hinduism in favor of a new form of Buddhism that he called "Neo-Buddhism."[14]

A lasting damage done by the Orientalists who studied the Indian society and religion was that they focused on a hegemonic reading of the sacred scriptures by selecting only those texts that ensured power to the upper-caste people in a patriarchal set-up while ignoring the more radical texts that too were available. For example, while discussing the marginalization of women in Indian society, it is important to note that its roots go back a long way. The Hindu scripture *Ramayana* depicts Sita as the ideal wife, worthy of being emulated by all Hindu women. As the wife of Rama, she follows her husband when he is sent into exile for fourteen years.

---

12. Pankaj Mishra, "Another Incarnation," *The New York Times* (April 24, 2009).

13. Ajaz Ashraf, "Of Dead Cows and Dalits: Revisiting Babasaheb Ambedkar's Inconvenient History of Caste Conversion," in *F. India*. http://www.firstpost.com/india/of-dead-cows-and-dalits-revisiting-ambedkars-inconvenient-history-of-caste-conversion-2195582.html (Cited, September 11, 2015). The reference here is to B. R. Ambedkar's book, *The Untouchables: Who were They and Why They became Untouchables?* (New Delhi: Amrit, 1948).

14. See *Ambedkar and the Neo-Buddhist Movement*, eds. T. S. Wilkinson and M. M. Thomas (Madras: CISRS & CLS, 1972).

Ramayana depicts the patriarchal nature of the Indian society, which expects the wife to be the embodiment of all virtue even though no such duty is assigned to the husband. There are, however, alternative versions of the Ramayana, such as "Chandrabati Ramayana" that examines Ramayana from the woman's perspective. "It brings to light the emotional state of Sita as a result of the events that happened in Ramayana."[15] The reluctance of the scholars to highlight texts such as Chandrabati Ramayana is an indication of the lingering patriarchal forces at sway in India.

The Complexity of Caste

Caste is a concept that is fascinating, yet overwhelming due to its many layers, interpretations, and dramatic changes in recent years. Many volumes have been written about India's caste system.[16] Understanding this social phenomenon at its most basic level, and having a sense of how it tends to work in Indian society is critical for understanding Indian society. And while any attempt to describe caste in India will be woefully inadequate, it simply must be attempted when discussing Indian society.

The origins of the Indian caste system are debated even today. One major interpretation of the origins of caste goes something like this.[17] The Aryan people from the West, perhaps ancient Persia or Central Asia, began arriving in northwest India in waves, beginning around 1500 BCE. They discovered an

15. Ashay Anand, "Ramayana: A Feminist Critique," *Quora.* http://www.quora.com/Ashay-Anand/A-potpurri-of-Controversial-Writings/Ramayana-A-Feminist-Critique (Accessed September 11, 2015).
16. An excellent, recent book dealing with Christianity and caste is David Mosse, *The Saint in the Banyan Tree: Christianity and Caste Society in India* (Los Angeles: University of California Press, 2012).
17. One classic rendition of early Indian history is Romila Thapar's *A History of India*, vol. 1 (New York: Penguin, 1966). See chapter two, "The Impact of Aryan Culture."

agricultural people, which scholars today call the "Indus Valley Civilization," or "Harappan Culture." Over time, it began to be clear that the Aryans were gaining power. By the 800s BCE, they were using iron, expanding, settling, and either conquering or intermarrying with the locals. The Aryans were organized into three large groupings: warriors, priests, and commoners. According to the Aryan text, the *Rig Veda*, the indigenous people whom they encountered were known to them as "Dasas" or "enemies."[18] These local people were darker in their skin color, and were considered lower in social status. It was in this encounter that the roots of the caste system began to take shape. It is important to note that the Aryans brought the Sanskrit language with them, and in their language, the word *varna*—from which we get the word "caste"—meant color. In other words, the early caste system was based mainly on color.

The light-skinned Aryans considered themselves the "noble ones," and accorded themselves a status superior to the Dasas. In time, as the local people were subsumed into Aryan culture, a four-fold arrangement of people developed: Brahmins (priests), Kshatriyas (warriors), Vaishyas (professionals), and Shudras (laborers). The ancient *Rig Veda* describes the mythical origins of caste by stating that when the archetypal human was created, the Brahmin was the mouth, the Kshatriya was the two arms, the Vaishya was the two thighs, and the Shudra—the "servile class"—was the feet.[19] In practical terms, it was inherited servitude since Shudras were unable to transcend their lowly status.

There was a large chasm separating the top three groups from the Shudras since Shudras were religiously impure; they

---

18. The Vedas might well be "the earliest documents of the human mind that have come down to us." See Sarvepalli Radhakrishnan and Charles Moore, *A Sourcebook in Indian Philosophy* (Princeton: Princeton University Press, 1957), xxx.

19. Radhakrishnan and Moore, 19.

were not allowed to take part in Aryan (or Vedic) religious rituals. Indeed, the Aryan boys went through an initiation rite at puberty. Thus, the top three groups—Brahmins, Kshatriya, and Vaishyas—were known as being "twice born." This concept is not altogether different from the Christian idea of baptism, or being "reborn." The Shudras—dark skinned locals and those of mixed race—were given a second-class status. They could never wear the title of being "twice born" simply because they were considered impure, or polluted. This notion of pollution has come down all the way to the present. Pollution is perhaps the most important issue in understanding why Dalits (outcastes) are usually kept at some distance by upper-caste Hindus, and why the government has had to intervene in order to improve the dire situation for India's "untouchables." Indeed, the Dalits were far below the status of the Shudras because at least the Shudras were part of the system. Dalits were "cast out" of the system altogether.

For an analysis of the politics of caste, the grouping espoused above as high castes, intermediate castes, low castes, and Dalits (outcastes/untouchables) may be helpful. The social reality of caste, however, is more complex. The basic units of the caste system are the thousands of sub-castes or *jatis*. While the caste system with its hierarchy of classifications has numerous manifestations, the plight of the Dalits stands at the center of it all. Considering that the majority of the Indian Christians come from the Dalit background, it is important that we gain a clear understanding of the basic ideas, values, and perception of the Dalit identity and the emerging Dalit consciousness.

Dalit Consciousness

A key aspect of the dominant religious and social life in India was the virtual exclusion of the Dalits and tribals from any decision-making process in religion or society. Dalits are the "outcastes" in Hinduism (The word *dalit* comes from the Sanskrit term *dal*, which means the broken, oppressed, and bruised. The outcastes today prefer the term *dalit* over "scheduled castes" (as in the official records of the government) or *Harijans* (children of God), given to them by Mahatma Gandhi). While the society could not survive without the menial jobs being performed by the Dalits, they just did not count as legitimate members of the society. The tribals, on the contrary, were never part of the mainline social order, and hence were not oppressed in the way the Dalits were. However, they were historically on the periphery of the society, and today are the victims of the patterns of development that increasingly displace them from their traditional habitat—the mountains and the forests. There are other marginalized sections too—women in all societies, fisherfolk, the urban and rural poor, bonded laborers, and so on.

While the Dalits have been oppressed and marginalized within the Hindu fold for several centuries, there is a growing awareness among them that "they are members of an ancient primeval society disinherited and uprooted by the alien Brahminical civilization of their ancestral place in the society."[20] In the process, these indigenous people had become a people without their own history, without their own individuality even though they succeeded in maintaining a certain degree of cultural distinctiveness. The history of the

20. A. M. Abraham Ayrookuzhiel, "The Ideological Nature of the Emerging Dalit Consciousness," in *Towards a Common Dalit Ideology* (Madras: Gurukul, 1990), 81.

Dalits lies buried in their folk songs, stories, myths, religious symbols, and practices which reveal elements of ancient conflict.[21] The gigantic task facing the Dalits today is to collect and document these vast resources, thus virtually reconstructing their history and identity. Scholars often compare the search of the Dalits for their own identity to the struggles of Malcolm X in the United States.

Along with Nehru, B. R. Ambedkar played a crucial role in the formative years of independent India. Ambedkar was the architect of the Constitution of India, which ensured freedom and a life of dignity for all citizens, including the minorities. He was also the champion of the Dalits. Realizing that the Dalits would never get justice within Hinduism, he took the initiative to found the Neo-Buddhism movement, which a large number of Dalits joined. Ambedkar ranks, along with Jotirao Phule and Periyar E. V. Ramsamy Naicker, as the architect of the social revolution in India.

Conversations around castes and tribes within Christianity are robust today. There is extreme tension surrounding the topic because it is a classic case of clashing worldviews. Hinduism's caste consciousness has a long, centuries-old history that is deeply enmeshed in religion. In Christianity however, the idea of a caste system, or even class distinctions, is undermined. In Galatians 3:28, the apostle Paul states, "There is neither Jew nor Greek, neither slave nor free, nor is there male and female, for you are all one in Christ Jesus." All throughout Paul's epistles, there is a rather consistent opposition to dissension, hierarchy, and discrimination within the church. But Paul was not the first to dream up this radical egalitarian ethic; it was Jesus himself. Jesus often chastises the

---

21. D. D. Kosambi, *The Culture and Civilization of Ancient India in Historical Outline* (Delhi: Vikas Publishing House Pvt Ltd, 1997), 16.

religious elite, the rich, and the powerful, in what is often deemed "a preferential option for the poor" and marginalized. Jesus's famous "high priestly prayer" in John 17—just before he is crucified—is an explicit nod to unity among his followers. To claim that hierarchy and social ranking does not occur in Christianity would be absolutely wrong. But it seems patently obvious that the earliest ideals for Christianity, laid down by its founders, were that disciples of Jesus were to forego their social privileges in favor of communal equality.

Nevertheless, there are deep tensions here for Indian Christians. These are people who follow Christ, but like all humans, are not immune to the culture into which they are born. Indian Christians are, in many cases, just as prone as Hindus to assume a caste mentality. It is a problem that most Christians in India readily admit. Thus, on one hand, the church pays lip service to the condemnation of caste distinctions—especially the notion that Dalits are somehow polluted. On the other hand, it is hard to escape caste consciousness in India. It is ancient, it is assumed, it is simply there, like a worldview—people cannot easily change their worldview. It is a part of their heritage of being from a particular soil, brought up in a particular society, speaking a particular language, and being socialized by a particular people-group. Sometimes, Christians from the Western world go to India and express frustration that Indian Christians cannot seem to shake notions of caste. However, it would be like asking a Westerner to "sell all he has and give it to the poor." Westerners have deep-seated assumptions too, and living a life without possessions is not one of them.

Nevertheless, there have been lively attempts in recent years to curtail the practice of casteism in Indian churches, with moderate success. However, many Dalits simply start their own churches. In their minds, the church is irredeemably "casteist." The only way to avoid the implications of being an "untouchable" in the caste system is to move their churches outside of the caste system. Indeed, when some Dalits left Hinduism for what they thought would be a more egalitarian Christianity, they were rebuffed. V. V. Thomas writes, "To their utter discouragement they saw the existence of caste distinctions even within the Church. . . . In many places there was open oppression of the Dalit Christians by the upper caste Christians."[22]

Some claim that while it is clear its history goes back to before the time of Christ, it was the British who shaped it into the set of ideas it has become today.[23] In the introduction to his important book *Castes of Mind*, Nicholas Dirks writes:

> I will argue that caste (again, as we know it today) is a modern phenomenon, that it is, specifically, the product of an historical encounter between India and Western colonial rule. By this I do not mean to imply that it was simply invented by the too clever British. . . . But I *am* suggesting that it was under the British that "caste" became a single term capable of expressing, organizing, and above all "systemizing" India's diverse forms of social identity, community, and organization. . . . In short, colonialism made caste what it is today.[24]

While his attempt is, without doubt, one of the most nuanced and comprehensive attempts to deal with caste in all of its complexity, his central thesis, it seems to me, falls short. The Hindu caste system is much larger and much more durable of an institution than the two centuries of British rule

---

22. V. V. Thomas, *Dalit and Tribal Christians of India: Issues and Challenges* (Malapuram: Focus India Trust, 2014), 203.
23. See Nicholas Dirks, *Castes of Mind: Colonialism and the Making of Modern India* (Princeton: Princeton University Press, 2001), 5 (Italics are the author's).
24. Ibid., chapter 1: "Introduction: The Modernity of Caste." http://press.princeton.edu/chapters/s7191.html (Accessed October 26, 2015).

(1757–1947) that ended many decades ago. The British are gone. And while their influence on India has been profound, one could easily make the argument that its impact pales in comparison to the 331 years of Mughal influence (1526–1857). Nevertheless, irrespective of the many empires that had their chance with India over the millennia, the caste system predates them all, and continues to exert its powerful presence on the subcontinent.

Poverty and Inequality

As India became independent, the primary challenge before the new government was to address the problems of poverty, injustice, and inequality in the country. Under the leadership of Prime Minister Jawaharlal Nehru, the country drew out a massive program to tackle these issues. The "development model," based on the values of self-reliance, industrial growth, and economic planning for the establishment of a welfare state was seen by many then as the way forward. The Nehruvian path, rooted in these principles and on the values of democracy and secularism, had a great impact not only in the nation, but in the thinking of the Indian church as well. "Development Departments" sprung up under the churches and ecumenical institutions and they strove to mobilize the students, youth, and others to return to the villages (where, as Mahatma Gandhi put it, resided "the soul of India") and to work among the poor and needy, and thus rebuild the nation and the society.

From the beginning, however, there were people who questioned the development model that did not include a concomitant focus on righting the historic wrong of social injustice and structural violence. At a time when growth and development were considered the most essential tasks for emerging democracies, they affirmed that "the notions of social justice and self-reliance have to radically re-define the meaning of development."[25] One of them was Samuel L. Parmar, who questioned the argument that development was possible in the third world without tears. He affirmed: "Rightly understood development is disorder because it changes existing social and economic relationships, breaks up old relationships to create new, brings about radical alternations in the values and structures of society."[26]

These days, we hear much about India becoming a "world power" with the country's tremendous progress in the areas of science and technology, industrialization, military might, and so on. These are all true, but it is also true that stark poverty on a fairly widespread level continues to exist in India. While independent India initiated large-scale welfare programs, poverty continues to be a reality; while India made giant strides in industrialization, that did not remove mass poverty. The following table may provide us with a quick glance at the situation:

- 50 percent of Indians don't have proper shelter;
- 70 percent don't have access to decent toilets (which inspires a multitude of bacteria to host their own disease party);
- 35 percent of households don't have a nearby water source;
- 85 percent of villages don't have a secondary school (how can this be the same government claiming 9 percent annual growth?);
- Over 40 percent of these same villages don't have proper roads connecting them.[27]

25. Ignatius Swart, *The Churches and the Development Debate: Perspectives on a Fourth Generation Approach* (Stellenbosch: African Sun Media, 2006), 40.
26. Ninan Koshy, *A History of the Ecumenical Movement in Asia*, vol. 1 (Hong Kong: WSCF AP, YMCA & CCA, 2004), 173.
27. Source: "Effects of Poverty in India: Between Injustice and Exclusion." *Poverties.org;*

Statistics can be deceptive. Poverty is not merely the lack of money or food alone, but has a cascading effect on all areas of life. Lack of food will keep children away from schools, denying them a proper education and a brighter future; it will lead to the breakup of families when one member goes away in search of jobs; it means malnutrition, especially for women, children, and the elderly. All in all, it is important to note that there are *manifold dimensions of poverty*. Scholars are divided in their opinion on whether over the last few decades, the rate of poverty has risen or fallen in India. Concerted efforts by the Government of India soon after independence to address poverty did yield results and the rate of poverty fell in the next few decades, but thanks to the neo-economic policies, the trend seems to have been reversed in recent decades. "If the decline in poverty went from 60% to 35% between the 70s and the early 90s, globalization and liberalization policies have made this trend go backwards in the 90s."[28]

Economists and social scientists point toward the integral link between poverty and wealth. This is evident by looking at the distribution of wealth in India. "As long as the rights to life of the poor is a matter of chance, whereas the right to property of the rich is guaranteed this is crucial."[29] Numerous studies done in India in recent years have established that access—or the lack of access—of people to land, water, and other property will determine, to a large extent, who is poor and who is not.[30] As long as gross inequality and injustice exist,

Research for Social & Economic Development. http://www.poverties.org / poverty-in-india.html#sthash.PcOE0M9U.dpuf (Accessed September 5, 2015).

28. "Effects of Poverty in India: Between Injustice and Exclusion," www.poverties.org /poverty-in-india.html (Accessed September 5, 2015).

29. Gabriele Dietrich and Bastiaan Wielenga, *Towards Understanding Indian Society* (Tiruvalla: Christava Sahitya Samithi, 1997), 113.

30. See C. T. Kurien, *Dynamics of Rural Transformation: A Study of Tamil Nadu 1950–1975* (New Delhi: Orient Longman, 1981) and, V. S. Vyas/Pradip Bhargava, "Public Intervention for Poverty Alleviation: An Overview" in, *Economic and Political Weekly*, October 14/21, 1995.

mass poverty will be a growing reality. Very often, it is the mega developmental projects of the government that alienates the vulnerable people from the much-needed resources, in the process, pushing them further into poverty. India needs to turn from a "want-based" economy to a "need-based" one. As Mahatma Gandhi reminded us, "The world has enough for everyone's need, but not enough for everyone's greed."[31]

Secularism and Rise of Religious Fundamentalism

The term "secularism" denotes a social order separate from religion, but which allows different religious beliefs and non-religious ideologies to exist side by side.[32] Independent India adopted secularism as one of its guiding principles. The opening words of the Preamble of the country's Constitution states: "We, the People of India having solemnly resolved to constitute India into a Sovereign, Socialist, Secular, Democratic, Republic and to secure to all its citizens; Justice, social, economic, political; Liberty of thought, expression, belief, faith and worship; Equality of status and opportunity; and to promote among them all; Fraternity, assuring the dignity of the individual and the unity and integrity of the nation." The words "Socialist," "Secular," and "Integrity" were originally not there in the Preamble, but were added by the 42nd Amendment (1976) of the Constitution.

Since the terms "secularism" and "secularization" often have different meanings in India and the United States, a word of clarification is needed. Secularism is often used in a political sense and it refers to political arrangements that make separation between religious institutions and the state. It

31. Birister Sharma, *The Golden Words of Gandhiji* (Delhi: Birister Sharma, 2015), 102.
32. G. J. Holyoake, *The Origin and Nature of Secularism* (London: Watts and Co., 1896), 51.

stands for the strict separation of the state from religious institutions. The affairs of a secular state are not conducted in accordance with the principles of a religion, and, in that sense, the state has no special relation to any one particular religion. Secularization, on the contrary, refers to a widespread decline of religious belief and practice among ordinary people.

In the highly pluralist context of India, characterized by multiple religions and cultures, secularism was probably the only viable path. Secularism in the Indian context implies freedom to choose one's religion. While the state gives every citizen the right to practice and propagate a religion of his/her choice, and the right to reject all religions, the state treats all religions as equal. Democracy and secularism go hand in hand. In a democratic society, there cannot be the concentration of power in any one institution or group. If religious leaders began to exercise power in political matters in the secular realm, the democratic framework would be undermined. In the absence of democracy and social justice, secularism cannot exist as a positive value in society.

In the Indian context, where religion and society lie so interwoven together, the question whether it is possible to separate religion from politics is relevant. In such societies, it may be difficult to disentangle the religious from the non-religious, and therefore practically impossible to separate strictly every religious from every non-religious practice.

While the Indian Constitution envisages a secular state, such a vision can be ensured only with a sustained movement to safeguard the fruits of freedom, democracy, and social justice. According to Ninan Koshy, secularism was offered to the non-Western world after the end of World War II as part of a package, which included also modernization and development. "Modernization was equated with westernization and was rejected and development failed to attain its promised objectives. This considerably weakened secularism."[33] This is also what happened in India. The achievements of secularism were taken for granted and the commitment to build a secular base for the society waned in due course. The forces of sectarianism and religious fundamentalism, which were relatively dormant in the early decades of India's independence, slowly started gathering momentum. While such forces are active in both the majority and the minority religious groups, it is the sectarian and fundamentalist groups in the majority Hinduism that has a direct and immediate impact on the policy and direction of the country. By the end of the twentieth century, while Hindu groups such as Rashtriya Swayamsevak Sangh (RSS) and Bajrang Dal/Vishva Hindu Parishad gained momentum in civil society, political organizations such as the Bharatiya Janata Party (BJP) and Shiv Sena slowly began capturing power in various states and even at the level of the central government. As these lines are being written in 2015, the BJP government, under the leadership of Prime Minister Narendra Modi, is in power at the Centre. BJP is also in power in numerous states.

Social scientists are divided in their opinion on how to account for the popularity of Hindu nationalist, fundamentalist, and sectarian forces in a country that is wedded to the principles of secularism. According to Rajeev Bhargava, secularism is a complex and evolving idea, not a doctrine with a fixed content with a single meaning. Secularism has multiple interpretations, which change over time. Different societies need to work out their own distinctive conceptions of secularism and see which one of them is good

---

33. Ninan Koshy, "Secularism," in *Religion in Southeast Asia: An Encyclopedia of Faiths and Cultures* (Santa Barbara, CA: ABC-CLIO, 2015), 273.

for them.[34] M. M. Thomas, however, has a different theory. Indian secularism was the result of the attempt of Indian nationalism during the days of the struggle for independence among all sections of people of the country. He locates Indian secularism in the cooperation between two forces as the independence movement gathered momentum in the country, and later as they worked together for nation-building. These were: (1) the secular, democratic and socialist forces that stood for changes in traditional social structures and cultural values, even if they were sanctioned by religion, in order to bring about social justice to the vulnerable sections of the society such as the Dalits, tribals, and women and (2) the reformed religious and neo-Hindu movements that supported the struggles of the marginalized people for social justice, and yet affirmed that religion can be a positive force in this process. The cooperation between Mahatma Gandhi and Jawaharlal Nehru was symbolic of the cooperation between these two forces, especially as the former was a firm believer in religion while the latter was an agnostic, but both stood for secularism, democracy, and social justice. Thomas, however, argues that in the decades that followed independence, the two forces—the secular and the socialist on the one hand, and religious reform on the other—moved to two poles, became rigid and their cooperation slackened. Secularism became closed or dogmatic secularism which rejected any relevance of religion in public life and, on the contrary, the reformed religious movements were overtaken by fundamentalist forces. This situation has created "a spiritual vacuum which is now sought to be filled by religious fundamentalism and communalism."[35]

---

34. See Rajeev Bhargava, *Secularism and its Critics* (New Delhi: Oxford University Press, 1998).
35. J. John & Jesudas M. Athyal, eds., *Religion, State and Communalism: A Post-Ayodhya Reflection* (Hong Kong: Christian Conference of Asia, 1995), 13–14.

Religion in modern India is invariably linked to secularism. Indian secularism is a product of modern Indian history, evolved mainly during the days of the struggle for independence and later in nation-building. Secularism in India is defined as freedom from discrimination on the basis of religion, and also the promotion of renascent and reform movements in religions, especially those aimed at the liberation of the downtrodden sections of the society. The Neo-Hindu movement of the nineteenth and twentieth centuries was, in essence, the struggle of Hinduism to build up a religious humanism in active dialogue with the secular and socialist movements in the country. These reform movements, in the context of the awakening of the marginalized people and influenced by the nationalist and socialist idealism sweeping the country, contributed to the evolution of a common platform for dialogue between renascent religions and social reform movements—in the process, building up the foundation of a secular and democratic India.

Christian Participation in Public Life

Although the Indian Christian community forms only a small portion of the country's population, it has played an important part in social, educational, political, and religious spheres of the recent life of India.[36] A glance at the Indian Christian participation in national affairs during the twentieth century with several indigenous Christian lay leaders and movements providing the impetus for mission and unity in the country would be quite informative. The All India Conference of Indian Christians (AICIC), founded in 1914, is considered to be the

---

36. Abraham Vazhayil Thomas, *Christians in Secular India* (Cranbury, NJ: Associated University Presses, 1974).

earliest organized response of Indian Christians to the nationalist movement for independence. In response to Mahatma Gandhi's call to Indians for *swadeshi* (self-sufficiency), the AICIC passed in 1921 a "resolution urging that the *swadeshi* spirit dominate all aspects of Indian Christian life, that Christians wear clothes of Indian manufacturer."[37] S. K. George, an Indian lay Christian leader of that period saw in the *satyagraphis*[38] "willingness to suffer at the hands of the government for the sake of the poor of India something profoundly Christian."[39] The Madras Rethinking Group that symbolized the Indian church's creative potential for indigenous theological expression, and the Christian magazine *The Guardian* too provided the framework for a lay and indigenous Christian response to the nationalist movement.

Many Indian churches and the leadership of the National Christian Council of India (now called the National Council of Churches in India—NCCI), dominated in its early phase by Western missionaries, often took an ambivalent attitude to the nationalist movement. As K. Baago put it, ". . . the Council issued two statements on the political situation in 1917 and 1920, using a good number of words, but saying actually nothing. These statements were so vague, wooly and cautious in their choice of words, that they could be interpreted both ways."[40] Baago further stated: "It must be admitted, therefore, that the National Christian Council hardly lived up to the first word in its name at that time, particularly not when we consider what the word 'National' stood for in those days."[41]

---

37. John C. B. Webster, "Gandhi and the Christians: Dialogue in the Nationalist Era," in *Hindu Christian Dialogue: Perspectives and Encounters*, ed. Harold Coward (Maryknoll, NY: Orbis, 1989), 83.
38. Participants in the non-violent resistance or civil disobedience to the colonial rule.
39. Webster, "Gandhi and the Christians," 87.
40. K. Baago, *National Christian Council of India: 1914-1964* (Nagpur: NCCI, 1965), 28.
41. Ibid., 37.

Till 1936, P. O. Philip, an Indian Christian layman, was the only Indian staff in the NCCI.

When the leadership of NCCI was taken over by the Indians in the 1940s, however, the Council "came out unequivocally in support of the Congress" (the Indian National Congress Party) "and its demand for Indian Independence."[42] As India became an independent nation, the Indian Christian lay leadership could equip the indigenous Christian movement to rise to the challenges of autonomy. The NCCI, at that time under the leadership of Indian leaders, spoke up firmly that the Indian church should not be controlled by foreigners. Rajah B. Manikam assumed the responsibility of NCCI during the difficult post-war period, when the missionaries still held leadership positions, but under his leadership, "the Council changed from a kind of missionary institution to a truly indigenous organization."[43]

What is clear in this historical sketch is that there was an integral link between ecumenical initiatives and the nationalist movement in India and that the driving force for change came from Indians, not the Western missionaries. While Indian Christians agreed that mission and colonialism did not always go together, the growth of the modern ecumenical movement, to a large extent, was, on the one hand, the affirmation of the aspirations of the indigenous people for self-rule, and on the other, a clear rejection of Western domination not only at the political level, but also in the church.

According to the 2011 Census figures, the Christian population of India is 27.8 million or 2.3 percent of the country's population.[44] However, this figure is widely disputed

---

42. Ibid., 61.
43. Ibid., 62.

as, due to historical and cultural factors, it is difficult to officially tabulate the exact number of Christians.[45] Whatever be the real number of Christians, it is obvious that they have exerted an impact that is much greater than their numerical strength. During the long years of tension and violence between the Hindus and the Muslims, on the one hand, and Hindus and Sikhs, on the other, the Christian groups and churches often played a mediatory role, trying to bring peace and reconciliation between the warring communities. For the last several decades, however, the Christians themselves were often targeted by the majority community and accused of unfair proselytizing. Laws were passed in different states to restrict the freedom to convert from one religion to another. The ascendance of a Hindu nationalist government at the center has, once again, kindled fears that Christians will be targeted—especially in areas where they are a minority, such as North India.

At the time of India's independence, the Christian representatives in the Constituent Assembly gave the solemn assurance that the Christians of the nation will not demand any special privileges as a minority. In return, the government assured them that they will have the right to not only practice and preach, but also propagate their faith.[46] For the well-being and future of this secular and sovereign nation, it is essential that both parties abide by their solemn commitments.

44. "Population by Religious Community," Government of India, www.censusindia.gov.in /2011census/c-01.html (Accessed September 13, 2015).
45. Elsewhere in this book, the reality in India of secret believers, unbaptized Christians and people who owe their allegiance to more than one religion is acknowledged, leading to the possibility that the real number of Christians in the country could be much higher than the official figures.
46. The "covenant" between the Indian Christians and the rest of the nation at the Constituent Assembly is discussed in more detail below.

The Emergency and the Christian Response

The greatest test for both the civil society and faith communities in free India was when political Emergency was declared on June 25, 1975, when Indira Gandhi was the prime minister. Gandhi, the daughter of Nehru, the first prime minister was, like her father, a secularist, and she began her tenure on a positive note by nationalizing the banks. Later, she also ensured that the terms "secularism" and "socialism" were enshrined in the Preamble of the Constitution of India. The general elections of 1967 and 1971 gave her party and her near-absolute control over the government. Soon after she assumed power in 1971, India defeated Pakistan in a war that resulted in the independence of Bangladesh (formerly East Pakistan). In short, Indira Gandhi was at the peak of her power and the Indian National Congress party under her leadership enjoyed a huge majority in Parliament.[47]

Absolute power soon led to absolute corruption and there was an unprecedented concentration of power in the office of the prime minister, with not only elected officers, but also those without any accountability to the people or the Parliament wielding power. When the opposition parties started an anti-government movement in states such as Bihar, Gandhi sensed a threat to her absolute power and the Emergency rule was soon imposed. Under the Emergency regime, the civil liberties and democratic rights of ordinary citizens stood suspended. The freedom of the press was curtailed and censorship was imposed on all publications. Thousands of leaders of the opposition political parties were imprisoned across the nation. There was even a campaign

47. See Ramachandra Guha, *India After Gandhi: The History of the World's Largest Democracy* (New York: HarperCollins, 2008).

aimed at forced mass-sterilization under the guise of controlling population. The other leaders of the Congress Party, however, willingly went along with Gandhi's grab of power. The president of the party, D. K. Barooah even declared: "India is Indira, Indira is India!"

As the Emergency regime sought to control most areas of civil life, an underground movement spread across the country, resisting the draconian rules of the regime. Many Christian leaders affirmed, "what it means to be the Church in face of the fundamental ethical challenges of our time or, to put it differently, how church fellowship can be maintained in face of ethical conflicts."[48] The World Council of Churches and its Commission of the Churches on International Affairs (CCIA) and the Christian Conference of Asia (CCA) protested the Emergency regime.[49] The ecumenical response to Emergency, however, was not a unified voice; a good part of the official leadership of the established Indian churches of NCCI supported Gandhi's regime. In response to the widespread opposition from within and outside the country, the Emergency was lifted on March 21, 1977. In the general election that followed, Indira Gandhi and her Congress Party lost badly and power was captured by the opposition parties.

The Indian Emergency reminded us of how fragile the democratic fabric of the country was, but also provided the occasion for people of faith and others to rethink their priorities and come together to uphold the values of peace, justice, and freedom. During the Emergency, Metropolitan Juhanon Mar Thoma of the Mar Thoma Church wrote a letter

---

48. Konrad Raiser, "Ecumenical Discussion of Ecclesiology and Ethics," *The Ecumenical Review* 48:1 (January 1996): 7.

49. WCC General Secretary Philip Potter wrote a letter to Prime Minister Indira Gandhi on October 9, 1975 that expressed the anguish of the ecumenical community at the Emergency regime in India, under which freedom of expression and other democratic rights had been suspended.

to Prime Minister Gandhi, "advising her to withdraw the emergency in stages, to release political detainees and not to hold elections or make constitutional changes during the emergency."[50] Another Indian Christian leader, M. J. Joseph, resigned his job as the Development Secretary of NCCI and started organizing faith-based groups against the Emergency regime. The Political Detainees Family Distress Relief Fund during that period too was an ecumenical response to the situation. The coalition of the religious and secular people that had come together to fight the Emergency recognized the potential of a common platform for solidarity and fellowship and decided to stay together even afterwards in order to address the problems of poverty, inequality, and injustice faced by the people. Considering social activism as their vocation, they initiated social action groups in different parts of the country working with the rural poor, women, Dalits, tribals, fish workers and the victims of mega-development projects.

Freedom of Religion: A Christian Perspective

I have repeated the story of how the Constituent Assembly came to accept the inclusion of freedom of religious propagation in the Constitution's clause on the fundamental right of religious freedom in response to the Indian Christian community voluntarily giving up the communal representation proposed by Britain as safeguard for the Christian minority. . . . H. C. Mookerjee and Jerome de Sousa were the spokesmen for this secular nationalist cum Christian approach in the Constituent Assembly. "The immediate outcome was an offer by Sardar Patel and accepted by the Assembly that religious freedom in its full sense including the right to propagate religion should be written

---

50. M. M. Thomas, *Response to Tyranny* (New Delhi: Forum for Christian Concern for People's Struggles. 1979), 65.

into the Constitution, not as a minority right but as a fundamental right of the human person."[51]

The statement by M. M. Thomas quoted above is an indication of the deliberations on the topic freedom of religion in the Assembly that drafted India's Constitution. Freedom of religion for all is a fundamental right guaranteed by Article 15 and Article 25 of the Constitution of India. Every citizen has the right to practice and promote their religion. People may also choose to be non-religious, atheists, or agnostics. Even though Hindus constitute the overall majority in India, there are states and regions within the country where other religious groups are in the majority.[52] Even Hindus are divided into numerous sects and sub-sects, making it difficult for all of them to stand under one banner.

For all these reasons, freedom and flexibility in the practice of religion was, perhaps, the only viable option for the country. As India became independent and a Constitution was being formulated, such a contract was worked out between various religious groups and the Union of India in order to ensure the harmonious relationship of the various religious communities in the country. The statement of Thomas, quoted above, "was a sort of covenant between Christians and the nation on the part of Christians that they will not use their numerical strength for the purpose of their communal interest in politics and that the state would not restrict their evangelistic freedom and the growth of the Christian fellowship."[53] The right to propagate one's religion, which was included in this agreement, was interpreted to include the right to convert as well. This has

---

51. J. John & Jesudas M. Athyal, eds., *Religion, State and Communalism: A Post-Ayodhya Reflection* (Hong Kong: Christian Conference of Asia, 1995), 102–3.
52. In Jammu and Kashmir, the Muslims; in Punjab, the Sikhs; and in Mizoram, Nagaland, and Meghalaya, the Christians constitute the majority.
53. John and Athyal, 103.

been a contentious issue ever since independence and both the parties have been responsible for its violation. The laws restricting religious conversion passed by the states of Orissa and Arunachal Pradesh and the O. P. Tyagi Bill that was introduced in the Indian Parliament during the time of Prime Minister Morarji Desai in 1978 were in clear violation of the covenant on the part of the state. The Christians also seemed unhappy to give up "minority rights" that gave them some privileges over the majority community. All in all, there have been numerous instances when the letter and the spirit of the freedom of religion have been violated during the last few decades.

Along with the rise of Hindu nationalism in India, there has been an attempt to bring large parts of the country under anti-conversion laws in order to make any conversion extremely difficult. Christians are, of course, not the only religious group for whom religious conversion is important. The very birth of Buddhism and Jainism in ancient times can be seen as revolt movements against Hinduism. Even in independent India, B. R. Ambedkar led a large number of people out of Hinduism in order to found the Neo-Buddhist movement.[54] The Christian Mass Movements a century ago also resulted in the conversion of a large number of people. For all these reasons, and in the absence of any concrete evidence of religious conversions under fraudulent or coercive means in any part of the country, the recent attempts of the Hindu nationalists at widespread legislation to curtail all conversions call for a closer scrutiny.

Several secular scholars have gone beyond general discussions on conversion as a Constitutional right, and have focused on the dynamics of conversion in the Indian context.

---

54. See *Ambedkar and the Neo-Buddhist Movement*, eds. T. S. Wilkinson and M. M. Thomas (Madras: CISRS & CLS, 1972).

A few historians of the Delhi University, in a booklet published under the title, *Christian Conversions*, stated: "A sustained programme of violent attacks on Christian missionaries is a new element in the history and tradition of Indian life."[55] They conceded that forced conversion or conversion under fraudulent means is illegal, but added that there is little evidence that Christians (or any other minorities in India) have been indulging in large-scale conversion. On the contrary, by failing to act decisively against the Hindu nationalist groups which are targeting Christian priests and missionaries in Rajasthan, Maharashtra, and elsewhere, the government is only increasing the likelihood of similar attacks in other places too. As the Delhi University historians put it, the recent demand of the fundamentalist group for a "national debate" on conversion is not an innocuous one, but one that is orchestrated by the Hindutva forces bent on fomenting communal tension in the society.

Under these circumstances, how do we account for the enthusiasm of Hindu nationalists to pass legislation curtailing conversion? Gabriele Dietrich and Bastiaan Wielenga, in their study of the Indian society,[56] point toward a number of social and economic factors that contribute to religious tension. The rising economic strength of a section of Muslims and the growing number of Muslim proletariat in some towns are perceived as an economic and political threat by a section of the Hindus who traditionally held economic power. This situation provides fertile ground for communal tensions to flare up. In places such as Bihar, Jharkhand, and Chhattisgarh, the work of Christian social activists among the marginalized

---

55. Sumit Sarkar, Tanika Sarkar, & Pradip Datta, *Christian Conversions* (Kolkata: Alap, 2004), 38.
56. Dietrich and Wielenga, *Towards Understanding Indian Society*.

sections has resulted in the Dalits and Adivasis shaking off their yokes of oppression and marginalization. While few conversions have been registered in such contexts, communal riots often occur there—not over religious questions, but are precipitated by upper-caste Hindus who are threatened with the loss of their traditional control over the power structures in society.

Discussions on freedom of religion and religious conversion in modern India are invariably linked to the concept of secularism. Secularism in India can be seen as the freedom from discrimination against any religion, and also the advancement of progressive and renascent movements in all religions. As noted earlier, Indian secularism evolved primarily during the days of the struggle for independence and later through nation-building, and therefore is a product of modern Indian history. The neo-Hindu movements of the nineteenth century can be understood as a struggle within Hinduism to build up a religious humanism that is in dialogue with the secular and socialist movements of the country. The role of the Christian mission, and especially the freedom the downtrodden and marginalized people enjoyed to convert to Christianity and thus escape oppression, cannot be undermined. It is important in the current discussion on freedom of religion and religious conversion to listen to the perspective of the Dalits and tribals and to acknowledge that they are not mere objects of conversion, but are people with freedom and dignity, capable of chalking out their own destiny.

Has Christianity Failed in India?

There has been much discussion in recent years, especially

in the West, on why Christianity failed in India. In World Christianity, India has a unique place as the heritage of Christianity in the country goes back all the way to the first century CE, when St. Thomas is believed to have preached the gospel and established several churches there. While the roots of the ancient St. Thomas Christianity community are in Kerala, St. Thomas churches in the diaspora can be found in most cities of India and abroad—notably, in the Middle East, North America, Malaysia, and Singapore. Apart from the St. Thomas Christians, there is, in India, a strong presence of the Catholic, Protestant, and Pentecostal churches founded by various missionary organizations from the West. Under the British rule in the country, Christianity thrived, with church steeples soaring to the sky in most Indian cities. Even in independent India, which was committed to being a "secular democracy," Christianity flourished. Few other countries with a minority Christian population such as in India can boast of such a favorable environment for the church to grow.

The question, however, is often posed: why, despite such positive settings, did Christianity fail in India? The arguments for such criticism are quite persuasive. Tony Joseph, in his article in *Outlook*, narrates in detail the favorable climate Christianity enjoyed in India for a long period, and then states rather bluntly:

> The fact is, the story of Christianity in India is a story of dismal failure, demographically speaking . . . what does Indian Christianity have to show for its humongous effort in terms of men, money and material, over two millennia? Almost zilch—or somewhere between two and three per cent of the population. And that number is on the way down, not up—from 2.6 per cent in 1971 to 2.3 per cent in 2001.[57]

57. Tony Joseph, "Why Christianity Failed in India," in *Outlook* (April 13, 2015).

In India, Joseph pointed out, Christianity is doing far worse than in most parts of the world, while Hinduism is booming. Presently, he declared, around 78 percent of Indians are Hindus.

In a rejoinder to Tony Joseph, Philip Jenkins referred to Joseph's dependence on the official census figures regarding the demography of Indian Christianity and asserted that the Indian national census was "one of the world's great works of creative fiction" since the official records on Indian Christian population "has nothing whatever to do with actual numbers on the ground." A more realistic estimate reached by independent scholars, according to Jenkins, "would put it closer to four percent, say 45 million people. The reason for the suppression of the real strength of Christianity in India," as he put it, "is because of systematic and widespread persecution by Hindu extremist sects, often operating in alliance with local governments and police authorities — violence that receives virtually no publicity in the West."[58]

What more can be added to this debate? Tony Joseph's mistake is in considering proselytization as the yardstick to measure the success or failure of a religion. The situation in India is, of course, far more nuanced. As several theologians and sociologists have pointed out, the Christian "influence" or "culture" in India is far greater than the numerical strength of the community. Every major city in India has at least one school run by the Christians and many of the current key leaders of the country (including Hindu nationalists) have studied there. Second, it can also be stated that conversion or proselytization was not the primary objective of most

http://www.outlookindia.com/article/why-christianity-failed-in-india/293895 (Accessed September 14, 2015).
58. Philip Jenkins, "Has Christianity Failed in India?," in *Aleteia* (May 11, 2015). http://aleteia.org/2015/05/11/has-christianity-failed-in-india (Accessed October 27, 2015).

Christian missionaries in India. Joseph points out the case of Kerala, where Christianity is believed to have been in existence since the first century CE. All possible evidence points to the fact that the Kerala Christians, during the long period before the Western missionaries arrived there, hardly attempted to convert anyone. As has been pointed out elsewhere in this book, the Kerala Christians understood their vocation as *permeation*—living in harmony with their Hindu neighbors, but as the salt of the society.

Yes, following the work of the Western missionaries (Catholics—from the sixteenth century and Protestants—from the eighteenth century onwards), many people from the lower rungs of the society—particularly, Dalits and tribals—joined the Christian faith, but, in most cases, the initiative for conversion came from them, not from the missionaries. But "permeation" continued as a model for many missionaries—notably, C. F. Andrews, Ralph R. Keithan, Pakenham Walsh, Bede Griffiths, and several others. There is hardly any dispute over the fact that Mother Teresa—the most visible face of Christianity in modern India—or her missionary movement never attempted to convert anyone. Their focus, and the focus of most missionaries, was on charity work, social reform, and education. Yes, many of them also preached the gospel (evangelization), but generally shied away from any attempts at conversion.

Comparing the history and numerical growth of the Hindus and Sikhs in the United Kingdom to the history and number of Christians in India, as Joseph does in his article is, of course, comparing apples to oranges. We know that the last century has seen the heavy migration of Indians (mostly Hindus and Sikhs) to the UK whereas there has hardly been any migration from UK to India. And, almost all the Hindus and Sikhs in the UK are of Indian origin, which means there is hardly any addition to their numbers by religious conversion; the numerical growth seems largely due to the normal biological process apart from continuing migration.

For all these reasons, there are serious discrepancies between the official and actual figures on the demography of Christians in India. However, Tony Joseph's thesis on the failure of Christianity in the country is problematic for other reasons as well. As noted earlier, the impact of a community on the larger society is not always proportionate to their numerical strength. While the number of Zoroastrians in India (around 69,000) and Jews in the country (around 5,000) may be seen to be minuscule, their impact, especially in the areas of culture and commerce, far outweigh their numerical strength. Whether Christians constitute 2 percent or 6 percent of the total Indian population, the schools, colleges, and hospitals run by them are among the finest in the country and serve the whole society. While assessing whether a movement has "failed" or not, one needs to take into account the total picture, not merely the figures the government wants us to believe.

The Gender Divide and Human Sexuality

The waves of modernization and secularization in India have influenced traditional patriarchal structures as well; many Indian women are venturing out of their homes into the professional sphere. At least in principle, Indian women today enjoy an equal status with men in most areas of life. The religious structures, however, is where the age-old traditions are still reinforced and solidified. Even the Indian Christians who live in the United States and lead highly successful and professional lives in the secular world, are seen to fall back on tradition—translated here as casteist and patriarchal values—in the religious sphere. Women's marginalization from most leadership positions in religion, segregated seating on gender lines for religious ceremonies, and the insistence that women should cover their heads in the worship place are all part of an archaic tradition that has been successfully relocated in the diaspora. As George Zachariah pointed out, "the association between Patriarchy and Casteism based on notions of purity and pollution has influenced the doctrines and the ecclesial practices of the Indian churches."[59] Religious structures seem the last domain where age-old traditions are reinforced and where the hegemonic role of men and the subservient role of women are solidified.

Discussions on the increased participation of women in the church have often centered on questions of ordination—can women be ordained as priests and bishops?—but there are deeper questions facing women. Women have been serving, for the last few decades, as preachers, priests/presbyters, and even bishops in several Western Protestant churches, but the Eastern churches have been slower in welcoming women to leadership positions. In India, the Church of South India (CSI) and the Lutheran churches have gone ahead with the ordination of women as priests and even bishops. The St. Thomas Christians of Kerala and their congregations in the diaspora, have, however, not yet seriously addressed the matter. For these churches, the very entry of women in the sacred space of the high altar is considered taboo. Even the Pentecostal churches of the St. Thomas heritage are reluctant to include women in leadership positions!

59. Keynote Address presented at the seminar of the American Academy of Religion in Chennai (India) on the theme, "Identity and Social Distinctions among Indian Christians, at Home and in the Diaspora: Some Theological Reflections," on July 19, 2014 (unpublished).

While the question of women's participation in all realms of the church seems to be a settled matter in most mainline Protestant churches, this continues to be debated vigorously in the Roman Catholic and Orthodox churches. Like the churches of Kerala origin, the Catholic and Orthodox churches too do not ordain women as priests, though they follow a less rigid approach with regard to the leadership of women in corporate worship. Both the traditions have a long history of women serving as acolytes, and, in certain cases, as deacons. According to the Catholic scholar Phyllis Zagano, women as deacons is not a concept for the future, but "for the present, for today."[60] Pope Francis also has emphasized that women's participation in the Church cannot be limited "to the acolyte, to the president of Caritas [and] the catechist." Instead, what is needed today is "a more profound theology of women."[61] The Orthodox churches in many parts of the world, till a few centuries ago, had the practice of female deacons though, for a number of reasons, it fell into disuse. It is, however, important to note that the practice has neither been abolished by canon or a council nor completely disappeared. The Inter-Orthodox Theological Consultation that met in Rhodes, Greece in 1988 noted that deaconess were ordained within the sanctuary during the Divine Liturgy with two prayers: she received the orarion (the deacon's stole) and received Holy Communion at the altar. The consultation affirmed the need to revive the practice of women deacons.[62]

60. "A woman on the altar: Can the church ordain women deacons?" http://www.uscatholic.org/church/2011/11/woman-altar-can-church-ordain-women-deacons (Accessed September 14, 2015).
61. "Pope's Remarks on Women in the Church Call for Deeper Theology, Says Expert" in, *National Catholic Register* http://www.ncregister.com/daily-news/popes-remarks-on-women-in-the-church-call-for-deeper-theology-says-expert (Accessed September 14, 2015).
62. "Orthodox Deacons: Frequently Asked Questions," http://orthodoxdeacons.org/node/15 (Accessed September 14, 2015).

While sections in the Roman Catholic and Orthodox traditions have been open to the increased participation of women in the church, it is a relevant question as to why the Indian churches, with their long heritage, have been negative to the full participation of women in the church. Even the churches that accept, at the theological level, the equal participation of women are reluctant to take administrative steps to include women at least as deacons. The challenges before the Indian churches today include the need to review their position on women's increased participation in the church.

Posing an effective challenge to the forces of discrimination and marginalization has been one of the hallmarks of reformed Christianity. The Christian missions led the way in the struggles against slavery and racism in the West and in its opposition to *sati*[63] and child marriage in India. The liberation of women from oppressive structures emerged from the realization that their exclusion from the sacred space was an affront not merely to human dignity, but to the very core of the Christian faith as well. As Miroslav Volf put it: "As agents of reconciliation, people in general and Christians in particular must choose to make space for the other to enter in. A way to embrace the identity of self while also understanding that identity to be connected to the other for the sake of belonging needs to be made."[64] When the liberative and inclusive streams of the past blended with the current realities that were ready for a breakthrough in the tradition, a change was possible.

Equally important is the church's position on human sexuality. Perhaps the most explosive topic in the global

---

63. The burning of the widow at the funeral pyre of her husband.
64. Miroslav Volf, *Exclusion and Embrace: A Theological Exploration of Identity, Otherness, and Reconciliation* (Nashville: Abingdon Press, 1996), 49.

church in recent times is the issue of the acceptance of homosexuality within the fold of the church. An openness among the Protestant churches in the North to embrace people of diverse sexual orientations has been angrily denounced by several churches in the rest of the world, particularly in Africa, where today, Anglicanism is stronger than in any other continent. In the Indian society, there is a general reluctance to even discuss the matter of human sexuality. However, increasingly, the voices for sexual inclusion are being heard in the society, and therefore the trend seems to be in favor of at least discussing this matter.

One should also note that the current crises in the churches in the North over gender-sexuality issues have prompted the churches elsewhere to ask the question, how far should these issues be *our* priorities? In the West, while it is the question of sexual orientation that is shaking the foundations of the Anglican fellowship, it is the issue of sexual abuse by the clergy that is rocking the Roman Catholic Church. The churches and communities in India, on the contrary, are confronted by the existential problems of poverty, economic inequality, and political instability. For them, *these* are their priorities. While they recognize that gender and sexuality are issues that are relevant for every society and faith community, it is also important to note that there is no universal formula for addressing these, and each society should have the space and time to grapple with these in accordance with their own priorities.

Singing the Lord's Song in a Strange Land

"Indian Christianity" is not confined to India alone! For over a century, Indians have been migrating to the other parts of the world and they carried with them the faith, heritage, and traditions of their home land. Along with the general population, the Indian Christians were also part of this migration process. Initially, the migration was to the neighboring countries, primarily Ceylon (now Sri Lanka) and Burma (now Myanmar).[65] In the early decades of the twentieth century, Indians migrated to Malaysia and Singapore as well.[66] The middle of the last century witnessed the heavy migration of Indians to the Middle East—primarily, the various Arabian Gulf countries.[67] And from the 1960s onwards, Indians traveled to the West—the United States, Canada, United Kingdom and the rest of Europe.[68] Second, Indian Christianity traveled outside the country also because many Indian churches are missionary churches that sent missionaries to other countries. While these missionaries primarily serve the local community, they offer pastoral assistance to the Indian Christians too in the diaspora. All in all, today a significant number of the Indian Christians live in the diaspora.[69]

Among all these different locations of migration of Indian Christians, the North American context is unique in several

65. From 1947, when the Church of South India (CSI) was inaugurated, one of the dioceses under the Church has been the CSI Diocese of Jaffna, located in North Sri Lanka. The diocese comprises primarily Christians who migrated from Tamil Nadu, in the early decades of the twentieth century, to Sri Lanka primarily as plantation workers, and their descendants.
66. Mar Thoma Church (MTC) has been active in Malaysia since 1911, and in 1962, a Diocese of Malaysia and Singapore was established.
67. Today, some of the largest parishes of the Indian denominations are in Kuwait, Dubai, Abu Dhabi, and the other places in the Middle East.
68. Among Indian churches, the Indian Orthodox Church, Jacobite Syrian Christian Church, Syro-Malankara Catholic Church, and the Mar Thoma Church each have today dioceses and resident bishops in North America.
69. Several examples can be cited for the missionary work of the Indian Christians. In 1960, the missionaries of the Mar Thoma Church took the initiative to build the Putali Sadak Church of Christ in Nepal in the heart of the Kathmandu city, as the first church building in that erstwhile Hindu Kingdom. Another example is from the Mizo Presbyterian Church which, according to a church report in 2014, supports more than one thousand missionaries, inside and outside of Mizoram.

respects, mainly because this is where there has been the heaviest flow of Indian Christians in recent decades. Also, unlike several other contexts (notably, the Middle East, Malaysia, and Singapore), assimilation to the local culture and community has been much more rapid in America. It is here that the Indian Christians are taking roots, settling down, and a second and third generation are now growing up as hybrid Indian Americans exhibiting characteristics of both the cultures. For all these reasons, we need to take a closer look at the Indian Christians in the American context.

First of all, Indian Christianity in North America needs to be located in the context of the shifting center of gravity of world Christianity. Scholars of religion are convinced that unprecedented and momentous changes are happening in world Christianity right before our eyes. Their thesis, stated in simple terms, goes like this: due to secularization, migration to New Religious Movements, and the sheer fall in population, Christianity is rapidly declining in America and Europe. On the contrary, due to missionary work, the Christian faith is galloping in Africa and Asia. Let us listen to the findings of some of these scholars: *The Atlas of Global Christianity*, published in 2010, focused sharply on the significance of the shifting center of gravity of Christianity to the global South. It corrected, "the false impression that Christianity is a Western religion" and affirmed that "Southern Christians can rediscover the theological, ecclesiastical and missiological trajectory of the first Christian millennium, when Southern Christians were in the majority and the center of gravity was in Western Asia."[70] About the European context, Kim Cain added: "A century ago 66 percent of the world's Christians lived in

---

70. Todd M. Johnson and Kenneth R. Ross, eds., *Atlas of Global Christianity 1910–2010* (Edinburgh: Edinburgh University Press, 2010), 51.

Europe, but today it accounts for only 26 percent of the world's Christian population."[71] According to Philip Jenkins, during "the past half century the center of gravity of the Christian world has moved decisively to the global South."[72] Due to all these changes, Dana Robert of Boston University affirmed: the "story of Christianity as a worldwide faith is being written before our eyes."[73] In short, while several sections of the traditionally Anglo-Saxon Northern communities are today shifting culturally to post-Christianity and undergoing varying degrees of secularization, intense and growing religiosity in the South is keeping the Christian faith vibrant.

The studies on the decline of Christianity in the Northern hemisphere was applied by other scholars to the specific context of America. In an issue of *Newsweek* published a few years ago, Jon Meacham argued that Christians now make up a declining percentage of the American population and that this trend would eventually lead to the marginalization of Christianity in the United States.[74] According to him, several Christians—the mainstream religious group in the United States—are drifting away from organized religion into either new religious movements or to a secular humanist worldview. Al Mohler, the President of the Southern Baptist Theological Seminary, in his article in *Newsweek*, endorsed Meacham and lamented what he perceived to be a disturbing trend. Mohler believed that "the historic foundation of America's religious culture was cracking."[75] He is particularly disturbed by the

71. Kim Cain (2011), "World Christianity has a New Address, a New Look and Many Names." http://www.pcusa.org/news/2011/10/17/world-christianity-has-new-address-new-look-and-ma (Accessed September 11, 2015).
72. Philip Jenkins, "Christianity Moves South" in *Global Christianity: Contested Claims*, eds. Frans Wijsen and Robert Schreiter (Amsterdam: Rodopi, 2007), 15.
73. "Report from Global Christian Forum 2011," http://www.bu.edu/cgcm/2011/10/12/report-from-global-christian-forum-2011 (Accessed October 27, 2015).
74. Jon Meacham, "The End of Christian America," in *Newsweek* (April 4, 2009).
75. Al Mohler, "Newsweek—The End of Christian America" in *Newsweek* (April 6, 2009).

decline of Christianity in New England, the cradle of the faith in the New World. With the rise of a secular culture in New England—an area where Puritanism, Protestantism, Roman Catholicism and Judaism, have all historically had influence—the region has ". . . emerged in 2008 as the new stronghold of the religiously unidentified."[76] In short, many scholars agree that the future of Christianity in North America, and in particular in places such as New England, is bleak.

There have, however, been counter-voices as well. In a rejoinder to Meacham's article, Soong-Chan Rah questioned the narrative of the decline of Christianity in the United States and argued that what is declining in the country is not so much the Christian faith as *Europeanized* Christianity. He, in fact, went a step further and argued that "American Christianity may actually be growing, but in unexpected and surprising ways." Soong-Chan's primary thesis is that immigrant Christian groups are rapidly replacing the space traditionally occupied by the Christians of European descent. Coming back to Al Mohler's point about the decline of Christianity, particularly in New England, Soong-Chan noted:

> Let's take for example the Northeastern city of Boston in a region of the country that Mohler believes we have "lost." In 1970, the city of Boston was home to about 200 churches. Thirty years later, there were 412 churches. The net gain in the number of churches was in the growth of the number of churches in the ethnic and immigrant communities. While only a handful of churches in 1970 held services in a language other than English, thirty years later, more than half of those churches held services in a language other than English.[77]

76. Ibid.
77. Soong-Chan Rah (2013), "The End of Christianity in America?," www.patheos.com/Resources/Additional-Resources/End-of-Christianity-in-America.html (Accessed Sept. 11, 2015).

Participating in the debate on the "coloring of American Christianity," Stephen Warner also noted that a large number of the recent immigrants to the United States are Christians. While the immigrants from Central and Latin America are predominantly Catholic, the Asian Christian immigrants are mostly Protestant and evangelical: "This means that the new immigrants represent not the de-Christianization of American society but the de-Europeanization of American Christianity."[78]

In short, as the North is rapidly ceasing to be a "Christian context" in the traditional sense, the immigrant groups in the diaspora are rapidly re-defining the meaning of world Christianity. It is in this larger context that we need to locate the story of Indian immigrant Christianity in America. As one of the fastest growing Christian groups in North America, the Indian church communities in the diaspora provide interesting and significant transnational linkages across the North–South divide from which much can be learned. They are part of both the resurgence of Christianity in the South and the emergent immigrant Christianity in the North, and consequently their presence in the diaspora provide transnational bridges across the North–South divide.

As the Indian Christians migrated to North America from the 1960s onwards, they were called upon to strike a balance between the social and cultural realities of their new homes and the values they brought along with them. The resultant conflicts often gave rise to cultural, social, and religious tensions which became particularly pronounced as the immigrant groups settled down in their new homes and second and subsequent generations were born and brought up in the

---

78. Stephen R. Warner, "Coming to America: Immigrants and the Faith They Bring," in *The Christian Century* 121:3 (February 10, 2004): 20–23.

diaspora. A dominant response to such challenges was for the immigrant Christians to create their own ecclesiastical and cultural havens in an alien context, in the process, evolving islands of familiarity. As the fledgling migrant groups took roots and became part of the local community, however, their religious institutions also underwent radical changes.

Indian Christians in America are generally known to self-segregate into linguistic and caste associations. Marriage alliances outside the denomination and ethnic community are generally frowned upon. Even church gatherings are seen by some as places to facilitate matchmaking without disrupting the caste codes. "The traditional family values of the Indian Churches and the patriarchal theology of American Christian Right groups provide theological sanction to patriarchy among the Indian Christian Diaspora in the US. Hierarchy, patriarchy, and casteism are ingrained in the DNA of the Indian Diaspora, and people faithfully internalize them and transmit them with religious zeal."[79] For long, Indians had taken for granted the "sanctity" of their marriages and believed that their family relationships were morally superior to that of the rest of the world. This assumption is, of course, questionable as they tend to ignore the anomalies in their own system, especially, the oppression and marginalization of women within a highly patriarchal family set up. Nor do they often consider that they were historically the beneficiaries in a caste-based and feudal-oriented social relationship.

The first generation Indian Christian immigrants in the United States are now aging and are rapidly being replaced by a second and third generation, who were born and brought

79. George Zachariah, "Identity and Social Distinctions among Indian Christians, at Home and in the Diaspora: Some Theological Reflections" (Paper presented at the meeting of Indian Christian theology in Chennai on July 19, 2014. Unpublished.).

up in North America as Indian Americans and they reflect the cultures of both the contexts. The new generation is now raising significant questions about the values and priorities of their elders. While institutions in India have traditionally been patriarchal at the social as well as religious levels, women are increasingly assuming positions of leadership in the diaspora churches. Caste—another major factor shaping the social and religious life in India—too is getting blurred in the American context. Do these gender-caste dynamics point to a more inclusive social and faith community in the American context? What are the contours of these differences and what is the direction of the changes? How is the ethnic and religious distinctiveness of the Indian Christians shaping their responses to the other Indian and American faith communities, and in particular to other forms of Christianity in the region? It is in seeking answers to these and other questions that we find our own identity and mission as hyphenated Christians in the diaspora.

In the ultimate analysis, it needs to be noted that a community's urge to settle down in a desirable location and build religious institutions around it to reflect its identity and prosperity can lead to stagnation. We know that the churches of European origin—both in Europe and in North America—despite their enormous resources and elaborate institutions are today in a state of decline, both in terms of membership and momentum. This can be the story of any immigrant community that seeks to settle down and prosper without addressing fundamental questions of identity and mission. Like most other immigrant groups, the Indian Christians in the diaspora too are today at the cutting edge of the rapid changes in culture, religiosity, and social values with questions and challenges of their own. The story of Christianity is the account of adaptability as the faith moved from one context to another. As a faith community, the church's identity and ministry should ultimately be linked to the mission of God.

Conclusion

Religion in any context is a social institution, but all the more so in a society like India, where private faith and public life are so interwoven. The challenge was, however, to ensure that all religious communities, even the numerically smallest one, would have their place in the sun. The tradition of secularism and religious harmony goes a long way back in the history of India, to the legacy of the Mughal Emperor Akbar's spirit of accommodation, Mahatma Gandhi's principle of non-violence, and Jawaharlal Nehru's commitment to a fair deal for all. The Indian Christians were certainly part of this heritage and they contributed richly to building up a secular and democratic India. And, yet, this journey was never a smooth one. Religious fundamentalism, sectarianism, and intolerance crept into India, like in all other societies. At times the Christians were the victims of this process, but at other times they too contributed to feeding the passion of hatred. The process of building a social order rooted in the values of peace, justice, and freedom calls for eternal vigilance and clarity of vision on the part of all.

India is like a well-worn palimpsest—a manuscript that has been written on by many different people throughout the generations. Each time a writer wants to compose a new message, she scrapes off the previous one in order to record a message of her own. In spite of her efforts to erase the previous one, it remains, just under the deceptively clean surface. But in reality, all of the messages ever written on that palimpsest are hidden just underneath a previous layer of parchment. Scholars who work with ancient texts can discover various messages composed throughout history by carefully deciphering the contents of previous authors.

Such is the case of India. Many civilizations have come and gone, using this beautiful landscape for their own purposes. And while empires fall and scatter, there are remnants, messages, and ideas left behind. By scratching a bit at the surface, we are often able to see that there is another message, perhaps many other messages, hidden just underneath. India's sociopolitical context is multilayered, haunted by messages from the past. But when observed carefully, those distant voices begin to be heard anew.

4

Geographical

Where Are India's Christians?

The Diamond Nation: An Overview of Indian Geography

Before the age of globalization, technology, and air travel, it was not easy for travelers to access India due to its protected geography: vast oceans in the south, the Thar Desert in the northwest, the stupendous Himalayas in the north, and the dense, nearly impenetrable forests of the extreme northeast. Northeast India's Naga and Khasi Hills are the rainiest places oxn earth.

India is nearly in the shape of a diamond, or like a kite. The southernmost point extends toward the Indian Ocean—that large body of water between Africa's east coast and Australia and Indonesia's west coasts. India's southwest side borders the Arabian Sea, and the small Laccadive Sea separates South India

from Sri Lanka and the Maldives. On India's southeast side is
the Bay of Bengal, shared by Bangladesh, Burma, and Sri Lanka.

Map of India's States (Created by Daniel Spencer).

On the northwest border of the Indian diamond is Pakistan,
which until 1947, was part of India. India's Independence Day
is August 15, 1947. That is also Partition Day, when India and
Pakistan split into separate countries. Between 1947 and 1971,
Pakistan was a nation consisting of two land masses: modern-
day Pakistan and modern-day Bangladesh. In 1971, Bangladesh

seceded from Pakistan, leaving the geographical situation as it stands today.

India's northernmost tip is a hotly contested region of the world that has led to three recent wars (1947, 1965, and 1999) and frequent, often violent, conflicts. This region is usually called Kashmir, although that is an imprecise term. The larger Kashmir region is split into three parts—administered by India, Pakistan, and China. The India-administered region is known as the Indian state of Jammu and Kashmir. It sits way up high on the western edge of the Himalayas.

The northeast border of India's diamond-shaped land consists of China, Nepal, Bhutan, Myanmar (Burma), and Bangladesh. The defining feature of this northeastern side is the Himalayan mountain range, the world's highest. Led by Mount Everest, these mammoth peaks reach nearly 30,000 feet into the sky.

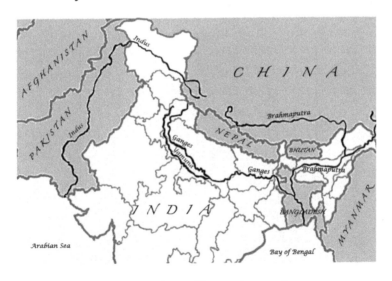

Map of India's four main rivers (Created by Daniel Spencer).

Land of Sacred Rivers

In terms of area, India is about a third the size of the United States. It is a land blessed with natural resources, especially an abundance of water coming down the rivers of the Himalayas, as well as a dependable monsoon season. Rivers play a major role in India. Not only are they considered sacred, and therefore revered by Hindus, but they also nourish India's billion plus citizens, provide electricity, and make for convenient transportation.[1]

The four great rivers of north India are the Ganges, the Yamuna, the Brahmaputra, and the Indus. The Ganges flows from the state of Uttarakhand in the Himalayas, across the northern states of Uttar Pradesh, Bihar, Jharkhand, and West Bengal, and empties into Bangladesh's portion of the Bay of Bengal. It is considered the holiest of India's rivers, passing Hinduism's most sacred city: Varanasi (formerly known as Benares).

India's second holiest river is the Yamuna, and it is entirely in India. It, too, flows from Uttarakhand. It then passes through or near Uttar Pradesh, Haryana, Himachal Pradesh, and Delhi. The confluence of three rivers: the Ganges, Yamuna, and the (mythical) Saraswati takes place at Allahabad (Prayag), in Uttar Pradesh. Prayag—the traditional Hindu name for the city—is one of four holy sites for the rotating Kumbh Mela festival, said to be the largest gathering of humans on earth. The festival gathers four times during a twelve-year span, based on zodiacal positioning. It is believed that this holy confluence of rivers has the power to remove sins from people so that they may have a good rebirth, or perhaps, even achieve

1. A good resource is Diana Eck, *India: A Sacred Geography* (New York: Three Rivers Press, 2012).

moksha—full liberation and cessation from the cycle of rebirth (*samsara*).

The third major river of north India is the Brahmaputra, meaning "son of Brahma." Brahma is the creator in Hinduism, and is part of the Hindu trinity (or Trimurti), consisting also of Vishnu (the sustainer) and Siva (the destroyer). The Brahmaputra River flows from Tibet into the Himalayas, where it travels through some of the world's most rugged mountain terrain, consisting of gigantic mountains and breathtaking canyons. It begins its Indian journey in the far northeastern state of Arunachal Pradesh. It plunges south into Assam, flows into Bangladesh, and finally, empties into the Bay of Bengal. Today, only two of India's states are host to the Brahmaputra, but before the 1947 Partition, Bangladesh was part of India.

The fourth major river of India's north is the Indus. Originating in Tibet, it runs down the length of Pakistan. The Indus has sustained human civilization for over five thousand years. One of the world's most ancient civilizations—the Indus Valley Civilization, also known as Harappa—flourished because of the Indus and its many distributaries. Scholars have yet to decipher the Harappan script, which would undoubtedly reveal a treasure trove of information about this rather mysterious people. The primary recipient of the mighty Indus River has always been the Punjab region, an extremely fertile land politically rent into two by the Partition. The word "Punjab" means "five waters," referring to the chief tributaries of the Indus: the Jhelum, Chenab, Ravi, Sutlej, and Beas. While the Indus is located mainly in Pakistan, it dramatically crosses India's northernmost state—Jammu and Kashmir—from its southeast corner to its northwestern side. The Punjab region is closely associated with Sikhism, a religion founded by Guru

Nanak in the 1400s. Sikhism is the majority religion in the Indian state of Punjab, at around 58 percent.[2]

These four rivers—the Ganges, Yamuna, Brahmaputra, and Indus—and dozens of other major tributaries, bring abundant water to one of the most fertile swaths of land on the planet known as the Indo-Gangetic Plain, the massive stretch between the Indus and the Ganges rivers. About a billion people live there because it easily sustains them. Many huge cities exist in this geographical bread basket: Dhaka (Bangladesh), Kolkata, Allahabad, Delhi, Lahore (Pakistan), and Karachi (Pakistan). There is little doubt that this most densely populated region in the world will continue to swell in numbers because of its sheer ability to support life, as pristine and fresh waters continually flow down from the beautiful Himalayas.

South India: Land of the Deccan Plateau

Separating North India from South India is Madhya Pradesh, Hindi for "middle land." Set right in the heart of India, this state is second in size after Rajasthan, the great desert state of India. Madhya Pradesh (MP) is a land thick with forests and jungles. Over the ages, its almost impenetrable terrain has contributed to its underdevelopment. MP's lush landscape is home to hundreds of tribal groups in India. Collectively, the tribal peoples of India are known as Adivasis (aboriginal). Conversations about Adivasis in India are extremely sensitive. On the one hand, they are somewhat cut off from the rest of the country, partly by choice. On the other hand, attempts to bring them into the larger fabric of India are often perceived as a threat to their ancient lifestyle.

---

2. See the 2011 Census of India religion statistics, located at: http://www.censusindia.gov.in/2011census/C-01.html.

South India is a completely different space geographically. It is dominated by the Deccan Plateau, a 2,000-foot tableland, which dominates the terrain of Central and South India. The Deccan—a word which comes from the Sanskrit for "south"—takes the shape of a downward pointing triangle, like the southernmost half of the Indian subcontinent itself. The Deccan is bordered by two mountain ranges: the Western Ghats and the Eastern Ghats. They prevent the plateau from receiving too much moisture. The region is therefore relatively dry.

Map of Deccan Plateau (Created by Daniel Spencer).

In many ways, South India is a different world from North India. The bulk of India's southern population is referred to as

"Dravidians." This term has been commonly employed to refer to the people and languages of South India since the British missionary and linguist Robert Caldwell in the nineteenth century.[3] Caldwell theorized that South Indian languages were very different from the Sanskrit-based languages of the North. He argued that the Dravidian languages have a history of their own. In his view, the most primary South Indian language is Tamil, "the most highly cultivated . . . of all Dravidian idioms . . . in which nearly all the literature has been written."[4] In his view, several languages are undoubtedly offshoots of Tamil, such as Malayalam (Kerala), Kannada (Karnataka), and Telugu (Andhra Pradesh and Telangana).[5]

South Indians also have a sense that they represent a more pristine, more ancient Indian culture. They see their Dravidian language and culture as being indigenous to India, as opposed to the Sanskrit culture of North India. This is a very complicated and often controversial topic. But it has to do with the famous Aryan invasion theory that divides scholars who research India. Essentially, the theory is this: around 1500 BC, Aryan people—light-skinned, possibly coming from Persia—entered India and dominated because they were culturally and technologically advanced. They brought their language, Sanskrit, as well as their religion, Vedic Hinduism, with them. The proponents of this theory argue that Sanskrit is part of the Indo-European family of languages, thereby insinuating that Hindu culture has its origins in the West. As the dominion of the Aryans grew, the indigenous people—the Dravidians—migrated south into what are now the states of

---

3. See Caldwell's philological masterpiece *A Comparative Grammar of the Dravidian or South-India Family of Languages* (Chennai: University of Madras, 2000), originally published in 1856.

4. Caldwell, *A Comparative Grammar*, 47.

5. Frykenberg, *Christianity in India*, 30.

Karnataka, Tamil Nadu, Andhra Pradesh, Telangana, and Kerala. We should emphasize that this theory is contested, primarily by Indian nationalists, who want to stress that Sanskrit language and culture are indigenous to the subcontinent, and were not imported from the West at some time in the distant past. According to Indian historian Rowena Robinson, this debate is ultimately about separating "the rightful owner/inheritors of the land" from the "foreigner," "arriviste," or "parvenu." The discourse, and its resolution, has "enormous implications."[6]

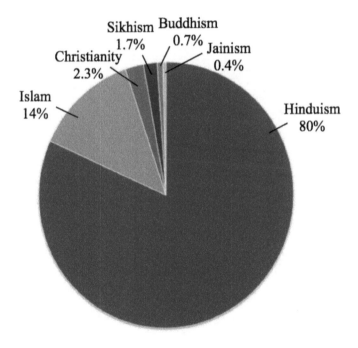

Pie Chart of India's Religions (Created by Daniel Spencer).

6. Rowena Robinson, *Christians of India* (New Delhi: Sage, 2003), 14. Robinson's discussion on pp. 13ff is extremely helpful.

India's Christians: By the Numbers

Although Christianity is the third largest religion in India, after Hinduism (80%) and Islam (14%) it claims the allegiance of around 2.3 percent of the population.[7] Officially, that is around 30 million Christians in India. The percentage of Christians in India is probably shrinking.[8] Why? The most obvious reason has to do with fertility and compounding numbers. It is difficult for Christians to catch up when 97 percent of the population is non-Christian. They would need a much higher fertility rate than the rest of the population if they were to gain any ground.

2001 Literacy Rates

Name of Religion	Literacy Rate (Total)	Literacy Rate (Males)	Literacy Rate (Females)
Hinduism	65.1	76.2	53.2
Islam	59.1	67.6	50.1
Christianity	80.3	84.4	76.2
Sikhism	69.4	75.2	63.1
Buddhism	72.7	83.1	61.7
Jainism	94.1	97.4	90.6
India	**64.8**	**75.3**	**53.7**

2011 Literacy Rates

Total	Males	Females
74.0	**82.1**	**65.5**

Graph of India's literacy rates by religion and gender (Created by Daniel Spencer).

---

7. See the 2011 India Census figures at: http://www.censusindia.gov.in/2011census/C-01.html.
8. See Fernando and Gispert-Sauch, xiii.

One major issue that impacts fertility rates is education, and in India, Christians are more educated than both Muslims and Hindus. In fact, the literacy rate for Christians (80%) is significantly higher than the literacy rates for Hindus (65%), Muslims (59%), Sikhs (69%), and Buddhists (73%).[9] In general, higher rates of education imply a decreasing fertility rate. It is crucial to note that Indian Christian women have relatively high literacy rates (76%) when compared with the women in India's other major religions: Hindus (53%), Muslims (50%), Sikhs (63%), and Buddhists (62%).

Another possibility for the apparently declining percentage of Christians in India is that Christians may hide their faith identity for fear of losing social and economic benefits, including employment, due to discrimination. It is a fact that some Christians in India are closet Christians. On a personal note, the authors of the present volume have encountered numerous situations where several people in a household are Christian, but the head of the household is not. The census does not account for these differences. Rather, the head of the household provides his religion, and the entire family is assumed to be members of his faith.

Is Christianity growing anywhere in India.[10] Yes, the Indian censuses show that Christianity is growing dramatically in four states: Arunachal Pradesh, Manipur, Sikkim, and Tripura. While their Christian growth has been remarkable, it should be noted that all of these are northeastern states, where a good number of Christians already exist. There can be little

9. See Census India, "Distribution of Population by Religions," http://censusindia.gov.in/Ad_Campaign/drop_in_articles/04-Distribution_by_Religion.pdf (Accessed October 28, 2014). It should be noted that Jains have the highest literacy in the nation; it is above 90% for men and women.

10. I have compared the 2011 census with the previous two, in 2001 and 1991, for this section. For the 1991 census, I relied on the excellent statistical analyses of Rowena Robinson in *Christians of India*, 34ff.

doubt that missionaries from the Christian-majority states of Nagaland, Mizoram, and Meghalaya have played a part in this evangelization process. However, these numbers must not be misinterpreted. After all, the population of northeastern India is tiny in comparison with the rest of India. The Christian states of the northeast have only two or three million people each. Assam is the only northeastern state with a significant population—around 30 million—but Christianity is small there, only about 4 percent.

Christianity stagnates in the well-populated states of Tamil Nadu (72 million) and Kerala (33 million), among others. It is contracting slightly in seven or eight states. In about half of India's 36 states and territories, however, Christianity sees continued growth, albeit very modest. But the fact that most of its growth has been in the smaller states means, overall, Christianity is probably losing a little ground.

Where are India's Christians?

India has 29 states and seven union territories.[11] Of these 36 geographical divisions, Christianity is a *majority* in three: Nagaland (88%), Mizoram (87%), and Meghalaya (75%).

In five of them, Christianity is a *significant minority*, meaning Christians comprise between 10 percent and 50 percent of the population: Andaman and Nicobar (21%), Arunachal Pradesh (30%), Goa (25%), Kerala (18%), and Manipur (41%).

In eight of them, Christianity is an *appreciable minority*, meaning Christians comprise between 2 percent and 10 percent of the population: Assam (4%), Jharkhand (4%),

---

11. Data is from the 2011 India census. See http://www.censusindia.gov.in/2011census/C-01.html.

Karnataka (2%), Odisha (3%), Puducherry (6%), Sikkim (10%), Tamil Nadu (6%), and Tripura (4%).

In 20 Indian states, Christianity is *tiny*, meaning Christians comprise less than 2 percent of the population: Andhra Pradesh, Bihar, Chandigarh, Chhattisgarh, Dadra and Nagar Haveli, Daman and Diu, Delhi, Gujarat, Haryana, Himachal Pradesh, Jammu and Kashmir, Lakshadweep, Madhya Pradesh, Maharashtra, Punjab, Rajasthan, Telangana, Uttar Pradesh, Uttarakhand, and West Bengal.

- **Christian *Majority* (over 50%)**

  - Nagaland (88%)
  - Mizoram (87%)
  - Meghalaya (75%)

- **Christianity is a *Significant Minority* (10%–50%)**

  - Andaman and Nicobar (21%)
  - Arunachal Pradesh (30%)
  - Goa (25%)
  - Kerala (18%)
  - Manipur (41%)

- **Christianity is an *Appreciable Minority* (2%–10%)**

  - Assam (4%)
  - Jharkhand (4%)
  - Karnataka (2%)
  - Odisha (3%)
  - Puducherry (6%)
  - Sikkim (10%)
  - Tamil Nadu (6%)
  - Tripura (4%)

- **Christianity is *Tiny* (less than 2%)**
  - Andhra Pradesh
  - Bihar
  - Chandigarh
  - Chhattisgarh
  - Dadra and Nagar Haveli
  - Daman and DiuDelhi
  - Gujarat
  - Haryana
  - Himachal Pradesh
  - Jammu and Kashmir
  - Lakshadweep
  - Madhya Pradesh
  - Maharashtra
  - Punjab
  - Rajasthan
  - Telangana
  - Uttar Pradesh
  - Uttarakhand
  - West Bengal

We could say that Christianity is on the outskirts of Indian geography. The two hotspots are the far northeast and the deep South, two regions often characterized as being outside the mainstream of Sanskritized India. The far northeastern states are in a class of their own due to their remote, tribal background, and their strong connections to Southeast Asia. The Dravidian Indians of Kerala and Tamil Nadu share a slightly different history than the people of the northern and central heartlands. Predictably, the former European strongholds of Puducherry (French) and Goa (Portuguese) in Southern India each have a good-sized Christian community.

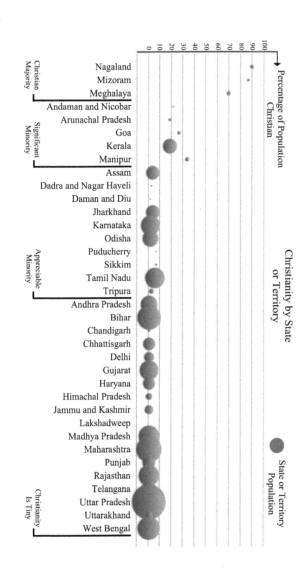

Graph of the percentage of Christians per Indian state (created by Daniel Spencer)

Indian Christianity in an Indian Way

Christianity does not exist outside of local, particular contexts. This is certainly the case in India, a gigantic non-Christian nation where the chief influences have been neither Christian, Jewish, Greek, Latin, or anything Western. While, in recent times, the Western world has made huge impacts on India through language (English), politics (especially democracy), and technology, Indian culture has remained comparatively unaffected by the *religion* of the Western world—Christianity. What we mean by this is that while Indians learn English, have adopted democracy—indeed, they are the world's largest—and integrate the technological advances of the Western world, they seem very reluctant to accept the Christian packaging that these three ideas arrived in. Indians seem content with their overarching culture. They prefer to pick and choose what aspects of the West they want to receive. Even India's Christians operate more by conventions and norms found in Hinduism than in the Western, supposedly Christian world. For the visitor, the *Indianness* of Christianity can be striking. While Indian Christians indeed follow Christ, they do so in profoundly Indian ways.

In recent decades, there has been much controversy over whether Christianity can possibly be considered an Indian faith.[12] On the face of it, there is no argument; Christianity is an Indian faith since it is present in India. However, there are those who consider any religion that originated outside India as being somehow non-Indian. The topic is controversial and the literature is vast, but suffice it to say that many Indian Christians are discriminated against because of their faith.

12. See Dyron Daughrity, "The Indianness of Christianity: The Task of Re-imagination," in *Re-imagining South AsianReligions*, eds. Pashaura Singh and Michael Hawley (Leiden: Brill, 2013), 245–70.

India's "Hindu code bills," passed in the 1950s, have been criticized for relegating Christians, Muslims, Parsis, and Jews to a second-class status since the origins of these religions are found outside of Indian soil. Hindus, Buddhists, Jains, and Sikhs, however, are granted more rights and privileges simply because these religions either began in India, or, as in the case of Hinduism, they have been in India for as far back in history as can be perceived.[13]

Christianity in India takes many forms, and the situation on the ground is extremely complex. On the one hand, since Christianity is such a small presence in India—only 2.3 percent officially—it can go ignored in many parts of the nation. On the other hand, in Kerala, Goa, and the northeast, Christianity is crucial. Indeed, the Nagas and the Mizos of northeastern India cannot be understood apart from their relatively recent conversion to the Christian faith.

Contextualizing Indian Christianity, State by State

In this section, we discuss Indian Christianity using geography as our guide. By briefly assessing Christianity in each of India's 36 states and territories, the colorful tapestry that is Indian Christianity will emerge. It should be emphasized, however, that even India's states contain within themselves a breathtaking diversity of tribes, castes, languages, and subcultures that are baffling to outsiders. Bishop Lesslie Newbigin once commented on this diversity when he said, "Every village is different and has a different story."[14]

---

13. See Rowena Robinson, *Christians of India*, 18–20.
14. Bishop Newbigin said this to historian Andrew Wingate. See Wingate, *The Church and Conversion* (Delhi: ISPCK, 1997), 6.

Map of India's States.

Indeed, each district, each village, and each Indian Christian carries a complex story of how she/he/they came to Christianity, why they have remained Christian, and how they embody the message of Jesus Christ today. Even so, it is hoped that by homing in on each state, one at a time, we will, to some extent, avoid the mistake of missing the trees for the forest.[15]

15. An excellent and recent resource for understanding the state of Christianity in India today is *The Oxford Encyclopaedia of South Asian Christianity* (New Delhi: Oxford University Press, 2012), in two volumes, by Roger Hedlund (chief editor), Jesudas Athyal, Joshua Kalapati (associate editors), and Jessica Richard (editorial assistant). The

This section will be best read with a map of India's states on hand.

Andaman and Nicobar Islands

This territory of 550 islands is closer to Myanmar, Thailand, and Indonesia than it is to mainland India. The islands effectively separate the Bay of Bengal from the Andaman Sea. With around 500,000 inhabitants, the archipelago is among the smallest and least populated of India's states and territories. It was first evangelized in 1690 by a Portuguese Franciscan. French Jesuits arrived in 1711, but were martyred within a few years. In the mid-eighteenth century, Denmark sent some Moravian Brethren from the Tranquebar mission to work there. In the 1830s, another wave of Jesuits arrived.[16]

The British set up a naval base there in the late 1700s. Following the Sepoy Mutiny of 1857, the British used Ross Island as a penal colony, and for years, put political prisoners there. Its infamous cellular prison was created for those who threatened the rule of the British Raj. The prison was constructed in such a way as to keep each prisoner in solitary confinement. After World War I, the British stationed Catholic laborers there from Chotanagpur (West Bengal, Jharkhand, Bihar, Odisha, and Chhattisgarh) to work in the forests. In 1928, a Catholic priest from Rangoon, Burma, began to visit twice per year for pastoral duties. Perhaps the most effective missionaries to the islands were V. Solomon, an Anglican who

state and territory entries are often the most recent evaluation of Christianity in those contexts, and I have relied on them for detailed observations. Contributors are almost entirely Indian, and have on-the-ground knowledge that is hard to find in the Western world. I have also relied on the 2011 Indian Census.

16. See A. Jayakumar, "Andaman and Nicobar Islands," in *Oxford Encyclopaedia of South Asian Christianity*.

arrived in the 1880s, and a Nicobari convert of his, who took the name John Richardson.

Japan took control of the islands in World War II and inflicted severe persecution. John Richardson's leadership was superb during this period, and after Japanese defeat there was a mass conversion movement to Christianity. Most of those Christians are today part of the Church of North India (CNI)—an affiliate of the worldwide Anglican Communion. There are around 90,000 Christians on the islands today, split evenly between Catholics and CNI. Many small denominations exist there as well. Today, around 21 percent of the inhabitants of Andaman and Nicobar are Christians.

Andhra Pradesh

Andhra Pradesh (AP) is considered part of Dravidian South India and covers a large portion of India's eastern-central coast. In 2014, it was broken up when the new state of Telangana was created. Now, AP has a population exceeding 50 million and is nicknamed "the rice bowl of India." The main language is Telugu, although a significant number of people also speak Urdu—the national language of Pakistan. While Urdu is spoken widely across India, it is often associated with South Asian Muslims.

Christianity claims only about one or two percent of the population in AP. It is a strongly Hindu state—around 88 percent. The Muslim population is around 10 percent.

Christianity first arrived to AP when Louis de Salvador, a Portuguese ambassador to Vijayanagara, arrived in 1512. Vijayanagar was a Hindu empire covering much of South India in the fourteenth through seventeenth centuries. It was created to stave off the southward expansion of Islam during those centuries. The Hindu Vijayanagara rulers and the Muslim Deccan sultanates fought viciously for over a century on the Deccan Plateau.[17]

Numerous Catholic orders (Franciscans, Jesuits, Theatines, Augustinians) missionized AP during the sixteenth and seventeenth centuries. Irish Catholics began working near the Guntur district in 1875. Protestants from the London Missionary Society arrived in 1804 and made possible a Telugu Bible translation. The list of Protestant denominations that came in the nineteenth and twentieth centuries is long: Canadian and American Baptists, the (British) Society for the Propagation of the Gospel, American and German Lutherans, Salvation Army, Methodists, Assemblies of God, Mennonites, and many more. Many indigenous churches have risen up in the last century, such as The Gospel Band, the Independent Christian Believers Gospel Fellowship, the Bible Mission, and the Gospel Association of India. The Pentecostal movement is alive and well, with hundreds of churches being associated with the Indian Pentecostal Church. Many of the old Protestant mission stations have joined the CSI.[18] AP's Guntur district is a nerve center for Christian activity, partly because of its numerous educational institutions.[19]

Arunachal Pradesh

Arunachal, "the land of the rising sun," was not a state until

---

17. D. Venkateswarlu and V. Antony Raj, "Proselytism and Status Enhancement: A Comparative Study of Scheduled Castes and Christian Converts from Scheduled Castes," in *Emerging Social Science Concerns*, ed. Surendra K. Gupta (New Delhi: Concept Publishing Company, 2004), 392-93.

18. Dokibura Joseph Jeremiah, "Andhra Pradesh," in *Oxford Encyclopaedia of South Asian Christianity*.

19. Historian Robert Frykenberg studied this region carefully in the 1960s. See *Guntur District, 1788-1848: A History of Local Influence and Central Authority* (Oxford: Clarendon Press, 1965). This book is a classic in the field of Indian history due to its attempts to emphasize indigenous agency.

1987, but its history goes back about 2500 years, since it is mentioned in India's beloved epic poem, the *Mahabharata*. This extreme northeastern state is contiguous with India's easternmost border. Over a hundred tribes reside in this state, sharing a border with Bhutan, Myanmar, Tibet, and China. The people are mongoloid and rugged, and share much with other nearby Himalayan people.

Arunachal is a state that seems to be turning to Christ. Its population is around 1.5 million, and census data shows that between 1991 and 2001, its Christian population doubled, from about 10 percent of the population to about 19 percent. By 2011 it had increased to 30 percent. This increase may be linked to strong Christian influences coming from nearby states Nagaland, Manipur, and Mizoram.

Christianity entered Arunachal Pradesh in the 1840s, when French fathers Nicolas Krick and Augustin Bourry were making their way to Tibet, but were martyred by the region's Mishmi tribe. American Baptists established the Sadiya and Sibsagor (Sivasagar) mission stations in Assam in the late nineteenth century to reach the tribes of the region. They soon produced a vernacular dictionary, and in 1920, a translation of the Scriptures.[20] Two notable missionaries in the late nineteenth century were Rev. C. E. Petrick and Rev. John Firth.

Led by indigenous converts, Christianity spread widely across Arunachal in the twentieth century. Some of the leading figures were Nara Sensu, the first Nyishi Christian convert (in 1920); brothers Kholie Chiji and Kholie Lezee (teachers); Kop Temi (a translator); and Shri Tayi Bate, "the first formal apostle among the Nyishi."[21]

---

20. See Nadam Tadar Rikam, *Emerging Religious Identities of Arunachal Pradesh: A Study of Nyishi Tribe* (Arunachal Pradesh: Mittal, 2005), 83–86.
21. Nadam Tadar Rikam, 87.

In the 1970s, many from the Nyishi and Nocte tribes converted to Christianity. Roman Catholics established a mission station and school at Harmutty in 1977. Education was free, and many young evangelists came out of that endeavor.[22]

Assam

Right in the heart of northeast India, Assam touches all of the northeastern states. In fact, the whole of northeast India was called "Assam" until recently. This changed in 1963, when Nagaland was granted statehood, followed by the other northeastern states in the 1970s and 1980s. Today, Assam is the gateway to India's northeast. And with over 30 million residents, it has a population far higher than any of the other states in the region. Assam is usually associated with its prominent tea-growing operations. Assam tea has been famous in the West since British rule.

Assam, and the whole of India's northeast, had remained relatively undisturbed by outside political forces since time immemorial. The Mughal Empire made some inroads into the region, but never gained complete control. However, in 1826, Britain's East India Company decisively defeated the Kingdom of Burma in the First Anglo-Burmese War. Both parties signed the Treaty of Yandabo, which put Britain in charge of northeast India. This treaty signaled several things: the British began their political consolidation of the area, the fragmented tribes were brought together to some extent under British rule, and the traditional forms of power eroded with the commanding presence of the British. Frederick Downs writes,

Within one hundred years British administration was gradually

---

22. Ibid., 85.

extended throughout the region. It brought with it irreversible forces of economic, social and cultural change.[23]

With a new and foreign presence, the various tribes began to see what they had in common rather than what separated them from each other.

When the British began to establish themselves in Assam in the mid-nineteenth century, they brought with them tribal groups from the region of Chotanagpur to work the land, particularly the tea gardens. Some of these people were Adivasi Christians, and they are considered the first Christians of Assam.[24]

In northeast India, there is a distinction between the people of the plains and the people in the hills. It is the hill people who have embraced Christianity to a large extent. The plains people in the Brahmaputra and Barak valleys of Assam have been Sanskritized throughout the ages, and are thus resistant to Christianity.[25] There are major cultural differences between these people, too. Most plains people speak Assamese, a derivative of Sanskrit, whereas most hill tribes speak languages from the Sino-Tibetan family. The plains of Assam are extremely fertile, among the most fertile lands of the world. Thus, the plains people tended to settle and farm. The hill people hunted and gathered. As a result of geography, two distinct cultures developed in northeast India: plains people who were Hindu and Sanskritized, and the remote hill people who were fiercely independent, mysterious, and feared by the people of the plains.

It is surprising that Assam's Christian population remains so

---

23. Frederick Downs, *History of Christianity: North East India in the Nineteenth and Twentieth Centuries*, vol. 5, part 5 (Bangalore: Church History Association of India, 2003), 7.
24. See Baxla Zephyrinus, "Assam: Christianity Among the Adivasis," in *Oxford Encyclopaedia of South Asian Christianity.*
25. See Downs, 2–3.

small—only around 4 percent—considering it lies so close to states having strong Christian majorities. Around 62 percent of the Assamese are Hindus, and 34 percent are Muslims, making Assam the logical mission point for the Christians of northeast India.[26] Christianity's nerve center in Assam is Eastern Theological College, in Jorhat. It is one of India's finest theological institutions with a first-rate faculty.

Bihar

Bihar—India's third most populated state—is home to some of the greatest moments in the history of world religions. It is the home of Buddhism, since it was at Bodh Gaya that the Buddha achieved nirvana. Bihar was the seat of the famed Maurya Empire (322–185 BC), which was led by the powerful emperor Ashoka in the 200s BC. Ashoka became a Buddhist and played a huge role in the missionary expansion of Buddhism across Asia. Bihar was home to Mahavira—the twenty-fourth, and last, Tirthankara of Jainism. His ashes are buried at the holy Jain city of Pawapuri, Bihar. And Patna, Bihar's capital city, was home to Guru Gobind Singh, the last of the ten sacred Sikh Gurus.[27]

Bihar's Christianity community, however, has remained very small indeed—just a tiny fraction of the population, around 1 percent. It is not for lack of effort, as Catholic missionaries began working there in the 1620s. In the 1740s, the Bettiah mission was established by Capuchins and had some success.[28] Dalit "mass movements" toward Christianity, both Protestant and Catholic, began to occur in the late

26. For the expansion of Christianity in northeast India, see Elungkiebe Zeliang, *Charismatic Movements in the Baptist Churches in North East India* (Delhi: ISPCK, 2014).
27. Jose Kalapura, "Bihar," in *Oxford Encyclopaedia of South Asian Christianity*.
28. See Albert Battandier, "Bettiah," in *The Catholic Encyclopedia*, vol. 2 (New York: The Encyclopedia Press, 1907).

nineteenth century among the Santals, Dusadhs, and Chamars.[29]

Chandigarh

Chandigarh, known as "city beautiful," is home to over one million souls. It is a tiny union territory in the north of India on the border of Punjab and Haryana, serving as the capital city for both. It is known for its high levels of income and development. Its first Christian worship service was held in a tent in 1953. A church now stands at that location, associated with the CNI. The architect of the impressive church was Jaswant Singh Dethe, the Chief Town Planner, who happened to be a Christian. He also designed the Catholic cathedral in the city.[30]

Chhattisgarh

Home to over 25 million people, Chhattisgarh was carved out of Madhya Pradesh in 2000. Mentioned in both Hindu epics, the *Ramayana* and *Mahabharata*, Chhattisgarh is a land almost completely comprising Hindus.[31] Muslims make up around 2 percent of the population. There is a small Christian community of around 500,000 that has a well-documented history of persecution. The Christians are mainly from Adivasi tribes, such as the Oraons, Mundas, and Kharias.

Belgian Catholics evangelized the region in the late 1800s. Anglicans became involved by the early 1900s. In 1908, there was a horrific persecution that was related to the Chotanagpur

29. See Jose Kalapura, "Margins of Faith: Dalits and Tribal Christians in Eastern India," in *Margins of Faith*, eds. Rowena Robinson and Joseph Marianus Kujur (New Delhi: Sage, 2010).
30. Vidyasagar Dogar, "Chandigarh," in *Oxford Encyclopaedia of South Asian Christianity.*
31. See the government site for Chhattisgarh on "Know India," http://www.knowindia.gov.in/knowindia/state_uts.php?id=6 (Accessed October 30, 2014).

Land Tenancy Act. Adivasis were given property rights, guaranteed by the British Raj. This led to mass movements toward Christianity. Local Hindu rulers were threatened by these developments and unleashed a devastating campaign of killing, property destruction, and looting.[32]

To the present day, Dalit and Tribal (Adivasi) people must think twice before converting. Chad Bauman, a historian of Christianity in the region, articulated the problem well:

> Independent India has failed to eradicate the social stigma of lower-caste status, particularly in its rural areas. Some Dalits have therefore converted to Christianity in order, among other reasons, to live in a world (theoretically) free of caste discrimination. Yet doing so means relinquishing their eligibility for governmental and educational reservations, and facing minor or major forms of social censure. Beaten down and neglected by the religion to which they adhere, yet risking marginalization, harassment, or even violence should they convert, India's Dalits are caught in the middle—damned, as it were, if they do, damned if they don't.[33]

Dadra and Nagar Haveli

This small, landlocked territory sits on the border of Gujarat and Maharashtra. It belonged to the Portuguese until 1954. It is a curious fact that so few of its population of 350,000 people are Christians, especially since the Portuguese were there since the late 1700s.[34] A Catholic church was erected in 1889. In the 1920s and 1930s, Franciscan brothers and sisters began doing benevolent work. Today, the Society of Pilar (also known as the Society of the Missionaries of St. Francis Xavier) works there,

---

32. Gabriel Ekka, "Chhattisgarh," in *Oxford Encyclopaedia of South Asian Christianity.*
33. Chad Bauman, *Christian Identity and Dalit Religion in Hindu India, 1868-1947* (Grand Rapids: Eerdmans, 2008), 5.
34. This is the 2011 population, located at http://www.census2011.co.in/district.php.

operating schools, food banks, orphanages, and tribal relief efforts.[35]

Daman and Diu

Daman is located just north of Dadra and Nagar Haveli and Diu is just across the water to the west, both within the state of Gujarat. Daman and Diu are tiny regions on the east and west sides of the Gulf of Khambhat, the lower of Gujarat's two major inlets on the Arabian Sea. Daman and Diu were under Portuguese influence for over four hundred years. In 1961, the two regions were forcibly incorporated into India, against the wishes of Portugal.

The territory has a population of around 250,000, with Christians accounting for only about 2 percent. The vast majority is Hindu. Muslims outnumber the Christians by about four to one. Daman and Diu share history with Dadra and Nagar Haveli. Both of them were under the jurisdiction of Goa for many years, and both of them were ministered to by the Society of Pilar in recent years. For all intents and purposes, it is a Catholic mission point today, and Pentecostal movements such as Believers Church (under K. P. Yohannan) are now working in the area.[36]

Delhi

Formally called the "Government of the National Capital Territory of Delhi," this union territory is one of the most populated cities in the world, with around 17 million people.

---

35. Cosme Jose Costa, "Dadra and Nagar Haveli," in *Oxford Encyclopaedia of South Asian Christianity*.

36. E. R. Hambye, *History of Christianity in India*, Vol. 3: *Eighteenth Century* (Bangalore: Church History Association of India, 1997), 392–94. Cosme Jose Costa, "Daman and Diu," in *Oxford Encyclopaedia of South Asian Christianity*.

Conquered and rebuilt many times, Delhi is located on the border of Haryana and Uttar Pradesh, in the north.

Christianity is tiny in Delhi, less than 1 percent. The city's 146,000 Christians trace their ancestry to the Mughal Empire, when Emperor Akbar invited Jesuits to reside in his court in 1579. Akbar was culturally astute, and recognized the major contribution Jesuit knowledge would bring to his empire's headquarters. Their facility in language and geography, among other things, impressed him greatly, although he never converted. Akbar made one Jesuit, Catalan Antoni Montserrate, the tutor for his second son.[37]

Protestant missionaries arrived with British power, and thereafter various mission societies worked in Delhi. In 1911, the British decided to move their Indian capital from Calcutta to Delhi. In the 1920s, they constructed "New Delhi" on the south side of the city. It was completed in 1931 and became India's capital upon independence in 1947.

Goa

On the west coast, south of Mumbai, is India's smallest state (by area): Goa. The history of Christianity in India cannot be told without Goa playing a central role. While today, the Christian population in Goa is only about 25 percent, Roman Catholic influence is everywhere, such as in the impressive European architecture, or in the name of one of the state's largest cities: Vasco da Gama. Today, Goa is known for tourism and its high quality of life.

The Portuguese, led by Alfonso de Albuquerque, captured Goa in 1510 and made it their base of operations. They expanded through the centuries and later retracted,

---

37. Fernando and Gispert-Sauch, *Christianity in India*, 136–40.

eventually leaving India altogether in the 1960s. The height of Portuguese influence coincided with the expansion of Islam into Southern India. The Portuguese were a thorn in the side of Muslim rulers, essentially keeping Muslim expansion in check until the British began to consolidate control of South Asia.

Goa's population is small—around 1.5 million. Over two-thirds of the people are Hindu. Its religious composition is changing. Christianity continues to decline while Islam and Hinduism enjoy gains. In 1961, Goa's Christian population was 38 percent; in 1991, it was 30 percent; in 2001, it was 27 percent; and in 2011, it was 25 percent. This decline indicates the state's Christians have a declining fertility rate. And in India, more education means less fertility. Therefore, it can be assumed, Christians are getting educated, and having fewer babies. In addition, young and educated Catholics are leaving Goa at precisely the same time that people from other states immigrate into Goa for its high quality of life. These changes have "dramatically transformed the composition of the church and seriously challenged its mission today."[38]

Gujarat

The majority of the state of Gujarat, on the far west of India, is actually a peninsula: the Kathiawar, which juts out into the Arabian Sea. The two major inlets on either side of the Kathiawar are the Gulfs of Khambhat and Kutch. It shares its northern border with Pakistan. As is the case with the other Indian states bordering Pakistan—Rajasthan, Punjab, Jammu and Kashmir—the Christian church is extremely small there. Of the sixty million people who live in Gujarat, Christians constitute about half of 1 percent.

38. Desmond D'Souza, "Goa," in *Oxford Encyclopaedia of South Asian Christianity.*

A French Dominican named Father Jordanus (or Jourdain) was the first to evangelize within Gujarat. He worked in western India during the years 1321 and 1322. He was an optimist who believed that India was a field ripe for the missionary. He wrote: "Let friars be getting ready to come, for there are three places I know where they might reap a great harvest."[39] The London Missionary Society arrived in 1815, and soon published a Gujarati Bible. The British missionary J. V. S. Taylor published an influential Gujarati grammar book.

Over the years, Christians have rendered remarkable service to Gujarat in the form of schools and hospitals, but not without accusations that they are only trying to entice converts. In recent years, Gujarat has been associated with strong Hindu nationalism. India's fifteenth prime minister, Narendra Modi, a controversial member of the ultranationalist BJP (Bharatiya Janata Party), was the chief minister of Gujarat from 2001 to 2014. The 2002 Gujarat riots, which began in Ahmedabad, led to the death of hundreds of people, mainly Muslims, over the issue of whether a holy site in Ayodhya (Uttar Pradesh) should be considered Hindu or Muslim. Hindus believe Ayodhya is where the deity Rama was born, but in the sixteenth century, the first Mughal emperor—Babur—built a mosque on the site. It was destroyed by Hindus in 1992, and the controversy is known today as the "Ayodhya dispute."

Haryana

One of the most important literary pieces in human history takes place in Haryana: the *Bhagavad Gita*. Kurukshetra, a region in Haryana, is the location of the epic battle between the Kauravas and Pandavas, recorded in the great Indian epic,

39. See Stephen Neill, *A History of Christianity in India*, vol. 1, 73.

the *Mahabharata*. During that battle, the Lord Krishna advised Arjuna on whether he should commit violence against people he knows and loves during a time of war. No other Indian literature has impacted the Western world more than the *Gita*. Haryana is one of the wealthier regions of South Asia. It is the Indian version of Detroit due to its being the hub of manufacturing for automobiles, tractors, and motorcycles. Haryana is also home to the Panipat oil refinery, one of the largest in South Asia. It is a flat and fertile land, making it a prosperous agricultural state. Its affluence is also linked to its proximity to Delhi, India's capital, which is essentially carved out of the southeastern side of Haryana.

Christianity's presence in Haryana is tiny, less than one percent. Only Bihar and Uttar Pradesh have smaller percentages of Christians than Haryana. However, as in most cases in India, the Christian population does a disproportionate amount of good for the society in which it finds itself. Pentecostal churches, such as the Indian Pentecostal Church of God (IPC) have had success reaching out to Dalits. Haryana's Catholic population, around 15,000 people, runs "8 ecclesiastical institutions, 33 high schools, 12 welfare centers, 2 hospitals, 12 dispensaries, and 4 homes for the aged." In addition, the state's religious brothers and nuns run 84 centers that offer socio-pastoral aid.[40]

Himachal Pradesh

This beautiful state in the Himalayas was where the British escaped the heat. Serving as British India's summer capital from 1863 until independence, the city of Shimla became famous as a British playground, where the elites of British

---

40. Jose Kalapura, "Haryana," in *Oxford Encyclopaedia of South Asian Christianity*.

society were known to frolic. Today, the state is well-known for its famous Buddhist resident, the Dalai Lama—perhaps the most recognized religious leader in the world today. His home is in the city of Dharamsala. His presence draws many visitors and has led to a strong and vocal pro-Tibetan movement in Himachal.

Himachal is one of the least Christianized states in India. Of its seven million people, only about 13,000 are Christians. Even though so many elite European officers took residence there during British times, the Christian impact was minimal. During British rule, colonial officers typically had an unfavorable view of missionaries and their work. Perhaps the lack of Christians in a once-heavily British city such as Shimla sheds light on the great divide separating missionaries from colonial officers.

Jammu and Kashmir

India's northernmost state is perched up in the Himalayas. It is a very sensitive region of the world due to longstanding border disputes with China and Pakistan. Thousands have died over these tensions. Jammu and Kashmir is the only Indian state having a Muslim majority. However, it is a land precious to Hindus because of the sacredness of the Himalayas, where many Hindu pilgrimages take place. Tibetan Buddhism also has a presence in Jammu and Kashmir, in the region of Ladakh.

Of the state's thirteen million people, there are only about 35,000 Christians, associated chiefly with the CNI. Anglican missionaries began establishing educational work there in the mid-nineteenth century. Scottish Presbyterians, Moravians, and Roman Catholics came a little later, generally placing emphasis on education.[41]

Jharkhand

The state of Jharkhand was cut out of Bihar in 2000. It is a landlocked state in the east of India, sandwiched between Bihar, West Bengal, Odisha, Chhattisgarh, and Uttar Pradesh. The name means "hilly land" and it has been the home of Adivasis (indigenous tribes) for centuries due to its many inaccessible areas. The British called the region Chotanagpur. Today, Jharkhand is home to a strong Naxalite resistance movement—a Maoist, communist guerrilla group that frequently resorts to violence when protesting against the government.

Of Jharkhand's 35 million people, well over a million are Christians. Compared to the other states in north India (outside of the northeastern states), that is significant. Virtually all of Jharkhand's Christians are former Adivasis (tribals). The Munda people, in particular, have shown interest in Christianity.

Christianity is relatively young in Jharkhand, arriving only when German missionaries established a modest work in Ranchi around 1850.[42] Today, the Lutherans, Catholics, and CNI have a presence in the state, as do several smaller denominations.

Karnataka

Before 1973, the state of Karnataka was known as Mysore. Karnataka is the only state to share a border with all of the South Indian states: Kerala, Tamil Nadu, Andhra Pradesh,

41. Vidyasagar Doga, "Jammu and Kashmir," in *Oxford Encyclopaedia of South Asian Christianity*.
42. Nirmal Minz, "Jharkhand, Christianity in," in *Oxford Encyclopaedia of South Asian Christianity*.

Telangana, and Goa. Geographically, the terrain is dominated by the Deccan Plateau. The language of Karnataka is Kannada, from the Dravidian family.

Karnataka's population exceeds 60 million, but only about 2 percent is Christian. This is puzzling, considering India's southwestern coast—made up of Goa, Karnataka, and Kerala—received so many Christian missionaries throughout the last five centuries. It is also strange that Bangalore (Bengaluru), Karnataka's capital, is something of an axis point for India's Christian institutions. There are over 800 Christian ministries based in Bangalore, one of India's fastest growing cities.[43] The Bible Society of India, United Theological College—one of India's finest seminaries, and St. John's Medical College, are all based in Bangalore. It is also a city that has a strong Western influence due to its being India's IT (information technology) hub. It is perplexing why Christianity has not made more of an impact on the population.

Kerala

Known historically as the Malabar Coast, and to Keralites as "God's Own Country," Kerala has had a relatively strong Christian presence for centuries. Much of Indian church history takes place within the borders of the modern state of Kerala. The Syrian Christians, often called the Thomas Christians, have a history that goes back to the first-century church, when, according to local tradition, the apostle Thomas arrived to their shores in AD 52. Today, the Thomas Christians can be found in virtually all Christian denominations and

---

43. Jason Mandryk, *Operation World*, 7th ed. (Colorado Springs: Biblica, 2010), 429.

movements: Orthodox, Catholic, mainline Protestant, and Pentecostal.

With well over six million Christians living in the state, nearly 20 percent, Kerala claims more Christians than any other Indian state by far. While India's far northeastern states have high *percentages* of Christians, Kerala is much more *populated* than those states, with around 35 million inhabitants.

Kerala boasts a high standard of life. Its education and literacy rates are among the highest in India, it is considered exemplary on the status of women, it has a low fertility rate, it enjoys India's highest life expectancy, and it has less crime than anywhere else in India.[44] Could these positive indicators of a healthy society be due to the strong presence of Christianity? Undoubtedly, Christianity plays a critical role.

Lakshadweep

The smallest of India's seven union territories, Lakshadweep consists of thirty six islands, but only ten are inhabited. Of the 65,000 inhabitants, only about 300 of them are Christians. The government considers most of the residents to be from the Scheduled Tribes. Located about 200 miles from Kerala, most of the islanders speak Kerala's language, Malayalam. The vast majority of the islanders—around 95 percent—are Sunni Muslim.[45]

---

44. For literacy, see Census of India, "State of Literacy," 114, located at http://www.censusindia.gov.in/2011-prov-results/data_files/india/ Final_PPT_2011_chapter6.pdf. For crime rates, see "Incidence and Rate of Violent Crimes During 2011," http://ncrb.nic.in/CD-CII2011/cii-2011/Table 3.1.pdf. For life expectancy, women, and quality of life, see "India Human Development Report 2011," 29, 152, http://www.iamrindia.gov.in/ihdr_book.pdf. All the above accessed on November 4, 2014.
45. See Lakshadweep official website, http://lakshadweep.nic.in (Accessed November 5, 2014).

Madhya Pradesh

Geographically, Madhya Pradesh is nicknamed "the heart of India." Its capital city, Bhopal, is a center point for the entire nation. In 1984, the Bhopal disaster drew international attention, and it is considered the worst industrial calamity in human history. Hundreds of thousands of people were exposed to toxic chemicals when a pesticide plant failed. Several thousands died.

Madhya Pradesh is the second largest state in India. It is known for its dense forests, large tribal populations which live in them, and its relative backwardness with these people being virtually cut off from the rest of India. Poverty and hunger abound in the tribal communities, which constitute roughly 20 percent of the state's inhabitants.

Of the state's nearly 80 million people, only about 200,000 are Christians. In 1968, Madhya Pradesh passed an anti-conversion law that is at odds with the Indian Constitution's protection of religious freedom. However, anti-conversion laws continue to be passed in the state, giving it a reputation for religious intolerance. It is a stronghold for the BJP (Bharatiya Janata Party), known for its Indocentric policies. Converting to another religion in Madhya Pradesh requires official permission, and is an extremely volatile act. It is reported that some Christians are reconverting back to Hinduism, presumably under pressure or inducement.

Many Catholic orders evangelized the state throughout history, beginning in the late 1600s, during the days of the Mughal Empire. Since then, Fransalians, Franciscans, Sisters of St. Joseph, Capuchins, Divine Word Missionaries, and many others have worked in the area. Today, Roman Catholics,

Methodists, the CNI, and various Pentecostal groups are active in the state.

Maharashtra

Based in west-central India is the highly populated state of Maharashtra. Maharashtra is associated with Indian swaraj (self-rule) partly because it was the home of the famous Maratha Empire. Based in Raigad and Pune—both in Maharashtra—the Marathas are celebrated in India because of their unexpected rise to power and their stunning series of victories over the Mughals who were on the verge of dominating all of India in the eighteenth century. The Marathas stopped the spread of the powerful Mughals, drove them into retreat, and eventually claimed most of the old Mughal territory during the years of the Maratha Empire's existence, from 1674 to 1818. The Marathas were eventually defeated by the British, but their legacy remains, particularly through their language: Marathi.

Maharashtra's capital city is Mumbai (Bombay), the largest city in India and one of the largest in the world. Mumbai is the financial hub and entertainment capital of India. Known as Bollywood, India's Mumbai-based film industry is massive and global. It was in Mumbai that the Indian National Congress political party was born in 1885, and the state became the epicenter of the Indian freedom movement led by Tilak, and, later, by Mahatma Gandhi. More recently, in 2008, the world watched in horror for four days as terrorists from Pakistan stormed several public buildings in Mumbai, killing 164 people and wounding hundreds more.

There are about a million Christians in Maharashtra, but in a state of nearly 120 million people, it can seem like a drop in the bucket. Nevertheless, several giants of Indian Christianity are sons and daughters of the state, such as social reformer Pandita Ramabai and poet Narayan Vaman Tilak. The Maharashtrian cities of Pune and Nagpur are home to notable Christian institutions such as Union Biblical Seminary and the National Council of Churches in India, respectively. Several prominent Catholic institutions are based in the state, such as Jnana-Deepa Vidyapeeth, Ishvani Kendra, and St. Xavier's College.

Manipur

If any of India's states see a Christian surge in the near future, the far northeastern state of Manipur is a contender because of its two next-door neighbors: Nagaland and Mizoram. Both of those states are strongly Christian, around 90 percent. There is little doubt that missionaries from those two states will take the gospel into Manipur in the coming years. By no means, however, is Manipur un-Christian. Over 40 percent of its three million people are Christians already, mainly from the hill tribes. But Manipur's most prominent tribe—the Meitei, who account for about one-quarter of the population—follows Hinduism or the traditional religion known as Sanamahism. Manipur has a violent insurgency movement that resorts to kidnapping, extortion, maiming, and even targeted executions in their efforts to attain full autonomy.

Meghalaya

Known as "the abode of clouds," Meghalaya is considered the world's wettest land. In British times, the capital city of Shillong was called the Scotland of the East because of its rolling, green hills.

With a population of over three million, Meghalaya ranks

third in terms of Christian percentage and is one of only three states having a Christian majority (Nagaland, Mizoram). Around 75 percent of the population is Christian. Evangelized first by Baptists and Presbyterians in the early 1800s, Anglican and Catholic missionaries came later. Today, the largest denominations are Catholic and Presbyterian. There are several Christian colleges in Shillong, including Martin Luther Christian University, St. Edmund's, and St. Anthony's.

Like other far northeastern states, Meghalaya is a land of tribes, primarily the Khasis, Garos, and Jaintias. It is landlocked, and the only Indian state it touches is Assam. Sandwiched between Assam and Bangladesh, both having very few Christians, it is somewhat surprising that most Meghalayans embraced Christianity.

Mizoram

The far northeastern state of Mizoram is known for its Christian energy. Around 87 percent of Mizoram is Christian, and their worship is exuberant and sincere. It is the home of the respected Aizawl Theological College, located in a capital city built, amazingly, on the side of steep mountains.

Known historically as the Lushai Hills, Mizoram was evangelized first in 1890 by William Williams, a Welshman. In 1894, two English Baptist missionaries, J. H. Lorrain and F. W. Savidge arrived and produced impressive linguistic work. They reduced the Mizo language to writing, produced a grammar and a dictionary, and translated several books of the Bible.[46] It was Presbyterians, however, who made the greatest impact, particularly due to the work of Welshman D. E. Jones and his

---

46. See C. L. Hminga, "Lorrain, J. H. and Savidge, F. W.," in *Oxford Encyclopaedia of South Asian Christianity.*

Khasi assistant, Rai Bhajur, in 1897.[47] Incredibly, within fifty years, virtually the entire Mizo tribe accepted Christianity. Mizoram's cultural transformation has been profound. Formerly known as headhunters, they are today the great missionaries of India. Previously illiterate, Mizoram now boasts the highest literacy rates in India. One of the last places to modernize in India, Mizoram is now modernizing so quickly that it is cause of serious concern. In spite of a ban on liquor, alcoholism is reportedly growing, as is drug abuse. Mizos are concerned about the rapid changes that have happened in such a short amount of time.

When I (Daughrity) visited Mizoram in 2014, I was told that Mizo Christians have many concerns right now: substance abuse, a growing devil worship movement happening among the youth, broken families, high suicide rates, and rampant materialism that stems from people watching Korean television shows. They believe these problems to be linked to the sudden changes brought on by modernization and massive social transformation. Their plan is to transform children's ministry, as they believe their methods were inherited from the missionaries and are now outdated.

Nagaland

The far northeastern state of Nagaland is a land of Baptists. Nearly 90 percent of the residents of Nagaland are Christian, and the vast majority of them are members of one of twenty or so Baptist denominations, making it, very possibly, the most Baptist place on earth.[48] While Nagaland's two dozen tribes have some similarities, in other ways, they are very distinct.

47. See Frederick Downs, *History of Christianity: North East India in the Nineteenth and Twentieth Centuries*, 83–84.
48. Jason Mandryk, *Operation World*, 7th ed., 436.

Each has a unique language and culture, and sometimes their differences lead to feuding. Nagas, like other fiercely protective tribes in the northeast, are prone to insurgency movements against the Indian government.[49] What brings Nagas together is Christianity. However, they comment that a true sense of Christian ecumenism is lacking, even though they were all Christianized by American Baptist missionaries in the late nineteenth century. For example, new independent churches sprout up regularly, pulling members from the established denominations. Some Nagas argue this is a necessary phase in order to revitalize lackluster churches. However, Naga culture is fragile, so breakaway church movements can disrupt social harmony.

When I (Daughrity) visited far northeast India in 2014, I learned that Nagaland is a state in rapid transition. They have a 150-year connection with the United States, but today, there is also an increasing connection with Korea. They claim that Koreans look more like them physically, and Koreans have taken a keen interest in funding Naga church work, especially missions. Nagas are also dealing with major problems shared by other northeastern states: Satanic worship among youths, division among churches due to a rapidly expanding Pentecostal movement, a distrust of the Indian government, and a swiftly changing culture—such as the transition from arranged marriage to so-called love marriage. Some couples simply elope in order to circumvent the traditional approach.

Perhaps the most serious problems facing the Naga churches have to do with children. Changes in society have left them confused and in some cases deeply troubled. Prostitution, drug abuse, and AIDS are not uncommon. Churches are struggling

---

49. See Frederick Downs, *History of Christianity: North East India in the Nineteenth and Twentieth Centuries*, 27.

with how to address these crises, and some Nagas report that the youth are disengaging from church activities at precisely the time they need them most.

Odisha

Odisha (formerly, Orissa) is located on India's east coast, between Andhra Pradesh and West Bengal, along the Bay of Bengal. While there are many different tribal groups in Odisha, there is an overall Oriya culture, bound together by the unique Oriya language.

The Oriya people are strongly Hindu; reverence for the sun plays a central role in their religion. Christianity comprises around 2 or 3 percent of the population. In the early 1800s, Baptist missionaries sent by William Carey arrived in the area and began translation and relief work. In the 1860s, a severe famine occurred, and Christian missionaries offered aid. As a result, many people, especially orphans, became Christian, stirring the long-held belief that Christians are opportunists, making rice Christians out of extremely vulnerable people.[50]

The state of Odisha is known to be vehemently against religious conversion, passing a series of anti-conversion laws in the 1960s. Odisha is where the Australian missionary Graham Staines, and his two young boys (ages 6 and 10), were burned alive in their car while ministering to lepers and poor tribal groups in 1999. His killers were prosecuted and his wife received a reward from the Indian government for her work with lepers. Nevertheless, this famous case illustrates the point that Christian mission is highly sensitive in Odisha. In 2008, a Hindu Swami named Lakshamanananda was killed by an

---

50. See Anugraha Behera, "Orissa (Odisha)," in *Oxford Encyclopaedia of South Asian Christianity.*

unknown assailant and Christians were scapegoated, resulting in dozens killed and thousands displaced.[51] Frequent persecution against Christians continues in Odisha, including vandalism and destruction of church buildings.

Puducherry

India's French Riviera consists of four former French enclaves: Puducherry, Karaikal, Mahe, and Yanam. The regions did not enter into the Indian Union until 1954. Known historically as Pondicherry, these resort-like areas are spread out; Mahe is on the Malabar Coast (Kerala), while the other three are on India's eastern shore.

In the late seventeenth century, France began to string together its colonial possessions in India. Capuchin and Jesuit missionaries sent from Rome worked in these French strongholds until the government of France decided to replace them with missionaries of their own in the 1820s.[52] By providing jobs and favors, the French rewarded those who converted to Christianity while inhibiting Hinduism and Islam.

Puducherry has a high quality of life, an abundance of higher education institutions, a robust tourism industry, and a decent Christian presence of around 6 percent of the population. A French Catholic influence is still evident.

Punjab

Located in the far north of India, Punjab is known as the land of the Sikhs, although there is a significant Hindu minority. Rising up as a conciliatory peace movement to unite Hindus

---

51. This is a very complex episode. There are land disputes, deep political disagreements, and issues of identity involved. Most of the Christians in Odisha are Dalits, and when they assert themselves, they are often crushed.
52. See Hambye, *History of Christianity in India*, vol. 3: *Eighteenth Century*, 170ff.

and Muslims in the fifteenth century under Guru Nanak, Sikhism is today known as a religion of great strength, yet also, of determined peace. But peace was hard-earned for the Sikhs. After a long period of persecution from the Mughals and Durranis, Sikhs eventually began to defend themselves with the sword. They have never completely shed their reputation as warriors.

In the 1980s, many Sikhs rose up to establish self-rule (Khalistan) in the Punjab. After years of violent exchange with the Indian government—including the assassination of Prime Minister Indira Gandhi by her own Sikh bodyguards in 1984—peace was finally restored in the 1990s. Sikhism's holiest building is the Golden Temple of Amritsar, which was the site of "Operation Blue Star," a bloody attempt by the Indian government in 1984 to suppress the Sikh insurgency.

Christianity has never been strong in the Punjab. Indeed, today, Christians constitute a mere 1 percent of the population. The Christians of the Punjab are today a very diverse and scattered lot, which adversely affects their ability to unite for a common cause. Pentecostal and evangelical movements are mushrooming, but they lack stability and are dependent on the charisma of a pastor. The Catholics have institutional strength, but their priests tend to come from outside the Punjab, and are thus disconnected from the laity. The various mainline Protestant churches, now primarily under the CNI, struggle with maintaining their membership and staving off lawsuits from present and former members. Their once-prestigious institutions are becoming ". . . increasingly centralized in the hands of top officers who function as patrons of their churches' resources."[53]

---

53. See John Webster, *A Social History of Christianity: Northwest India Since 1800* (Oxford: University Press, 2007), 356.

Rajasthan

Rajasthan is India's largest state in terms of geographical area. And with over 70 million people, it is not small in population either. Just to understand the scale of population in India, Rajasthan—India's seventh most populated state—has more people than the nations of France, the UK, or Italy. Rajasthan's population is about the same as Turkey's. Rajasthan's growth rate, however, is much higher than any of those countries.

Rajasthan is the home of the famous Rajput Hindu princely states that fought against the Mughals, repelling them for centuries, and keeping them from overrunning the subcontinent. They were the first line of defense for the Mughals' westward expansion. They were eventually subdued, but the cost to the Mughals was very high, and weakened their empire beyond repair. Historian Stephen Dale writes, "Knowledge of the Rajput rebellion is important for those who try to understand how Mughal rule atrophied so quickly in the eighteenth century."[54]

Rajasthan is strongly Hindu, which is a bit surprising, considering it borders Pakistan. The Christians of Rajasthan amount to about one-tenth of 1 percent of the population. However, their contribution to society is immense. For example, about half of Rajasthan's 100,000 Christians are Roman Catholic, organized into three dioceses: Ajmer, Udaipur, and Jaipur (the capital city). This relatively small number of Catholics is able to run a hundred schools, twenty-seven hospitals, and twenty-three pharmacies. They also contribute to society through four social welfare centers, three publishing houses, and over fifty parishes/mission stations.

---

54. Stephen Dale, *The Muslim Empires of the Ottomans, Safavids, and Mughals* (Cambridge: Cambridge University Press, 2010), 261.

Catholic brothers and sisters run dozens of centers that serve the communities in myriad ways. The Mission Sisters of Ajmer and Prabhudasi Sisters of Ajmer run nearly fifty service centers between them.[55]

Sadly, as anti-conversion laws are passed and Hindutva ("Hindu-ness") ideology proliferates, the Christians of India become further marginalized and in some cases harassed. Rajasthan is one of the hot spots for anti-conversion legislation.[56] And while these laws are often directed more at Muslims than Christians, the fact of the matter is that many Hindus want to keep India as Hindu as possible for as long as possible. And there is a pressing fear of the Muslim fertility rate, which is comparatively high.[57]

Sikkim

Tucked in between Bhutan, Nepal, and historic Tibet is Sikkim, India's second smallest state after Goa, and the least populated. Its holy mountain, however, called Kangchenjunga, is huge. It is the third highest peak in the world after Everest and K2. That mountain is revered by the state's majority Hindu population. Sikkim also has a substantial Buddhist minority. Christianity is growing in the state. It already accounts for approximately 10 percent of the population, coming mostly from the Lepcha people, a Tibeto-Burman group. The larger denominations are Presbyterians and the CNI. K. P. Yohannan's Gospel for Asia,

---

55. For Roman Catholic work in Rajasthan, see Jose Kalapura, "Rajasthan," in *Oxford Encyclopaedia of South Asian Christianity*.
56. See the report by Christian Solidarity Worldwide, "Briefing India: Anti-Conversion Legislation: Summary of Concerns," November 2006, http://www.cswusa.org/filerequest/1125.pdf.
57. See "India's Muslims Growing, and Neglected: A steadily rising Muslim population continues to fall behind," in *The Economist*, March 2, 2013, http://www.economist.com/news/asia/21572785-steadily-rising-muslim-population-continues-fall-behind-growing-and-neglected (Accessed November 7, 2014).

the Bakht Singh movement, and several Pentecostal groups are also working in the state.

Tamil Nadu

Tamil Nadu, located on the southeastern coast of India, is one of the more populated states of India. The state has a storied past. The heart of Dravidian culture and Tamil language, it was home to several important ruling dynasties, such as the Cholas, Cheras, Pandyas, and Pallavas.[58] The Cholas, in particular, had a presence in South India since the 300s BC, reaching their zenith of influence in the eleventh century AD. Their influence extended up and down the entire eastern coast of India, Kerala, and Lakshadweep, Sri Lanka, and the Maldives to the south. Tamil culture is a proud one, reluctant to let go of its distinct, Tamil identity in favor of a pan-Indian one. To illustrate, it is common in Tamil Nadu to see signs written in three languages: Tamil, Hindi, and English. Occasionally, however, the Hindi words are crossed out.

There are roughly four million Christians in Tamil Nadu, about 6 percent of the state's population. Supposedly the apostle Thomas evangelized the region and is buried in Mylapore, on the south side of Chennai (Madras), India's third largest city after Mumbai and Delhi. Many famous missionaries have tried their luck with the Tamils, including Xavier, Robert de Nobili, Ziegenbalg, Robert Caldwell, Stephen Neill, and Lesslie Newbigin. Virtually all of the European colonial powers sent missionaries to the region. There are hundreds of Christian institutions of higher learning in Tamil Nadu, some huge and nationally renowned, others small and hardly noticed. Christian Medical College and Hospital in Vellore is

58. See Stephen Neill, vol. 1, 57ff.

highly respected. It was founded in 1900 by the American female missionary Dr. Ida Scudder. Other notable institutions are Madras Christian College, Gurukul Lutheran Theological College (Chennai), and St. Joseph's College in Tiruchirappalli.

The Roman Catholic Church is Tamil Nadu's largest denomination. India's largest Protestant denomination—the CSI—is based in Chennai. Pentecostal groups such as the Pentecostal Mission are growing in Tamil Nadu, generally among Dalits. Tamil Nadu has become a heartland for Dalit theology. Many Dalits converted to Christianity during the catastrophic famines of the eighteenth and nineteenth centuries, and they are now routinely courted by Hindutva groups trying to win them back to Hinduism.[59] There is a high price to pay because Dalits who are Christians or Muslims are ineligible for numerous social and welfare programs as well as government jobs.

Telangana

On June 2, 2014, Telangana became India's most recent state. It was carved out of Andhra Pradesh. Its capital city, Hyderabad, is one of the largest and fastest growing cities in India. It is a highly industrious city, particularly in the pharmaceutical and IT sectors. Its religious demography is similar to Andhra Pradesh: the vast majority is Hindu; there is a significant Muslim minority; and a tiny Christian population of around 1 percent is present.

---

59. See M. Christhu Doss, "Repainting Religious Landscape: Economics of Conversion and Making of Rice Christians in Colonial South India (1781–1880)," in *Studies in History* 30:2 (2014): 179ff.

Tripura

Nestled between Bangladesh, Mizoram, and Assam is the small, far northeastern state of Tripura. Only one highway connects this isolated state to the rest of India.

Over 70 percent of Tripura's four million people are Bengalis, a large people-group that also dominate in Bangladesh and West Bengal. All Bengalis share a history, language (Bengali), and identity. Tripura's remaining population, from the Scheduled Tribes, considers itself indigenous to the region. This is a source of deep tension in the region because a huge influx of Bengalis has occurred in recent years, radically altering the demographics; Tripuris have lost control of their homeland.

Baptists have been working in Tripura since the late eighteenth century. In 1818, Felix Carey—William Carey's somewhat troubled son—visited Tripura, but little came of it. Baptists from New Zealand tried to gain a foothold in the early 1900s. Christianity began to take root in 1912, when some Presbyterian Mizos migrated into Tripura. They had no pastor, but soon, invited the Welsh Mission at Aizawl (Mizoram) to send workers. This is an important point that illustrates how missionaries were, at times, called upon by indigenous Christians for help. Today, Tripura is only about 4 percent Christian, but due to mission work by nearby Mizos, it is growing among the tribespeople. Most Christians in the state are members of the Tripura Baptist Christian Union.[60]

Uttarakhand

Uttarakhand was carved out of Uttar Pradesh in 2000. It is

---

60. Rajani Kaipeng, "Tripura," in *Oxford Encyclopaedia of South Asian Christianity.*

a Himalayan state in North India bordering Nepal and the Tibetan region of China. Christians are only a tiny fraction of the state's ten million inhabitants. Most people in Uttarakhand are from the high castes: Brahmin and Rajput (Kshatriya). Thus, it is very difficult for Christianity to take root. The capital city, Dehradun, is home to three small Bible colleges: New Theological College, Presbyterian Theological Seminary, and Doon Bible College.

Uttar Pradesh

Uttar Pradesh (UP) has a mammoth population of over 200 million people. If it was a country, its population would rank fifth in the world after China, India, the USA, and Indonesia. Its population is almost exactly the same as Brazil's. Located in the north and bordering Nepal as well as eight Indian states, UP has a presence that looms large in virtually every aspect of Indian society.

Religiously, UP is strongly Hindu. However, it is also associated with Buddhism, Jainism, and Islam. The Buddha preached his first sermon at Sarnath, and he breathed his last breath at Kushinagar. Several of the revered Tirthankaras (enlightened conquerors) of Jainism, as well as some of the most important temples are associated with/located in the state. Islam's Mughal Empire was based in the UP city of Agra, where the splendid Taj Mahal stands. However, Hinduism is, by far, the major religion and some of the most important Hindu sites are located there: Ayodhya (birthplace of Rama), Allahabad/Prayag (one of the host cities for the Kumbh Mela, the largest gathering of humans on the planet), and Varanasi (Hinduism's most holy city).

Christianity is tiny in UP. The few Christians in the state are mainly Dalits; thus, Christianity is associated with the despised and rejected there. The higher castes and the culturally respectable people-groups have nothing to gain from associating themselves with India's rejects. Christian mission organizations consider UP to be "the most intense concentration of unevangelized people and groups in the world, and thereby the greatest mission challenge."[61]

West Bengal

At the partition of India and Pakistan in 1947, the people and region of Bengal became split into two: a mainly Hindu West Bengal and a mainly Muslim East Pakistan. In 1971, East Pakistan won its independence and became known as Bangladesh. West Bengal remains, however, an Indian state. In recent decades, West Bengal was coterminous with communism, as India's democratically elected Communist Party ruled the state from 1977 to 2011.

West Bengal's capital city is Kolkata (formerly, Calcutta), which was the seat of British power in India from the late eighteenth century until 1911, when the British moved their capital to Delhi. Kolkata, known to many as the City of Joy, is, in many ways, a very sad city, full of pollution, countless street people, and seemingly endless slum communities. One encounters despair and neglect at every turn. Today, it is hard to believe that Kolkata was once the seat of authority for Britain's Asian empire.

At around 100 million, West Bengal is India's fourth most populated state, after Uttar Pradesh, Maharashtra, and Bihar. It has a Hindu majority, although Muslims account for over 25 percent of the population. Christians are a very small minority,

---

61. Jason Mandryk, *Operation World*, 7th ed., 443.

less than 1 percent. However, Christianity's presence in the state is historic, beginning with the missionaries.

William Carey famously conducted his Bible translation work from Serampore in the early nineteenth century. Even today, the Senate of Serampore College is the main degree-granting body for India's theological colleges. Scotsman Alexander Duff (1806–78) was a strong and effective advocate for Western education. He was also an effective evangelist, counting the brilliant Krishna Mohan Banerjee as one of his many converts. Banerjee became one of the most important Indian Christians of the nineteenth century, converting many people himself. Mother Theresa (1910–97) is, of course, one of the most prolific Christ-followers of the twentieth century. Based in Calcutta, she became world famous for founding the Missionaries of Charity and ministering to street people.

It is odd that with such an excellent Christian pedigree, West Bengal has never responded to Christ the way other places in India have. Christian institutions are numerous and influential in West Bengal, but they struggle to gain converts.

Conclusion: English is India's Geographical Bridge

The lion's share of India's Christians can be found in the South and in the far northeast. In the South, Christianity has an important presence in Goa, Kerala, and to a lesser extent in Tamil Nadu. In the far northeast, Christianity is the dominant religion in Meghalaya, Mizoram, and Nagaland.

Where is Christianity growing in India? It is growing fast in Arunachal Pradesh, Sikkim, and Tripura. And it is growing modestly in Assam. Something very special is happening in these far northeastern states. We are watching a society

Christianize. While Christianity is already strong among the tribal people there, that trend should continue.

It should be sobering for Christians to know that the expansion of the gospel languishes or retracts throughout the rest of India, where hundreds of millions of non-Christians associate Christianity with the lowest of the low. Perhaps this should not be so discouraging to Christians since Jesus clearly has a preferential option for the poor and disenfranchised in the gospels. It is the crushed—the Dalits—who are exalted in the New Testament. The high and mighty, the pure-bred, the elite, the rich, and the privileged are all confronted by Jesus. It makes sense that Christianity would grow first among the marginalized in India, among the Dalits and the tribals.

Going forward, the greatest threat to Indian Christianity will likely be disunity. India's Adivasis are usually quite ethnocentric. They focus inward. There are reasons for this. India has never been an egalitarian society in the sense that different people groups are able to impact each other freely. No, in India, people are born with duties and roles. And often these roles have been defined for families and tribes for hundreds of years. Until very recently, the sweeper had virtually no chance of going to college to become an IT businessman. Some claim these trends have begun to change. It is very tough to break through to another social class in India. This is perhaps the greatest challenge to India's Christians as they attempt to reach the people around them with the love of Christ.

But Indian Christians do have bridges. And one of those bridges is English, the coveted language of India. It is the language of education and the future. It is the language of advance. But it is also the language that could unite the country. India's Christians realize this. English is a language that has a long and historic connection to Christianity. It is possible that as English flourishes and grows, new opportunities will appear. Christians will be able to use English to reach out to those around them, breaking the barriers of gender, class, caste, occupation, jati (birth), and varna (basic caste, rank, and color). English seems to be the *one way* a person can define herself, rather than being forced to accept the assignment that her birth has placed upon her. English is associated with liberation, education, and power in India. And these three ideas are sacred in Indian society. Robert Frykenberg has written at length about the impact of English on India:

> . . . the proportion of English speakers that can be found throughout the entire subcontinent is significant. They are the most modern and most highly educated. They are the ruling elites. . . . Because English has become the common speech of the educated throughout the entire continent, it is essential for preserving constitutional government, for civil administration, and for national unity. *Without a common knowledge of English, it is hardly possible for the peoples from various parts of India to talk to each other.* It gives enormous advantages to diasporas from India who have migrated throughout the world. Thus, ironically, like Sanskrit and Persian in previous ages, English is the language of learning. Ramifications of the role of English are not only enormous, but increasingly so.[62]

If anything promises to unite the tribals and Dalits with the twice-born, it is the English language. It is, therefore, not an overstatement to say that English is India's geographical bridge. Within the language of English are the seeds of national unity. And within the language of English are other seeds: Christian ones.

Will India's thousands of tribes, castes, and languages ever

---

62. Frykenberg, *Christianity in India*, 33–34. Italics are mine.

find a sense of unity amidst all the profound diversity? It seems highly unlikely at the present. But in the long term, English—and the values associated with it such as equality, freedom, and education—may provide the best reason for hope.

5

Biographical

Some Pioneer Indian Christian Leaders

Introduction

While discussing the two-thousand-year-old heritage of Indian Christianity, with its regional variations, numerous traditions, and confessional differences, it is possible to lose sight of individuals who played an important role in this process. They were the public faces of Indian Christianity. Dogmas and creeds can often be rigid, but committed individuals with their personal testimonies, warmth, and good humor add a human dimension. While being faithful to their own confessional traditions, these individual Christians often rose above denominational barriers in order to build ecumenical bridges across the divide and even across religious lines. Any account of Indian Christianity cannot forget the role of individual stories in this process. Yet, from among the thousands of faithful Christian leaders who served the Indian church through the centuries, how do we select a few representative names? This question proved to be most challenging, and any approach to address it can be found to be inadequate and criticized. In order to select a few names, therefore, the authors of this volume had to settle for certain criteria: one was to divide Indian Christianity into seven broad categories and discuss a few names in each. Second, while acknowledging the great many leaders who contributed in the past, for practical reasons, we decided to select only people who were active in the twentieth century. Another major concern was to include as many women as possible in this discussion, even while accepting that Indian Christianity all through had generally been a male enterprise. Finally, we also decided to include a few current names, including those who continue to be active at the time of this writing.

It must especially be acknowledged that the most difficult section to write in this chapter was the one on the independent Christian figures. From a plethora of independent leaders who served and continue to serve Indian Christianity, how do we select three figures? In the contemporary times, we have leading names—such as K. P. Yohannan, who has built up a mission work and church across South Asia; Ravi Zacharias, who has a teaching and preaching ministry that caters primarily to the intelligentsia; and Paul Dinakaran who, along with his late father, D. G. S. Dinakaran, built up the Jesus Calls ministry during the last few decades as a preaching and healing ministry. Their ministry continues at the time of this writing and we are sure that scholars in the future will evaluate their work. In the end, the editorial consensus was to select three names from the past—people who were pioneers in their own areas as independent Christian leaders.

The following twenty-five leaders are briefly introduced and discussed in this chapter:

- *Orthodox figures:*

  o Sarah Chakko

  o Paulos Mar Gregorios

  o Geevarghese Mar Coorilos

- *Roman Catholic figures:*

  o Raimon Panikkar

  o Mother Teresa

  o Mathias Mundadan

  o Michael Amaladoss

- *Protestant figures:*

  o Vedanayagam Samuel Azariah

  o Harendra Coomar Mookerjee

  o Kunchala Rajaratnam

  o Aruna Gnanadason

  o Roger Gaikwad

- *Mar Thoma figures:*

  o Madathiparampil Mammen Thomas

  o Annamma George

- *Evangelical Protestant figures:*

  o Ben Wati

  o Theodore Williams

  o Saphir Philip Athyal

  o Elizabeth Leelavathi Manasseh

- *Pentecostal figures:*
  - K. E. Abraham
  - Pastor Paramjyoti
  - Mary Kovoor
  - Ambakattuparambil Chacko George
- *Independent figures:*
  - Pandita Ramabai
  - Sadhu Sundar Singh
  - Bakht Singh

Orthodox Figures

Sarah Chakko (1905–1954)

Born on February 13, 1905, in Kerala, Sarah Chakko was an educationalist and the first woman to serve as a president of the World Council of Churches. After her studies in Madras, she moved to Lucknow in North India, where she spent most of her adult life working at the Isabella Thoburn College. She was primarily a member of the teaching staff, and later became the principal of the college. As a member of the Orthodox Syrian Church in India, she brought her Christian heritage and courage of conviction to be an active participant in the ecumenical movement.[1] In particular, she was closely associated with two ecumenical institutions in India—the Student Christian Movement (SCM) and the Young Women's Christian Association (YWCA). While she served as the chairperson of SCM of India, Burma, and Ceylon (now Sri Lanka), she was, for a while, vice-president of the World YWCA.

---

1. Mary Louis Slater, in her book, *Future-maker in India: The Story of Sarah Chakko* (New York: Friendship Press, 1958), narrates the ecumenical journey of Sarah Chakko.

In recognition of her services in the ecumenical movement, especially in India, Chakko was invited to attend the first assembly of the World Council of Churches (WCC) in Amsterdam in 1948. During the short period when she was on the international scene, she played several key roles.[2] She was entrusted with the task of presenting at Amsterdam the Baarn Report from the Life and Work of the Women in the Church. She subsequently became executive secretary of the Commission on the Life and Work of Women in the Church. And in 1951, when T. C. Chao of China resigned as a WCC president due to political reasons, she was chosen to succeed him—the first woman to hold that position.

Sarah Chakko was a shooting star that lit up the ecumenical horizon for a just a short while and then disappeared. She died young, at the age of 49, but within that short life, accomplished much.[3] With her participation in the various educational and ecumenical institutions within India and as a leader of WCC, she inspired generations of women across the world to play leadership roles in their churches and in the ecumenical movement. Her life may not be familiar to many in the current generation, but the impact she left behind is phenomenal. The ecumenical movement has broadly continued in the legacy of Sarah Chakko by becoming communities of women and men that are committed to the values of justice, unity, and fellowship.

Paulos Mar Gregorios (1922–1996)

Widely known and honored as a theologian, philosopher, and

---

2. Susannah Harris-Wilson, "Sarah Chakko 1905–1954," in *Ecumenical Pilgrims: Profiles of Pioneers in Christian Reconciliation*, eds. Ioan Bria and Dagmar Heller (Geneva: WCC Publications, 1995).

3. M. Kurian, *Sarah Chakko: A Voice for Women in the Ecumenical Movement* (Thiruvalla: Christhava Sahitya Samithi, 1998), 134.

bishop, Paulos Mar Gregorios was the first Metropolitan of the Delhi diocese of the Orthodox Syrian Church. He was born on August 9, 1922, in an Orthodox Christian family in Tripunithura, Kerala, India and was named Paul Varghese. He was a brilliant student at school, but could not afford to go to college because of financial difficulties at home. For a while, he worked with the government in the Post & Telegraph Department, and in 1947, went to Ethiopia to be a school teacher, where he came to the attention of Emperor Haile Selassie I. The relationship between the two enabled young Paul to occupy important assignments at various educational institutions in Ethiopia. He also served as personal advisor to the Emperor.

For higher studies, Paul went to the United States, where he studied at the Union Theological Seminary (NY), Princeton, and Yale. He did his doctoral studies in Oxford and Munster (Germany) and received a Doctorate in Theology from Serampore University, India. In 1954, he returned to India and taught at the Union Christian College, Aluva. He was also Associate General Secretary, Student Christian Movement of India.

He served his church in various capacities. In 1961, he was ordained a priest, and in 1975, as a bishop with the name Paulos Mar Gregorios. He served for long as the principal of the Orthodox Theological Seminary at Kottayam, Kerala and played an important role in building up the Seminary as an academic center of excellence.

He had a long and distinguished career in the ecumenical movement. While doing his doctoral studies in Oxford, he was invited to conduct five Bible studies at the New Delhi Assembly of the WCC in 1961.[4] He later served as the director of the Division of Ecumenical Action and associate general secretary of WCC. He chaired the World Conference on Faith, Science and the Future in Cambridge, USA in 1979[5] and was the vice-president of the Christian Peace Conference (1970–1990). During 1983 to 1991, he was one of the presidents of the WCC.[6]

In recognition of his services to church and society, a number of awards and honors were conferred on him. He is the author of more than a dozen books. Having made his mark at different levels as a thinker, scholar, theologian, visionary, orator, writer, and journalist, he passed away on November 24, 1996. He was endowed with a rare form of broad intellectual curiosity, and had a sincere quest for a just order of the world.

Geevarghese Mor Coorilos (1965–)

Geevarghese Mor Coorilos (birth name: George Mathew Nalunnakkal) is a bishop of the Syrian Orthodox Church and the Metropolitan of Niranam. He was born in Nalunnakkal, Kottayam, Kerala in 1965 as the son of P. C. Mathew and Marykutty Mathew, and was brought up in the Syrian Orthodox faith since his childhood. He passed his school final examination with first class and joined St. Berchman's College, Changanacherry, where he did his Pre-Degree and BA in English literature. After university studies, he joined the United Theological College, Bangalore for theological studies and completed his BD in 1990 with a first class. He subsequently traveled to the University of Kent at Canterbury, England to do his PhD in Eco-theology.

On completing his PhD, he returned to India and served

4. Paulos Mar Gregorios, *Love's Freedom- The Grand Mystery: A Spiritual Autobiography* (Kottayam: MGF, 1997), 22.
5. Paulos Mar Gregorios, "Why the Churches are Gathering at M.I.T.?," *One World* 42 (May 1979).
6. Paulos Mar Gregorios, *On Ecumenism*, ed. Fr. Dr. Jacob Kurian (Kottayam: ISPCK & MGF, 2006).

on the faculty of the Malankara Syrian Orthodox Theological Seminary in Kerala and the United Theological College, Bangalore. He was a senior faculty member at the Kerala Council of Churches and served the National Council of Churches in India as its executive secretary for Mission and Evangelism.[7] He was ordained a deacon in 2001 and a priest in 2002. He became a bishop in 2006.

Mor Coorilos had a distinguished career as a teacher of theology and ecumenical leader. As of 2015, he serves the WCC as moderator of its Commission on World Mission and Evangelism (CWME). He was nominated by the WCC to its Advisory Group on Economic Matters. He serves as the chairperson of the Student Christian Movement of India and as a consultant for the World Student Christian Federation. He is the working president of Mor Adai Study Center and the patriarchal vicar of the Malankara Congregations in the United Kingdom. He has attended several international consultations.

A prolific writer, Mor Coorilos has written a number of books and articles in both Malayalam and English.[8] Despite his busy schedule, he serves as the chairperson of the India Center for Social Change (Theeram centers), a charitable organization working for the welfare of mentally challenged children and adults in Kerala. He is deeply committed to translating his theological insights and ecumenical vision into praxis at the grassroots level. He envisions a Trinitarian society that is characterized by the values of justice, equality, sharing, inclusivity, hospitality, and interdependence.

---

7. Geevarghese Mor Coorilose, *Quest for Justice: Perspectives on Mission and Unity* (co-edited; Delhi: NCCI/GURUKUL/ISPCK, 2000).

8. Two significant books authored by Geevarghese Mor Coorilose in English are *New Beings and New Communities: Theological Reflections in a Postmodern Context* (Tiruvalla: KCC/EDTP, 1998) and *Green Liberation: Towards an Integral Ecotheology* (Delhi: NCCI/ISPCK, 1999).

Roman Catholic Figures

Raimon Panikkar (1918–2010)

Raimon Panikkar (also known as Raymond Panikkar and Raimundo Panikkar), Roman Catholic priest and scholar on interreligious dialogue, was born in Barcelona, Spain on November 2, 1918, to a Spanish Christian mother and Indian Hindu father. Due largely to his unique family background, he felt perfectly at home in diverse traditions, and often maintained that interreligious dialogue was not a mere academic exercise for him, but a lived reality. A genius, he earned PhDs in philosophy, theology, and chemistry. Ordained as a priest in 1946, he taught at the University of Madrid. Panikkar lived and taught in the United States from 1966 to 1987, working primarily at Harvard University and the University of California in Santa Barbara, where he was chair of Comparative Religious Philosophy from 1971 to 1987. In recognition of his services, the University of California awards a prize every year—"The Raimundo Panikkar Award in Comparative Religions"—to the philosophy student who completes his/her degree with the highest marks.

Panikkar lived and researched in India for long and he opened unique paths in interfaith dialogue by viewing issues in the real world through the eyes of two or more traditions. About himself, he often said: "I left Europe [for India] as a Christian, I discovered I was a Hindu and returned as a Buddhist without ever having ceased to be Christian."[9] In interreligious relations, he argued, what was needed was "dialogical dialogue," which recognized differences and yet affirmed what we have in common. The ability to *listen* is an

---

9. This has been so often quoted that a source is no longer given.

important part of dialogue. For him, dialogue is not merely a human exercise, but has cosmic dimensions as well, and he affirms the sacredness of life as "sacred secularity." We live at a time when sensitivity toward the sacredness of matter has been lost and he calls upon our generation to affirm the truth that because everything is sacred, everything is inviolable. He condemns our "obsession with certainty" and pleads for the need for polysemy, ambiguity, and openness.

Panikkar has written dozens of books, papers, and articles and has received numerous prizes and awards.[10] In 1960, he was one of the founders of the NGO Pax Romana—with consultative status at the United Nations—which protects the rights and dignity of people all over the globe. He took part in international consultations for UNESCO and several other academic institutions and was a special envoy for the Indian government on cultural missions to South America. He died on August 26, 2010 in Tavertet, Spain.

Mother Teresa (1910–1997)

Roman Catholic nun and missionary to India, Mother Teresa was born on August 26, 1910, as Agnes Gonxha Bojaxhiu in Skopje in the Republic of Macedonia to parents, Nikola and Dranafile Bojaxhiu, people of Albanian descent. Hers was a devoutly Catholic family, and, after the sudden death of her father in 1919, the little Agnes became very close to her mother, who instilled in her daughter a deep commitment to help the poor and the needy. There is little doubt that her

---

10. Some of the best known books of Panikkar are *The Unknown Christ of Hinduism: Towards an Ecumenical Christophany* (Maryknoll, NY: Orbis Books, 1981); *The Trinity and the Religious Experience of Man: Icon-person-mystery* (Maryknoll, NY: Orbis Books, 1973); *The Silence of God: The Answer of the Buddha* (Maryknoll, NY: Orbis Books; revised edition June 1989); and *A Dwelling Place for Wisdom* (Louisville: Westminster John Knox Press, 1993).

mother had a profound impact on Agnes's decision to set aside her life for social and charitable service.[11]

Agnes Bojaxhiu studied at a convent-run primary school, and was convinced at the age of twelve that she was being called by God for a religious life. In 1928, at eighteen, she decided to become a nun and joined the Loreto Sisters of Dublin, Ireland. While in Dublin, she took the name "Sister Mary Teresa"—after the French Discalced Carmelite nun, Saint Thérèse of Lisieux.

After making her Profession of Vows, Sister Teresa traveled to Darjeeling, India in 1931 for the novitiate period. She subsequently went to Calcutta, where she was assigned to teach at Saint Mary's High School for Girls, a school dedicated to educating girls from the city's poorest Bengali families. She became dedicated to the education of girls which, she believed, was a means to alleviate their poverty.

In 1937, Teresa took her Final Profession of Vows to a life of poverty and obedience and, in accordance with the practice of Loreto nuns, took on the title of "mother," thus becoming known as Mother Teresa.[12] In 1946, she took the decision to leave teaching so as to work in the slums of Calcutta with the city's poorest and most needy people. In 1950, she won canonical recognition for a new congregation, the Missionaries of Charity, for the work among the poor. In the 1950s and 1960s, the work of her organization grew and a number of nuns joined her. In 1965, Pope Paul VI bestowed the Decree of Praise upon the Missionaries of Charity and Teresa's work spread internationally. By the time of her death in 1997, the

---

11. See Kathryn Spink, *Mother Teresa. A Complete Authorized Biography* (New York: HarperCollins, 1997).
12. Mother Teresa, *No Greater Love* (Novato, CA: New World Library, 1997).

Missionaries of Charity numbered in the thousands and had a presence in over one hundred countries around the world.

Mother Teresa received numerous awards and honors for her tireless work. She was awarded the Jewel of India, the highest honor bestowed on Indian civilians, as well as the Gold Medal of the Soviet Peace Committee. In 1979, she was awarded the Nobel Peace Prize in recognition of her work of bringing help to the suffering masses. The beatification of Mother Teresa was conducted by Pope John Paul II in 2003, thus bestowing on her the title "Blessed." Mother Teresa can easily be counted as one of the greatest humanitarians of the twentieth century.

A. Mathias Mundadan (1923–2012)

Anthony Mathias Mundadan, a priest of the Carmelites of Mary Immaculate (CMI) in the Syro-Malabar tradition of the Roman Catholic Church, a renowned theologian and scholar in the history of Christianity, was born at Karingamthuruth, North Parur Taluk, Kerala on November 12, 1923. After his basic studies in Kerala, he did courses in philosophy and theology at St. Joseph's Pontifical Seminary, Mangalore and De Nobili College, Pune. Ordained as a Priest in 1953, he received his MA in theology the next year. For advanced studies, he went to Rome and specialized in church history at the Gregorian University, from where he took, in 1957, the licentiate in Church History, and in 1960, completed his PhD. Returning to India, he taught at Dharmaram College/Dharmaram Pontifical Institute (now Dharmaram Vidya Kshetram) for several decades, and in 1976, became president of Dharmaram. He also served his Carmelites of Mary Immaculate Congregation as the Provincial Superior during 1972 to 1975 and 1990 to 1996.

Mundadan was primarily a theologian who could offer valid insights in interpreting historical developments and milestones in such a way that his contributions to the history of Christianity are rated to be significant contributions in Indian Christian theology as well. He wrote extensively on topics such as the history of Christianity in India, the arrival of the Portuguese in India, the Thomas Christians, Indian Christians' search for identity and struggle for autonomy, and an overview of the Syro-Malabar church.[13] He wrote in both English and Malayalam.

Apart from his individual study and research, as a scholar and priest, he believed that historians cutting across the denominational divide should come together for corporate study and research. He was instrumental in founding the Church History Association of India (CHAI) as a common forum for historians of Christianity in India. Under his leadership, CHAI undertook a number of projects and publications.[14] Mundadan served for long as the general editor of "Indian Church History Series" and as chief editor of *Church History Association of India Review*. He was the member of a number of national and international associations. To sum up, Mundadan was an eminent historian, a great theologian, an effective teacher, an able administrator, and, above all, a holy priest. He died on August 31, 2012.

Michael Amaladoss (1936-)

Michael Amaladoss, an Indian Jesuit and liberation theologian was born on December 8, 1936, in Dindigul, Tamil Nadu. He

---

13. See Mathias Mundadan, *The Arrival of the Portuguese in India and the Thomas Christians under Mar Jacob 1498-1552* (Bangalore; Dharmaram College, 1967).
14. In particular, Mathias Mundadan authored *History of Christianity in India*, vol. 1 (Bangalore: TPI for CHAI, 1984).

entered the novitiate of the Jesuits in 1953 and was ordained a priest in 1968. He took on specialized study in liturgy and received a doctorate in sacramental theology at Catholic Institute of Paris. Back in India, he taught at St. Paul's Seminary in Tiruchirapalli (Tamil Nadu) and Vidyajyoti College of Theology in Delhi (1973–1983). In Delhi, he facilitated the starting of Regional Theological Centers for Jesuits, where theology was taught in the local Indian language and people were in close touch with the living situation of the people, but academically associated with the college at Delhi. Along with the British Benedictine Bede Griffiths, he also founded an interreligious dialogue group in Delhi.

During the 33rd General Congregation of the Society of Jesus in Rome in 1983, Amaladoss was elected as one of four assistants of Peter-Hans Kolvenbach, the new Superior General of the Jesuits and he had the special responsibility of all matters that concerned mission in the Society of Jesus. During this period, he was also a consultant to the Pontifical Council for Interreligious Dialogue and a Vatican representative in the Commission for World Mission and Evangelism of the WCC. He worked in Rome till 1995, and since 1999 has been living in Chennai, acting as director of the Institute for Dialogue with Cultures and Religions of the Loyola College.

During his work in Rome, Amaladoss was recognized as a missiologist and he was elected as president of the International Association of Mission Studies. He has, however, confessed that he dislikes being identified as a missiologist and prefers being called an Indian theologian who is interested in mission and dialogue, inculturation and liberation. He has written extensively. In his book, *The Asian Jesus*, he explores the images that Asians perhaps would have used to understand

Jesus if Christianity had spread toward Asia rather than toward the West.[15]

Amaladoss is a versatile scholar. He is trained in South Indian classical music and has composed about one hundred hymns and *bhajans* (repetitive devotional chants for prayer) for worship, a "teach yourself" book on South Indian music for beginners, and songs on Christian themes for the South Indian classical dance form, Bharathanatyam.

In recognition of Amaladoss's contributions, the Regis College of Toronto (Canada) conferred on him an honorary doctorate degree. In 2014, his writings and speeches were being investigated by the Vatican, with the possibility of censure, for allegedly espousing unorthodox beliefs on the uniqueness of Jesus and the Catholic Church.[16]

Mainline Protestant Figures

Vedanayagam Samuel Azariah (1874–1945)

Vedanayagam Samuel Azariah, the first Indian bishop in the churches of the Anglican Communion, a pioneer on church unity and the first bishop of the diocese of Dornakal, was born to devout parents on August 17, 1874, at Vellanvilai in Tamil Nadu. After his education, Azariah worked as an evangelist under the Young Men's Christian Association (YMCA) and served the association in several capacities, including as an associate general secretary. Convinced of the importance of indigenous forms of Christian ministry and witness, the interdenominational National Missionary Society was founded

15. Michael Amaladoss, *The Asian Jesus* (Maryknoll, NY: Orbis Books, 2006).
16. "Fr. Michael Amaladoss SJ under investigation by Rome," *Metamorphose* (May 14, 2014), http://ephesians511blog.com/2014/05/29/fr-michael-amaladoss-sj-under-investigation-by-rome (Accessed September 21, 2015).

in 1905, with Azariah as its secretary. During this period, he also traveled abroad, to Jaffna in Sri Lanka, to attend the World Student Christian Federation Conference in Tokyo, and the YMCA conference in Shanghai. He was ordained in 1909 as an Anglican priest and consecrated in 1912 as the first bishop of the new Diocese of Dornakal in Telengana.

Azariah delivered a memorable speech at the International Missionary Conference in Edinburgh in 1910, asking the foreign missionary in the non-Western world "to show that he is in the midst of the people to be to them not a lord and master but a brother and a friend."[17] While his speech and interventions at the Edinburgh Conference were criticized by many missionaries and mission bodies, it came as a boost to the efforts of the Asian African churches that were striving to be indigenous. Azariah also attended the missionary conferences in Jerusalem (1928) and Tambaram (1938). From 1929 to 1945, he was the chairman of the National Christian Council of India.

Azariah was, first and foremost, an evangelist and he contributed richly in the area of the theology of evangelism within the context of an emerging Indian nationhood and with a deep concern for the rural millions in India who had not yet heard the gospel.[18] He wrote many books and spoke extensively on the need for the Indian church, in its expression of the gospel, to take seriously the country's cultural traditions and to contribute its share in the creation of a new India. He believed that disunity among Christians was sinful and that the task of Christian witness to such a vast nation by a small minority Christian community, fragmented by many

17. World Missionary Conference (WMC), *History and Records of the Conference, Together with Addresses Delivered at the Evening Meetings* (Edinburgh: Oliphant, Anderson & Ferrier; New York: Fleming H. Revell, n. d. [1910]), 306–15.
18. See Susan Billington Harper, *In the Shadow of the Mahatma: Bishop V. S. Azariah and the Travails of Christianity in British India* (Grand Rapids & Cambridge: Eerdmans, and Richmond, Surrey, UK: Curzon Press, 2000).

denominations, cannot be done effectively. While he did not live to see the inauguration of the Church of South India (CSI) in 1947, the "Tranquebar Manifesto" compiled under his creative leadership in 1919 laid a laid a strong foundation for Christian unity in India and for the formation of the CSI. He died on January 1, 1945.

Harendra Coomar Mookerjee (1887–1956)

H. C. Mookerjee was a prominent Indian Christian leader at the time of the nation's independence and he served as vice-president of the Constituent Assembly and governor of West Bengal. Born in a Bengali family in Bengal, he did his studies in Calcutta (Kolkata) and was the first Indian to receive a PhD from the University of Calcutta. From 1936 to 1940, he served as a professor of English at the Calcutta University. He was a nominated member in the Bengal Legislative Council and was elected to the Bengal Legislative Assembly. From 1951 to 1956, he served as governor of West Bengal. He died in office on August 4, 1956.

As the vice-president of the Constituent Assembly that drafted the Constitution of the country and as chairman of the Minority rights sub-committee and Provincial constitution committee, Mookerjee played an important role in defining the meaning of "minority rights" in India. He argued for reservation (affirmative action) for the minorities in all fields, including politics. In particular, he had a clear vision of the role and place of the minority Christians in public life. As the British left India and the reigns of the government moved to indigenous hands, he advised the Christians: "We have to demonstrate by every word we utter and by every act we perform that the professing of a different religious faith has not tended in the least to make us less Indian in our outlook than our non-Christian brethren, that we are prepared to play our part and to shoulder our share of the responsibility in every kind of work undertaken for the benefit of our country as a whole."[19]

Mookerjee called himself a Christian Indian nationalist.[20] He argued that the condition of the poor Christian Indian was no different from the condition of an equally poor Hindu Indian or Muslim Indian. He was against communal representation for Christians in the legislative bodies and believed that the majority Hindus can be trusted to be fair to minorities such as the Christians. The gesture of goodwill expressed by well-intentioned Christian leaders such as Mookerjee was duly reciprocated by the Hindus and the right to not only preach and practice, but also "propagate" one's religion was enshrined in the Indian Constitution. Mookerjee also served as the president of the All India Council of Indian Christians that represented all Indian Christians, except the Anglo-Indians.

Kunchala Rajaratnam (1921–2010)

Kunchala Rajaratnam was an economist, social scientist, Lutheran theologian, and one of the leading theological educators of India in the twentieth century. Born in 1921, he studied at various schools and colleges, including Madras Christian College and the University of Madras. He completed his PhD from London School of Economics on the topic, "A History of Economic Thought and Analysis—Lord Lionnel Robbins." For over two decades, he taught economics in

---

19. "Happy Gestures," *Hindu Books Universe*, http://www.hindubooks.org/Retrospect _of_Christianity/ch4.htm (Accessed September 21, 2015).
20. "Explain the Contribution of Christians to the India's National Movements" (Paper Presentation on the History of Christianity in India), http://system46.blogspot.in/ 2012/04/history-of-christianity-in-india.html (Accessed September 21, 2015).

various colleges in India. He has also lectured in universities around the world.

In 1992, Rajaratnam established the Centre for Research on New International Economic Order (CReNIEO) as a place of advanced study and action in the areas of economic trends, social action, and rural development. Under his initiative, CReNIEO undertook a number of projects and programs, including a training center for development economists, the Integrated Rural Development for Weaker Sections, Integrated Fisherfolk Development Project, and others. During this period, Rajaratnam served as the chairperson of Orissa Development Action Forum, which was a network of eleven non-governmental organizations in Orissa. He also pioneered cutting edge academic research. CReNIEO is an accredited research institute under the University of Madras and a number of research projects, leading to major publications, emerged under his leadership.

Rajaratnam was an outstanding Lutheran theologian and church statesman. He served as the Asia Secretary of the Lutheran World Federation in Geneva and the executive secretary of the United Evangelical Lutheran Churches in India. He built up the Gurukul Lutheran Theological College as both the major theological institution of the Lutheran churches in India and as a major ecumenical institution, with the faculty and students drawn from diverse Christian backgrounds.[21] He served for long as the director of Gurukul.

During his long years of service, Rajaratnam also provided outstanding leadership to ecumenical theological education, the ecumenical movement, and leadership development in Indian churches. He was the president of the National Council

---

21. Prasanna Kumari, ed., *Adventurous Faith, Bold Theological Vision & Commitment to Service: Dr. Kunchala Rajaratnam as Testified by Others* (Chennai: UELCI, 2000).

of Churches in India and the Master (chancellor) of the Senate of Serampore University. He gave new dynamism to the Indian Christian Dalit movement and was instrumental in initiating ecumenical endeavors to highlight Dalit liberation within international ecumenical and ecclesiastical circles. He wrote a number of books and articles in the areas of economic development, Lutheran mission, theological education, and the ecumenical movement.[22] In recognition of his services, several awards and honors were conferred on him. He died in 2010.

Aruna Gnanadason (1949–)

Aruna Gnanadason, born in Bengaluru in 1949, is a feminist theologian, church worker, and activist for the rights of women, other marginalised groups such as Dalits, tribals, and Adivasis as well as the earth itself. She was deeply influenced by a strong Christian upbringing in a family committed to the education of women and men. In the Student Christian Movement and as an active member of the women's movement in church and society, she developed a consciousness about patriarchal and casteist India and the critical role the subaltern can play in healing relationships between people and between people and the earth.

In the church, in particular during her years on the staff of the Ecumenical Christian Centre (Whitefield in Bengaluru) and in her work with the All India Council of Christian Women of the National Council of Churches in India (Nagpur), the Women's Programme and in the Justice Peace and Creation work of the WCC (Geneva, Switzerland), she recognized the potential of the churches and theology to raise questions about

22. Two of Rajaratnam's major writings are *Development and Environmental Economics: The Relevance of Gandhi* (Chennai: CReNIEO, 1993) and *Structural Crises of National and Global Economics: Relevance of Received Economic Theory Questioned* (Chennai: CReNIEO, 1981).

injustice and all that fractures community and to act for justice and peace.[23] Her educational background in English literature and theology prepared her to be a prolific writer in many international publications and speaker in forums in many parts of the world.

An earned doctorate of ministries (from the San Francisco School of Theology in USA), and three honorary doctorates (Madras, Serampore Senate, and Matanzas, Cuba), all recognized her role in challenging patriarchal structures in church and society and her specific interest and contributions to eco-feminist theologies. She proudly calls herself an Indian Christian feminist as she sees feminism as a movement not just for a transformed world for women, but for all men and women in society and for the earth itself.[24] She believes that we need to move into a new wave of the feminist movement in India that will draw together various struggles against poverty, caste, ecocide, patriarchy, and heteronormativity—all of which have an impact on the lives of women. She also believes that feminism's potential to become a transforming force in church, society, and in all of creation cannot be underestimated.

Roger Gaikwad (1953–)

Born on February 13, 1953, Roger Gaikwad is general secretary of the National Council of Churches in India and a minister of the Mizo Presbyterian Synod under the Presbyterian Church of India. He completed his theological studies at Serampore

23. For a detailed discussion of Aruna Gnanadason's ecumenical theology, see her writings, "Nameless and Silenced No Longer, We Will Overcome Violence!," *In God's Image* (Asian Women's Resource Centre) 24:1 (March 2005): 3–8; and "Introduction," Aruna Gnanadason, Musimbi Kanyoro, and Lucia Anna McSpadden, eds., *Women, Violence and Non-Violent Change* (Geneva: WCC, 1996), vii–xi.
24. See Natalie Maxson, *Journey for Justice: The Story of Women in the WCC* (Geneva: WCC, 2014).

University and holds a doctorate in theology. In 1976, he was ordained a deacon in the Methodist Church and served the church for a while. From 1978, he has been working in Mizoram, primarily as a teacher at the Aizawl Theological College, and in 1981, he was ordained as a minister in the Mizoram Presbyterian Synod, Presbyterian Church of India. During 2008–2010, he served as principal (president) of Aizawl Theological College.

Gaikwad has been a leader of the ecumenical movement at the national and global levels. During 1996 to 2001 and 2003 to 2005, he served as chairperson of the Student Christian Movement of India. He has also been chairperson of World Student Christian Federation of the Asia-Pacific Region and president of the Lutheran World Service India Trust. In 2002, he was appointed as director of the Extension Program in the Senate of Serampore College, a position he held with distinction for six years. In recognition of his rich contribution in the church, the ecumenical movement, and theological education, he was invited, in 2010, to be the 10th General Secretary of the National Council of Churches in India (NCCI), the ecumenical forum of the Protestant and Orthodox churches in the country. Under his leadership, the centenary celebration of NCCI was held in 2014.

Gaikwad has traveled widely and has ministered and lectured in churches and colleges in India, Bangladesh, Nepal, and Bhutan. In 2000, he was visiting fellow at University of Bristol, UK, and in 2004, he delivered the Teape Lectures in Cambridge, UK.[25] He has written several articles for magazines, journals, and books. His spouse Zomuani is the first Mizo

25. Roger Gaikwad, "The Interplay of Religion, Politics and Communalism in India" (Teape Lectures in Cambridge, UK, 2003; unpublished).

woman to earn the theological degree, BD (Bachelor of Divinity).

Based on his long years of experience in the church and in the ecumenical movement, Gaikwad visualizes Indian Christianity as consisting of vibrant grassroots ecumenical communities of integrity, transparency, and accountability. Such communities would be in solidarity with all who are engaged in struggles for life, livelihood, justice, and peace. And they would be communities where there is space for everyone, and where all partner together and in doing so bear witness to the truth that the Gospel is for all.

Mar Thoma Figures

Madathiparampil Mammen Thomas (1916–96)

Born on May 15, 1916, into a devout Mar Thoma Church family in Kozhencherry in Kerala, M. M. Thomas was an outstanding social theologian and ecumenical leader of the twentieth century. The primary arena of his work was India, where he was closely associated with the Christian Institute for the Study of Religion and Society (CISRS) in Bangalore, India. Under his leadership, CISRS undertook a number of study programs and publications in the areas of nation-building, interreligious dialogue, and Christian social responsibility. Along with group studies, Thomas's personal research during this period on the meaning of Christian mission in the context of renascent religions and secular ideologies set the pace for theological reflections in this area in post-independent India.[26] Prior to the founding of CISRS, he was closely associated with

---

26. M. M. Thomas's books, *The Acknowledged Christ of the Indian Renaissance* (London: Student Christian Movement Press, 1969) and *Secular Ideologies of India and Secular Meaning of Christianity* (Madras: CLS, 1976), are considered classic works in these areas.

Youth Christian Council of Action (YCCA), a springboard in the 1940s and 1950s for ecumenical youth.[27] He also served the Mar Thoma Church as youth secretary.

Thomas was a key participant in the ecumenical movement at the Asian and global levels. Beginning in 1947, he served for three years as secretary of the Geneva-based World Student Christian Federation, the first Asian to hold that position. He was part of the team that built up an ecumenical network of Asian churches, which in 1957 led to the formation of the East Asia Christian Conference (now, the Christian Conference of Asia). He was closely connected to the WCC from the 1940s onwards. The primary arena of his work in WCC was the Department on Church and Society. He chaired the World Conference on Church and Society in Geneva in 1966, a path-breaking event that brought together social thinkers and theologians from around the world. In 1968, at the fourth Assembly, Thomas was elected the Moderator of the WCC Central Committee, the first lay person and non-Westerner to hold that position. Under his leadership, the WCC took crucial steps to support the anti-apartheid struggle in South Africa and established relations with the churches in China.[28] As Alf Tergel, the Swedish church historian noted, along with Visser't Hooft, M. M. Thomas has had the greatest influence on the modern ecumenical movement.[29]

After retirement, Thomas settled down in his home in Kerala and participated actively in the social and religious life of the state and the country. A study man to the core, he wrote and edited several dozens of books during his life time.[30] During

---

27. See George M. John, *Youth Christian Council of Action, 1938-1954: The Story of a Dynamic Movement of Christian Youth* (Bangalore: CISRS, 1972).
28. See M. M. Thomas's autobiographical book of this period *My Ecumenical Journey* (Trivandrum: Ecumenical Publishing Centre, 1990).
29. Paul Abrecht, "In memoriam: M. M. Thomas," *The Ecumenical Review* 49:1 (January 1997): 111.

1991 to 1993, he served as the governor of Nagaland and grappled, administratively and intellectually, with the challenges faced by the indigenous people.[31] His vision and vast experience enabled him to be the elder statesman of that state. Thomas died on December 3, 1996, during a train journey on his way home.

Annamma George (1923–2012)

Born in 1923 in Kerala, Annamma George is one of the pioneers of the women's Christian movement in India. She was among the few Asian women present at the inaugural Assembly of the WCC in Amsterdam in 1948. She was a member of the Mar Thoma Church and she served, for a long duration and with rare dedication, Sevika Sanghom, the women's fellowship of the church. For fourteen years, she was the organizing secretary of Sevika Sanghom.

George was deeply committed to women's full and creative participation in the ministerial and theological life of the church. She was closely associated with the All India Council of Christian Women (AICCW), the women's department of the National Council of Churches in India. As one of the first theologically trained women in India, she was also committed to re-defining tradition from a theological perspective. Annamma was deeply troubled by the fact that several Indian churches—including her own—deny ordination to women. As the number of theologically trained women grew in the country, she and the others took the initiative in founding the Association of Theologically Trained Women in India (ATTWI). She served for two terms as the president of ATTWI.

30. Thomas wrote twenty one Bible commentaries in Malayalam during this period. Several of them have since been translated into English.
31. See M. M. Thomas, *The Nagas Towards A. D. 2000* (Madras: CReNIEO, 1992).

George was an able theologian and she authored and edited a number of books.[32] In 1964, she became the executive secretary of the Theological Literature Council (TLC) in Kerala, a position she held with distinction for a quarter of a century. Under her leadership, TLC published 84 theological books in Malayalam, thus making available rich theological literature to the common people in their language.

George's good sense of humor, added to her timely delivery and wit, has many a times embarrassed the bishops and priests, but she was deeply loyal to her church. She had a vision of a just community of women and men in the church and society and she was prepared to stand up to her convictions.

In recognition of her services to the church and society, the Senate of Serampore College and the Academy of Ecumenical Indian Theology and Church Administration awarded her honorary doctorates. She died in 2012.

Evangelical Figures

Ben Wati (1920–2012)

Ben Wati, an internationally renowned evangelical Christian leader of northeast India, was born on December 18, 1920, in Impur, Nagaland. After his school and university studies, he traveled to the United States for higher studies. He is reputed to be the first person from North East India to earn a BD (Northern Baptist Theological Seminary, Chicago, 1948) and an MA (Wheaton College, Wheaton, Illinois, 1949). In 1970, Wheaton College conferred on him the honorary degree DD.

Ben Wati's long association with the World Evangelical Fellowship (WEF—now world Evangelical Alliance, WEA) began

---

32. Most of Annamma George's books and other writings are in Malayalam and are yet to be translated into English.

in 1956. He served as vice-president (1962–1968) and president (1968–1974) of WEF. In India, he was closely associated with the Evangelical Fellowship of India (EFI) and the Union Biblical Seminary (UBS). He joined EFI in 1953 and worked in various capacities. He served as executive secretary of EFI (1957–1976)[33] and became, in 1957, founder chairman of the EFI Commission on Relief and Development (EFICOR), an organization that undertook emergency relief and development in various parts of India. Under his initiative and with Tear Fund's assistance, EFICOR extended its ministry into Bangladesh as well. He served as the chairman of the UBS Board for 16 years and as officiating principal during 1994 to 1995.[34]

Ben Wati was deeply rooted in the context of North East India. Ordained as a Baptist minister in 1973 by Ao Baptist Church Association, he was instrumental in translating the first Naga Bible. He played an important role in founding some key theological institutions in North East India, such as the Eastern Theological College, Jorhat and Clark Theological Seminary, Nagaland. Even while being an international leader, at heart, he remained a Naga and oversaw Naga associations abroad.

Even in retirement, he continued the ministry of counseling, Bible teaching, and writing. He authored a number of books and traveled around the world several times, teaching and preaching. He died on June 14, 2012, at his younger brother Colonel Maken's residence in Dimapur, Nagaland.

Ben Wati has left an indelible mark on the evangelical movement at the national and global levels. He believed that

33. See Ben Wati, *Whither Evangelicals? : The Evangelical Movement in India* (New Delhi: Evangelical Fellowship of India, 1975).
34. Ben Wati, "A Pilgrimage in Theological Education," *UBS Journal* 3 (March 2005): 66–74.

the Holy Spirit has guided him through uncharted grounds to give the best of his ministry to the church in North East India, India, and around the world. He mentored a generation of leaders to serve God and love people. He was courageous to speak the truth in love. His life and witness will continue to be an example for the worldwide body of Christ.

Theodore Williams (1935–2009)

Born on February 24, 1935, in the town of Nazareth in Tuticorin District of Tamil Nadu, Theodore Williams was a renowned preacher, Bible expositor, and church leader. His father was a school teacher and grandfather, an Anglican priest. Born in a devout Christian family, Williams regularly attended church services. He had the habit of memorizing Bible verses and short prayers at Sunday school and would recite at home the sermon points. During his student days, he had a deep affinity toward Dravidian politics and he wrote stories in a Tamil monthly magazine. At a revival meeting in Emmanuel Methodist Church, Chennai, in 1953, he surrendered himself for God's work. After realizing his call for ministry and despite heavy objections from his family, he decided to pursue theological education and joined the South India Bible Institute (SIBI) in Bangarapet, Karnataka. He went on to do his advanced theological studies at Serampore University. After his studies, he worked for a while as a pastor at Immanuel Methodist Church, and, along with a few others, founded the Friends Missionary Prayer Band (FMPB), which is a leading missionary organization in India today. He served as the first president of FMPB. Subsequently, he became active in the EFI, and in 1965, he founded the Indian Evangelical Mission (IEM).[35]

---

35. "Dr. Theodore Williams: A Example to Modern Generation," in *Dust From Miry Clay*.

Theodore Williams was an excellent Bible expositor and preacher. His knowledge of the Word of God and his preaching skills were well-known. He had an English broadcast of back to the Bible and "Satyavasanam," a Tamil program through which he influenced many people to turn to God. He has authored a number of books, which have been published and translated into many languages. For several years, he was a speaker at the world-famous Maramon convention. He died on December 29, 2009.

Theodore Williams set an example of how to completely obey God. He was indifferent to fame or prestige in this world. Rather, he craved for the love of Christ and eternity. He believed in standing for Christ in any situation, with humility and complete obedience to God.

Saphir Philip Athyal (1931–)

Born on April 12, 1931 (an Easter Sunday), Saphir Athyal belongs to the Christian community in South India that dates back its origin to a tradition that Apostle Thomas founded it. As a young boy, he had a strong Christian upbringing, high moral standards, and a fairly good understanding of the Bible. After his studies in English literature, political science, and philosophy at Allahabad University, he went to Princeton Theological Seminary, where he earned his PhD (with *cum laude* honors) as the first and only Indian national at that time with a doctorate in the Old Testament.

He joined the faculty of the Union Biblical Seminary (UBS) at Yavatmal in central India, and served there for 24 years, including as its principal (president) for 14 years. During his

https://spiritualwhip.wordpress.com/2011/05/27/dr-theodore-williams-a-example-to-modern-generation (Accessed September 22, 2015).

leadership, he more than doubled the size of its student body, brought in highly qualified Indian staff, and added post-graduate programs, including Doctor of Theology (DTh) studies. As the seminary grew rapidly, he led the shifting of the total seminary to the cosmopolitan city of Pune.

He has been one of the leaders of the Lausanne Movement at the Asian and global levels.[36] He served on the Planning Committee of the 1974 Lausanne Congress on World Evangelization, and then, as its deputy chairman for ten years. In the two main Lausanne global events, he was the program director for the 1980 Consultation on World Evangelization in Pattaya, and program chairman for 1989 Lausanne II Congress in Manila.[37] He was one of the founders of the All-India Association for Theological Education by Extension (TAFTEE) and the Asia Theological Association, which is the largest accrediting body for the Asia-Pacific region.

After retirement from UBS, he was invited by the World Vision International to serve as the director of Holistic Mission and Christian Witness at their global office in California for seven years, and later as director of Christian Commitments and senior advisor of World Vision-Asia-Pacific Region.

Back home in Kerala, he conducts a Theological Academy he founded and does some writing. He believes resolutely that Christians need only one central thing: our bond of love with our Lord. This bond is our ultimate freedom. He has always been wary of the use of the terms "evangelical" and "ecumenical." To him, only those who truly accept and serve Christ as their Savior and Lord are Christians and Evangelicals.

36. The volume edited by Saphir Athyal, *Church in Asia Today: Challenges and Opportunities* (Asia Lausanne Committee, 1996), discusses the most noteworthy present-day trends of the church in each country of Asia, its critical challenges, and opportunities ahead.
37. See Saphir Athyal, *How Shall They Hear? Consultation on World Evangelism, Official Reference Volume* (1980).

He has authored and edited a number of books and booklets, and has lectured in universities and seminaries around the world. In recognition of his services, an honorary Doctor of Divinity degree was conferred upon him by Serampore University (India) and Asbury Theological Seminary (USA).

Elizabeth Leelavathi Manasseh (1954-)

A well-known evangelical leader and the first Indian woman to obtain the Master of Theology degree through the Association of Theological Education by Extension (TAFTEE) from Oxford University, Elizabeth Leelavathi Manasseh was born in Bangalore on April 17, 1954. At the age of eight, she accepted Jesus Christ as her Savior, and at a Youth For Christ meeting in Bangalore, at the age of seventeen, she surrendered her life to Christ.

After obtaining the degree Bachelor of Science (Hons) from Bangalore University and teaching for three years, in response to God's call, Manasseh resigned her job and joined the Union Biblical Seminary, Yavatmal for theological studies. In 1978, she completed the course, Bachelor of Religious Education, and has ever since been serving Jesus Christ all over India and abroad.

In 1978, she joined the Evangelical Fellowship of India (EFI), and during the next three decades, held several positions in that organization. For thirteen years, she worked in the EFI Christian Education Department and served further as the general secretary of India Association for Christian Education. From 1991 to 2007, she was the secretary of EFI's Department of Women Ministries, during which period she provided leadership to the Women's Commission of Evangelical Fellowship of Asia as well.

Since 1991, Manasseh has been closely associated with several programs of the World Evangelical Fellowship (now, World Evangelical Alliance—WEA). She served as the first Asian Vice Chairperson and Director of WEF's Commission on Women's Concerns (1992–1998), as a member (1999–2009), and as the first Asian Chairperson of WEA's Women's Commission (2010–), and as a member on WEA's Anti Human Trafficking Task Force. She is the global evangelical voice on gender issues, pioneer for Empowerment of School Dropouts, Widows, Suffering Women and Commercial Sex Workers. She is firmly convinced that the power of God will enable the church to be liberated from all forms of inequalities and discrimination such as gender, race, caste, class, and rank.[38] She is the first woman chairperson of Union Biblical Seminary and ACTS Institute. Since 2007, she has been serving as the National Director of the Department of Church Relations and Resource Mobilisation of the Bible Society of India (BSI) and is the first woman director of BSI.

Manasseh is sought after for boards, preaching, training, teaching, counseling, and curriculum construction. She has served on various boards of Christian institutions and organizations, including the Lausanne Movement (Prayer Mobilisation). In recognition of her services, an honorary doctorate was conferred upon her by the International Council of Higher Education, Switzerland, through ACTS Academy of Higher Education.

---

38. Elizabeth Leelavathi Manasseh, "Where the Spirit of God is there is liberty," in *Evangelical Fellowship of India.* http://www.efionline.org/wisdom-theology/267-where-the-spirit-of-god-is-there-is-liberty (Accessed September 22, 2015).

Pentecostal figures

K. E. Abraham (1899–1974)

Pastor K. E. Abraham is the founder of the Indian Pentecostal Church, the largest indigenous Pentecostal denomination in India. Born on March 1, 1899, in an Orthodox Christian family in Mulakuzha, Kerala, as a young man, he dedicated his life for full-time Christian work. After his studies, he worked for a short period simultaneously as a teacher and an evangelist. In his younger days, he moved from one church to another and evangelized along with foreign missionaries, but in 1923, Abraham was baptized in the Holy Spirit—an event that is considered to have laid the foundation of the Indian Pentecostal Church of God. He became convinced that evangelism in India must be done primarily by indigenous Christians, not overseas missionaries. Consequently, he dissociated with the foreigners and started the South India Pentecostal Church of God. He became a well-known preacher and evangelist, and because of his work many joined the Pentecostal Church. The first Pentecostal church founded by his ministry was in his native village of Mulakuzha. Soon, the number of Christians and churches under his ministry grew. To train people for Christian ministry, he established in 1930 the Hebron Bible School in Kumbanad, and to propagate the Pentecostal faith, he founded a journal named *Zion Trumpet* and served as its chief editor. In 1935, along with a few others, he founded the Indian Pentecostal Church (IPC), and in the following year he became the president of the Church.[39] Until

---

39. K. E. Abraham's autobiography in Malayalam, titled *Yesu Kristhuvinte Eliya Dasan* (Kumbanad: K. E. Abraham Foundation Publications, 1965), has the details of his faith journey.

his death in 1974, he continued to be the moving spirit behind the IPC.

Pachigalla Lazarus Paramjyothi (1921–1996)

Pachigalla Lazarus Paramjyothi (P. L. Paramjyoti), a pioneer of the Pentecostal movement in India, was born on March 2, 1921, in Vuyyur, Krishna District in Andhra Pradesh, to a minister's family. His grandfather, Pachigalla Samuel, had become a Christian after hearing the gospel preached by some Western missionaries. Paramjyothi's father, Lazarus, was a pastor and teacher in the Canadian Baptist Mission field in Krishna District.[40] As a young man, Paramjyoti had a vision in which he heard the voice of Jesus asking him to become a full-time Christian worker, and consequently by a young age he became a well-known preacher. While engaged in gospel preaching, "Paramjyothi met Apostle P. M. Samuel and was baptized by him into Pentecostal faith and received the Holy Spirit."[41] Apart from being a good preacher, Paramjyothi also translated the sermons of visiting Christian leaders into Telugu. In 1944, he married Esther, who was a source of great support for him in his ministry. The couple had ten children and all of them have become active in Christian work.

As Pentecostalism was taking roots in India in the middle of the twentieth century, Paramjyothi was a pillar of great support, both in Andhra Pradesh and at the national level. Even when many Pentecostal leaders in South India began working with the World Missionary Evangelism (WME), he remained steadfast in his relationship with the Indian Pentecostal

---

40. Rachel Jyothi Komanapalli, *A Man Sent From God: Life Story and Messages of Apostle P. L. Paramjyoti* (Bangalore: Manna Ministries, 2012), 11.
41. P. Solomon Raj, *The New Wine-Skins: The Story of the Indigenous Missions in Coastal Andhra Pradesh, India* (Delhi: Indian Society for Promoting Christian Knowledge (ISPCK) for Mylapore Institute for Indigenous Studies (MIIS), Chennai, 2003), 52.

Church,[42] and believed that the primary responsibility for the mission of India should be with the Indians. He served for over twelve years as the National President of the Indian Pentecostal Church of God. He also trained and sent out three hundred pastors from his local church, who established many more churches.

Paramjyothi was a highly respected Christian leader in Andhra Pradesh. He maintained a friendly relationship with all the denominational churches. He served on the Executive Committee of the Bible Society of India and was a great support for the Bible Society movement. In recognition of his service, in 1961, he was invited to be one of the speakers at the World Christian Conference in Los Angeles. He has also traveled on preaching tours to Lebanon, Canada, Sweden, France, Germany, Holland, Norway, Singapore, the Middle East, and various places in the United States. He died on the day of Pentecost on May 26, 1996.

Mary Kovoor (1932–)

Mary Kovoor is, perhaps, the best-known woman Pentecostal leader in India. She was born on October 8, 1932, in Mavelikara, Kerala, as the daughter of T. T. Mathai (who was the headmaster of a school) and Mariamma. Mary had her school education in two Christian schools in Kerala. A brilliant student, she was the best outgoing student of her school. She earned a BA degree from St. Mary's College, Trichur, and at the age of 18, joined the Mar Ivanios Convent School in Nangyakulankara (Kerala) as a teacher.

During her childhood, Mary was greatly inspired by the

---

42. Michael Bergunder, *The South Indian Pentecostal Movement in the Twentieth Century* (Cambridge: Eerdmans, 2008), 97.

saintly lives of her grandfather, Rev. Father M. C. Thomas of the C. M. S. church, her aunt, Saramma Kochamma, and several others. Realizing that God was calling her also for full-time Christian ministry, Mary resigned her job as a teacher and became a preacher at the age of 19. It was an uphill task since she began her public ministry in the 1950s, when there were hardly any women in full-time Christian work. Soon, in obedience to God's call, she accepted adult baptism and began working as an independent Pentecostal preacher.

In 1960, Mary married Kuruvilla Kovoor, who came from a family of distinguished church leaders, rationalists, and other intellectuals. After marriage, the couple worked together as a team in God's ministry. A church was started in their house, where hundreds of people would come together on Sundays. Apart from preaching, she was also known for her healing ministry, and because of her work, several people were restored to full health in body and mind.

In her public ministry spanning over half a century, Mary Kovoor has preached over five thousand sermons. Her husky voice, coupled with her knowledge of the Word of God and her exemplary spiritual life, made her ministry a great success. She proved with her life that women could be successfully used by God. As P. I. Abraham (Kanam Achen) notes in his introduction to the autobiography of Mary Kovoor: "there are some small minded people who think that ladies should not speak in public. Let these people read about the great women who guided the destiny of the world."[43] Apart from preaching all over Kerala and in many places in India, Mary has also traveled to Kuwait, Bahrain, and the United States to preach

---

43. Mary Kovoor, *Taste of God's Love: Autobiography of Sr. Mary Kovoor* (Venmony: George Abraham, 2012), 7.

the Word of God. She continues to be used by God as an exceptionally gifted woman.

Ambakattuparambil Chacko George (1935–)

Ambakattuparambil Chacko George (A. C. George), a renowned Pentecostal scholar, historian, author, and missionary, was born in Kerala on September 20, 1935. Tragedy struck him at a young age as both his parents died before he was ten years old. George had a childhood of meager resources and had to walk over four miles every day to attend school. He came from a Syrian Orthodox Christian background, but as a child was led to a Pentecostal church that had a Sunday school. It was here that he had the experience of salvation, and he soon became a member of the Pentecostal church.

George's long academic career began when he joined the Sharon Bible College, Tiruvalla, Kerala as a student. Subsequently, he was admitted to the three-year-course in Theology program at the South Asia Bible Institute (SABI), Bangalore. His arrival in Bangalore was the beginning of his life long journey on a route marked by scholarly pursuits. After studies, he was appointed as a teacher at SABI, an association that lasted for over half a century until his retirement in March 2013. With the addition of advanced theological courses in 1975, SABI's name was changed to Southern Asia Bible College—SABC.[44]

George is one of the first Indian Pentecostal leaders to earn high academic degrees from American institutions. He finished the degree of Master of Theology at the Asbury Theological Seminary, Kentucky and a Master of Arts from Brandeis

---

44. A. C. George, *Trailblazers for God: A History of the Assemblies of God of India* (Bangalore: SABC Publications, 2004), 309.

University, Massachusetts. He subsequently earned a doctorate in theology from the Westminster Theological Seminary, Pennsylvania on the topic, *"Martin Luther's Doctrine of Sanctification with Special Reference to the Formula 'simul iustus et peccator': A Study in Luther's Lectures on Romans and Galatians."* Considering his humble and difficult childhood days, such high degrees at a young age was an extraordinary achievement for George. Though he received several attractive offers of appointments from other Bible Colleges and denominations, he was singularly focused on serving the students in India. He returned to India and continued his teaching ministry at SABC.

On August 26, 1965, George was ordained by the South India Assemblies of God.[45] A prolific writer, he has authored a number of scholarly books, including *Study Guide for Hebrews, Dimensions of Spirituality, Trailblazers, A Text Book on Hebrews, In Rome but not a Roman,* and *Reflections on Theology.* He has also raised his voice against social injustices such as the dowry system and caste discrimination in India.[46] He emphasizes that Christian parents should be careful not to deprive their daughters of the right to education and property rights. He continues to be a voice of prophetic witness and bold reformation in both church and society.

Independent Figures

Pandita Ramabai (1858–1922)

Pandita Ramabai, an educator, social reformer, devout Christian, and campaigner for women's rights was born in Karnataka on April 23, 1858, in a Hindu family. As a child,

---

45. See *Trailblazers for God.*
46. See Sudhir Kakar, ed., *Identity and Adulthood* (New Delhi: Oxford University Press, 1998), 90.

she learned the Hindu way of devotion. Having been orphaned at a young age, she came to Calcutta (Kolkota) in 1878, and because of her expertise in Sanskrit and the Hindu sacred texts, the Senate of Calcutta University honored her with the titles *Pandita* and *Saraswati*. At a young age, her husband died, and along with her young daughter, Ramabai moved to Poona (now known as Pune), where she joined the Brahmo Samaj, a reformist Hindu movement.

In Pune, Ramabai met Nehemiah Goreh at the Cowley Father's Mission and had discussions with him on Brahmo Samaj and Christianity. Along with her daughter, she traveled to England and stayed at the Community of Anglican Sisters at Wantage. She was baptized as a Christian in the local Anglican Church in 1883. From England, she traveled to the United States to canvas support for starting an institution in India for women in distress. Back in India, she founded the Mukti Mission in Kedgaon near Pune as a haven for such women. Ramabai died in 1922 and the institution she built up continues to serve the wider society as an interdenominational ecclesial community with the name, Pandita Ramabai Mukti Mission. While Ramabai is primarily known for her pioneering leadership in the movement for the liberation of Indian women, her significance for Indian theology lies in the fact that her upbringing as a Hindu and her quest for spiritual freedom led her to question the relevance of denominational Christianity.[47] Her concern was for a Christian faith that was rooted in the Indian culture and is committed to service humanity.[48] Based on her own life story, she argued that to

---

47. Clementina Butler, *Pandita Ramabai Sarasvati: Pioneer in the Movement for the Education of the Child-widow of India* (London & Edinburgh: Fleming H. Revell Company, 1922).

48. See Roger E. Hedlund, Sebastian Kim, and Rajkumar Boaz Johnson, *Indian & Christian: The Life and Legacy of Pandita Ramabai* (Madras: ISPCK/MIIS, 2011). The book focuses on different facets of Ramabai's remarkable life and includes several retellings of her life story.

an already caste-divided Hinduism, Christianity adds denominational divisions. Therefore, she believed that till all the divisions had ceased, the Christian convert should continue to struggle for the truth of Christ.

Sadhu Sundar Singh (1889–1929[?])

While indigenization and contextual Christianity are fashionable terms in the Indian Church today, the first person who lived indigenous Christianity as its true follower was Sadhu Sundar Singh ("Sadhu" means "holy," "Saint," or "ascetic" and is often used within the Hindu tradition). Sundar Singh was a Christian convert from a Sikh background. He was born in Punjab in 1889 in a Sikh family, and his mother, a devout lady, hoped that he would become a *sadhu*, serving God by renouncing the pleasures of the world. However, she died when he was 14 years old, causing him to face a major religious crisis. His religious traditions did not bring him any peace. He was sent to a mission school in Ludhiana, but he hated the Christian missionaries there who preached the gospel. Restless, frustrated, and disappointed, he resolved one night that if spiritual peace did not come to him during the night, he would commit suicide in the morning by placing himself on the railway lines in front of a train which passed by his village each day at five o'clock. Shortly before the appointed time, a vision of a bright cloud filled his room, and in the cloud, he saw the radiant figure of Jesus asking him, "Why do you persecute me? See, I have died on the cross for you and for the whole world."[49] At that moment, an inner peace (*shanti*) filled Sundar Singh and he decided to become a Christian.

---

49. Phyllis Thompson, *Sadhus Sundar Singh: A Biography of the Remarkable Indian Disciple of Jesus Christ* (Singapore: Armour Publishing, 2005), 18.

The vision of Christ was the turning point of Sundar Singh's life. He dedicated his life to Christ, but his family rejected him. He was baptized as a Christian on September 3, 1905, at Simla. Almost immediately, he started traveling as an evangelist and an itinerant preacher. He traveled all over India, preaching the gospel. Sundar Singh was baptized an Anglican, but he gave up the preacher's license so that he could preach Christ wherever people invited him. He partook of the Holy Eucharist in all churches that welcomed him. He believed that he belonged to the body of Christ, the true Church which transcended all denominational barriers.[50]

Sundar Singh traveled several times to Tibet for missionary work, returning each time, but in 1929, he set out again for Tibet with some Tibetan traders and never returned. All searches failed to determine what had happened. Did he die in an accident or illness? Or, did he die the death of a martyr?

Here I will add a "personal touch" to this chapter. In 1917, Sundar Singh was a speaker at the Maramon Convention, a gathering organized every year by the Mar Thoma Church on a dry river bed in Kerala where millions of people gather for a week to listen to the Word of God. Sundar Singh preached there about the need for parents to dedicate their children for missionary work in places such as Nepal and Tibet. Among his listeners was a woman from rural Kerala who dedicated her unborn child for mission work in Nepal. That child—C. K. Athialy (my father)—entered Nepal in 1950 and is believed to be the first Indian to enter Nepal as a missionary.[51] The church Athialy and his team built in Nepal—Church of Christ (Putali

50. Among the several books on Sadhu Sundar Singh, two, written by renowned Christian leaders, are C. F. Andrews, *Sadhu Sundar Singh: A Personal Memoir* (New York: Harper & Brothers, 1934) and A. J. Appasamy, *Sundar Singh* (Cambridge: Lutterworth, 1958).
51. Rev. C. K. Athialy, *Kanyakumari to Kathmandu: The Faith Journey of Rev. C. K. Athialy* (Ernakulam: Rev C. K. Athialy Family, 2011), 15–16.

Sadak church) in the heart of Kathmandu—is the first church in that country and continues to be a vibrant church to this day.

Bakht Singh (1903–2000)

Bakht Singh was a Christian evangelist, revival preacher, and author.[52] Born to Sikh parents in 1903 in the Punjab area (now part of Pakistan), as a young man he traveled to England, and later to Canada for higher studies. While abroad, he was attracted to the Christian faith and became a Christian by baptism. He returned to India in 1933, and soon became popular as a speaker and revivalist.

After serving as an itinerant preacher for a few years in different parts of India, in 1941, Bakht Singh built in Madras his first church, called Jehovah Shamma. Other churches were soon established throughout Andhra Pradesh and in different parts of India. Within a period of two decades, more than two hundred local assemblies were formed. In 1950, Bakht Singh and his associates established the headquarters of their ministry in Hyderabad. During the following few decades, the local churches established by Bakht Singh and his co-workers multiplied rapidly in India, especially in Andhra Pradesh. He died in 2000.

A defining aspect of the ministry of Bakht Singh was his Bible-centered preaching and teaching. Throughout his work, he gave priority to scripture. In his worship services, the Bible always occupied a position of central prominence. Every believer was expected to own and carry a Bible everywhere. Exposition based on scripture took up a central place in the Sunday worship of the Assemblies.

---

52. "Bakht Singh Movement/Assemblies," in *Oxford Encyclopedia of South Asian Christianity* (New Delhi: Oxford University Press, 2012), 55.

The Assemblies started under the initiative of Bakht Singh followed a de-centralized structure of administration. Elders were the leaders at the local levels and every group became active in preaching in the streets and adding more believers. The annual All-India Holy Convocations brought together thousands of believers from across the country for fellowship and spiritual nurture.

At a time when Christianity in India was identified with the Western culture and was hierarchically organized as denominations, Singh followed a unique style of Christian leadership, adopting a structure that was culturally indigenous. The church in India has gained much from this stalwart of Christian faith. He believed that the Indian church should reflect the values of Jesus Christ. "This reflection of Christ in the church needed to be expressed within the cultural and linguistic background of the people so that the 'foreignness' of the church might be removed without changing the distinctiveness of the church."[53] Along with indigenization, Bakht Singh's highly decentralized pattern of administration appealed to many people. It is also important that in a country where all religions, including Christianity, functioned largely within the framework of the established caste and linguistic dividing lines, Bakht Singh welcomed into his fellowship and treated as equals people of all caste, language, and regional backgrounds.

Conclusion

Our purpose in this chapter was to provide the readers with an insight into the lives of some leading Indian Christians. It

---

53. T. E. Koshy, *Bakht Singh of India: The Incredible Account of a Modern-Day Apostle* (Colorado Springs, CO: Authentic, 2008), 4.

is virtually impossible to cover all the key people in Indian Christianity that is so ancient, diverse and dense. As was outlined at the beginning of this chapter, this is a selected, but also a representative, list of names. The Indian and world church have been richly blessed in the past by these stalwarts of the Christian faith. Some of them—especially those who have contributed richly to world Christianity—are already famous outside India, but some others are not so well-known. With regard to all, it needs to be emphasized that what we have provided here are mere short biographical notes. It is, however, our hope and prayer that these notes will inspire the more serious readers to dig deeper into the lives of these pioneers of Indian and world Christianity.

6

Theological

Some Theological Trends in Indian
Christianity

Trying to write in a chapter about the "theology" of Indian Christianity is like a child sitting at the Kanyakumari shore with a teaspoon, trying to drain the Indian Ocean! Countless number of scholars and church fathers and mothers in the past have spent their lifetime studying the various theologies of Indian Christianity. This writer does not have the competence to be even their student! Yet, we cannot discuss religion in a particular context without considering the theologies implied in it for those are the faith affirmations that shape their beliefs, lifestyles, and the very core of their lives. What is attempted in this chapter, therefore, is merely a pointing toward *some* theological trends in Indian Christianity. The discussion here, by no means, is an exhaustive one, but can be the starting point for a more thorough study on what should—and should not—be included in such a discussion.

This chapter is in nine sections: (1) St. Thomas Christians: Permeation as Mission, (2) De Nobili's Path of Accommodation, (3) Protestantism as Liberative Theology, (4) Roman Catholic Mission: Indigenization and Liberation, (5) Orthodox Perspective, (6) Pentecostal, Neo-Pentecostal and Independent Movements, (7) Marginalized People Theologize, (8) Hindu Christians and Non-Baptized Believers, and (9) Indian Presence in the Ecumenical Movement. This framework too can be problematic, as a confessional–denominational divide may not be the most feasible way to discuss theological trends. It becomes more complicated when we consider that most of the Christian scholars discussed here theologized in an ecumenical milieu, along with scholars of other Christian confessions, and often with the adherents of other religions and even secular humanists. This has been especially the characteristic of the modern ecumenical movement. It, therefore, needs to be emphasized that the framework followed here is *only* for the sake of including as many names as possible in this discussion and does not, in any way, set limits to the content or impact of their work.

St. Thomas Christians: *Permeation* as Mission

There is a strong tradition of linking the origin of Christianity in India to Apostle Thomas, who is believed to have landed on the Malabar Coast (currently a part of Kerala) in the first century CE. While there is little documentary evidence of the early few centuries of Christianity in India, what remains are oral traditions and secondary evidences, such as the habits and practices of the people, the architecture of places of worship, trade and commerce, and so on. "We know very little about the history of the Malabar Church in the first few centuries. The historical evidences are fitful and inconclusive and once again we derive from tradition what we cannot get in history."[1]

While "outreach"—evangelization—was an integral part of the spread of Western Christianity from the early days, what were the patterns of Christian witness for the ancient Indian Christians? Again, we are not sure, but we have glimpses of the past. We are not aware of the development of any systematic theological schools during that period and the faith practices of the Christians then was invariably linked to the customs of the wider society. In a context where Christianity was a minority religion in a highly pluralistic context, the St. Thomas Christians developed their faith and modes of evangelization in relation to their Hindu neighbors. Philipose Mar Chrysostom, who was Metropolitan of the Mar Thoma Church, argues that the mode of Christian witness of our ancestors was not preaching, but *permeation*. As he put it,

> They went and lived with the people. That is the incarnation principle. The outside society would often say about our forefathers: 'In business, he will be honest, because he is a Christian.' That was a form of witness. This was our missionary pattern till recently. . . . Evangelism is possible only by permeation.[2]

Permeation was understood as both the preference for the lived experience over verbal proclamation and the preference for upholding "Christian values" over proselytization in a largely Hindu culture for which interreligious conversion was an alien practice. Chrysostom understood mission as

1. Juhanon Mar Thoma Metropolitan, *Christianity in India and a Brief History of the Mar Thoma Church* (Tiruvalla: CSS, 2011), 13.
2. Jesudas M. Athyal and John J. Thatamanil, eds., *Metropolitan Chrysostom on Mission in the Marketplace* (Tiruvalla: CSS, 2002), 49.

transformation and permeation of this world by showing forth the presence of God in everyday life. Basic mission, therefore, is to follow the lead of God's incarnation and self-emptying in Christ. Today, however, he fears, the missionary work follows an efficiency mode, where we have strategies and targets. The impression that evangelism is the program of a specific department of the church assigned that task, was alien to the ancient Indian Christians. Evangelism, for them, was possible only by permeation. It may also be added that this was a characteristic of Eastern Christianity, which generally moved closer to what in Greek is called *apokathastasis ton panton*, the redemption of all.[3]

As a distinct socio-religious community and as part of the larger milieu, the St. Thomas Christians were inherently a part of the social life of the region from the early centuries onwards. The experience of the early Indian Christians living in close relation with people of other faiths and cultures is often cited as one of the earliest examples of religious harmony in India. They were generally favored by local non-Christian authorities and they "enjoyed a high degree of civil autonomy, and were regarded as the second highest caste."[4] However, it may also be noted that the identity of the St. Thomas Christians as a privileged upper-caste group considerably hampered their potential for any viable missionary outreach, especially in relation to the lower castes. It was the arrival of missionaries from the West—Catholic and Protestant—and their message of the universality of the Christian gospel that challenged the unjust caste privilege of not only the upper-caste Hindus, but also the St. Thomas Christians and opened the doors of the

---

3. Gabriele Dietrich, "Political Aspects of the New Humanity in Christ" (Unpublished article).

4. John C. England, *The Hidden History of Christianity in Asia: The Churches of the East before 1500* (Delhi & Hong Kong: ISPCK & CCA, 2002), 61.

church for all, including the outcastes.[5] The sixteenth and seventeenth centuries, which saw the heyday of Portuguese power in India, was a period also of great missionary activity. It would, therefore, be no exaggeration to maintain that the missionary era profoundly influenced the course and content of Christian witness in India.

De Nobili's Path of Accommodation

The work of Roberto de Nobili,[6] the Italian Jesuit missionary, in India was markedly different from that of his predecessors who had, more or less, carried out on the prescribed pattern approved by the church hierarchy in the West. De Nobili reached Madurai in 1606 and joined Gonçalo Fernandez, a Portuguese Jesuit who had been working there for several years. While Fernandez had worked among both the local people and the Portuguese diaspora community, his work did not lead to any direct results, such as conversions to Christianity. De Nobili inferred that his senior colleague's failure to attract converts was because his work was concentrated among the outcaste people there. Accordingly, he crafted out a methodology rooted in the principle of *accommodation*—adopting the local customs to present the gospel. De Nobili's study of the complex social realities of the context convinced him that unless the upper-caste Brahmins, the influential section of the society, is attracted toward the gospel, Christianity would not have any direct impact on the larger society. Accordingly, he crafted out a strategy starting

---

5. Outcastes are the people who fell outside the Hindu caste system. They are also called untouchables—the lowest section in the Indian society.
6. While the discussion in this chapter deals primarily with the work of *Indians* in Christian theology (and not the work of Western missionaries), we will make an exemption in the case of de Nobili because of the deep impact his approach had on charting out a fresh course in mission work and interfaith relations in India.

at the top of the caste ladder. In order to attract the Brahmins to his message, he changed his lifestyle and habits and adopted the garb of Brahmins (the spiritual leaders in Hinduism), gave up meat, and, like the Brahmins, wore the sacred thread across his chest. He "professed to be an Italian Brahmin who had renounced the world, had studied wisdom at Rome and rejected all the pleasures and comforts of this world."[7] De Nobili also realized that the future of Christianity in India lay in the hands of local leaders, not Western missionaries. Accordingly, he attempted to establish a theological seminary to train Indian converts to be clergy and sought the permission of the Vatican to allow the use of Sanskrit, and not Latin, as the liturgical language in the Indian church.

Realizing that the rich plurality of India's culture, religion, and philosophy was fundamentally different from that of the West, de Nobili stood for patterns of Christian ministry and witness that were indigenous to the local context. Having learned Sanskrit and Tamil and studied the Indian religious and philosophical streams in depth, he concluded that unless the Christian gospel is presented in the local idioms, it will not be intelligible to the Indians. There is no doubt that his methods were indigenous and highly original.

De Nobili's approach toward indigenization met with mixed reaction. With his work, he effectively challenged the work of generations of Portuguese missionaries before him, who believed that it was the mission of the Christian faith to stand with the low-caste people who were oppressed and marginalized in the Brahminical system, and thus challenge the evil practices in the society. De Nobili's superiors in the Church were sympathetic toward his attempts to broad base

7. S. Rajamanickam, "The Goa Conference of 1619 (A Letter of Fr. Robert de Nobili to Pope Paul V)," *Indian Church History Review* 2 (1968): 85.

the appeal of the Christian faith even though they did not permit him to depart radically from the traditional missionary strategy. Opposition, however, grew toward de Nobili's methodology, and in due course, the church hierarchy almost completely overturned his pattern.

History, in general, has not been kind toward de Nobili. While his approach was generally seen as one of the earliest forms of indigenous Christianity in India, how far he was true to the core of the Christian faith—or, for that matter, to the essence of Hinduism—is questionable. The severest criticism of de Nobili's approach in recent years has come from Dalit theologians, who argue that appealing to the goodwill of the Brahmins to evangelize India amounted to endorsing the caste structure that pushed the Dalits—the outcastes—to be the lowest rung of society. De Nobili "did not consider the Christian principle that all people are equal before God to be contradictory of the social hierarchy of caste."[8] By allowing his upper-caste converts to retain many of the rituals and practices of the Brahmins, he legitimized several of them as mere cultural practices unrelated to the core of Hinduism.

The impact of de Nobili's approach far outlived his lifestyle and laid the foundations for a Christian mission work that too was segregated on caste lines. Francis Clooney, a Jesuit like de Nobili, criticized the method of de Nobili as an "odd combination of external adaptation (the effort 'to shift from one society to another' for the sake of communication) and internal rigidity."[9] In the immediate decades after de Nobili's death, the Jesuit missionaries in the region divided their work broadly along caste lines, with particular missionaries working

---

8. Zoe C. Sherinian, *Tamil Folk Music as Dalit Liberation Theology* (Bloomington, Indiana University Press, 2014), 74.
9. Francis Clooney, "Roberto de Nobili: Adaptation and the Reasonable Interpretation of Religion," *Missiology* 18 (January 1990): 32.

exclusively among either the lower caste or Brahmin converts. In the long run, however, the overwhelming majority of not only the Catholics, but also the Protestants among Indian Christians came to comprise the Dalit or lower-caste sections, once again challenging de Nobili's notion that evangelizing the lower-caste sections will not lead to a cascading effect toward Christianization in the entire society.

De Nobili lived during a period when the caste stratification of the Indian society was firmly in place and when clear voices of dissent or a sustained movement against such an unjust system were yet to emerge. He was definitely a child of his times and followed zealously a path of evangelization that took into consideration the permutations and combinations of the caste structure of the land. In that sense, it can even be argued that he was, perhaps, the first person whose method of evangelization and indigenization emerged from a clear analysis of the social realities. With the benefit of hindsight four centuries later, we can say that his pattern did not convey the message of the universality of the Christian gospel and that his methodology was inadequate and insensitive to the plight of the marginalized and outcaste sections of the society. De Nobili's primary contribution was as a trendsetter who set in motion a process of indigenization so powerful that, over the centuries, it threatened to devour the methodology of de Nobili himself. Yet, we need to recognize the significance of his pioneering work. In the words of Robin Boyd, de Nobili's

> achievement—and it was a great achievement—is to be seen in his understanding and adaptation of Hindu customs and ceremonies, in his pioneering study of Sanskrit and Tamil and in his initiation of the essential task of evolving a Christian theological vocabulary for Indian languages. For this contribution Indian Christian theology will always be indebted to him.[10]

Protestantism as Liberative Theology

It is difficult to study the theology of the Protestant churches in India, the primary reason being the difficulty to *define* what Protestantism is, in the Indian context. While the Catholic and Orthodox traditions have fairly well-knit hierarchical frameworks, there is no similarly clearly defined structure for the Protestants. Especially during the last century or so, numerous divisions have occurred in the traditional Indian Protestant churches, leading to the amoebic growth of groups and churches across the land. It is difficult to pinpoint whether they remain Protestant or not and whether they have well-defined theological positions. Due to all these limitations, this section will consider primarily the traditional and well-established Protestant groups that have, over a long period, evolved theological positions that have had an impact on the wider church, and on the other faiths and the larger society. This discussion, however, does not claim to be a comprehensive account of the theological positions of the Protestant churches in India. What is attempted here is merely to highlight certain theological trends that have been dominant.

The impact of Protestantism around the world has been variously defined. Lutheranism in Europe led to the theology of the two kingdoms and the theory of the separation of the church and state. Max Weber, on the other hand, argued that Protestantism played a major role in creating the capitalistic spirit.[11] The Protestant movement in the West often enjoyed a cozy relationship with the principalities and power—the colonizers and the oppressors. Protestantism in India, on the

10. Robin Boyd, *An Introduction to Indian Christian Theology* (Delhi: ISPCK, 1991), 14.
11. Max Weber, *The Protestant Ethic and the Spirit of Capitalism* (New York: Routledge, 2001).

contrary, followed a radically different course. The very genesis of several Indian Protestant churches can be traced back to Western missionaries who *protested* the highhandedness of their European political masters and church leaders and worked in India, primarily among the marginalized and the dispossessed people. From the very beginning, therefore, Indian Protestantism was, in particular, good news to the poor. Almost a century after de Nobili identified himself with the upper-caste Brahmins in Tamil Nadu (as the state is now called) in his effort to propagate the gospel, the German Lutheran missionaries Bartholomaeus Ziegenbalg and Heinrich Pluetschau also reached Tamil Nadu, landing in Tranquebar (Tharangambadi) on July 9, 1706, but they pursued an altogether different path of evangelization. Their work was primarily concentrated among the Dalits (the outcastes) in the society. As Lutheranism spread around India in the following decades and centuries, the focus on the lowest sections of the society too spread. As *Oxford Encyclopedia of South Asian Christianity* states, "About 85 per cent of the Indian Lutherans, who are members of eleven Lutheran Churches, came from Dalit and tribal backgrounds."[12]

It is, therefore, not surprising that Dalit theology, as a major branch of Indian Christian theology, emerged during the last few decades of the twentieth century primarily under Indian Lutheran patronage. In particular, Gurukul Lutheran Theological College, the major theological seminary of the Indian Lutheran churches, has played a key role in the promotion and interpretation of Dalit theology. The Dalit theology department of the college published some of the pioneering literature in this area, leading to a growing

---

12. Jacob G. J. Sundarsingh, "Lutherans in India," in *Oxford Encyclopedia of South Asian Christianity*, vol. 2 (New Delhi: Oxford University Press, 2012), 407.

sensitivity on understanding theology from the people's perspective. It can be stated without much exaggeration that Dalit theology during the last three decades or so has provided a virtual paradigm shift in theologizing in India since liberative ecclesiology and hermeneutics have been constant themes of Dalit theologians. M. Deenabandhu, an Indian Lutheran theologian, reflected thus on the challenges for Dalit theology:

> To some extent, one can say that ecumenical theology too, like Dalit theology, has been a counter-theological discourse, an alternative to the dominant ways of theological reflection that is often grounded in western denominational/confessional ecclesial settings. Likewise, it is also faced with the need to make itself relevant to the changed realities of the twenty-first century as it is cast in and remains in the methodological mould of the twentieth century western ecclesial reality.[13]

By the nineteenth century, Baptist, Anglican, Methodist, and other missionaries too were actively working in various parts of India. A significant area of their initial work was in translation. While the primary interest of several missionaries was the translation of Bible portions as part of their work of evangelization, the process of making literature available to the common people in their languages had a long-lasting impact on the education and liberation of the colonized and oppressed masses. In a different context, in Africa—Lamin Sanneh argued—translation and vernacular renewal played a crucial role in not only the spread of Christian mission, but in the liberation of the indigenous people as well. And in many places, the new converts were at the vanguard in resisting colonialism.

---

13. Deenabandhu Manchala, "Expanding the Ambit: Dalit Theological Contribution to Ecumenical Social Thought," in *Dalit Theology in the Twenty-first Century: Discordant Voices, Discerning Pathways*, eds. Sathianathan Clarke, Deenabandhu Manchala, and Philip Vinod Peacock (New Delhi: OUP, 2011), 41.

The translation work led by the missionaries was instrumental in the emergence of indigenous resistance to colonialism. Local Christians acquired from the vernacular translations confidence in the indigenous cause. While the colonial system represented a worldwide economic and military order, mission represented vindication for the vernacular. Local Christians apprehended the significance of world events, and as such the purposes of God, through the familiar medium of mother tongues, with subject peoples able to respond to colonial events in the light of vernacular understanding.[14]

The impact translation had on renascent movements in religion and society has been recognized in India too. Analyzing the work of William Carey and the Serampore Mission which he led, in relation to the Bengali cultural renaissance of the nineteenth century, especially for the development of the Bengali language, M. M. Thomas noted that they were vernacularists in the debate of that period about the medium of education, and unlike the Anglicists who suppressed the local cultures and languages and missed "a rare opportunity of constructive combination" of eastern and western cultures through dialogue.[15] Such suppression, Thomas noted, had devastating effects on the future course of the country, and holds a lesson for the church's mission today.

While the Western countries had commercial interests in promoting their languages in the colonies, their interest often clashed with the focus of the missionaries on translation that made *mother tongues* the centerpiece of Christian mission. True, evangelization and the numerical growth of the church were the primary concern of the missionaries, but the impact of their work went far beyond, into precipitating a renascent and

---

14. Lamin Sanneh, *Translating the Message: The Missionary Impact on Culture* (Maryknoll, NY: Orbis Books, 1989), 123.
15. M. M. Thomas, *A Diaconal Approach to Indian Ecclesiology* (CIIS, Rome & CSS, Tiruvalla, 1995), 65.

liberative movement in the wider society. Translation and vernacular renewal had an especially profound impact on the cultural and social renaissance of the indigenous people. The masses that had no place so far found a place under the sun. Their awakening to a new identity and self-dignity enabled the indigenous people to struggle against all forms of oppression.

The focus on secular education, especially through the medium of English, was also seen as an important aspect of the work of both the Protestant and Catholic missionaries in India. The nineteenth century saw the building up of colleges in the major cities of India, which provided avenues for the native people to gain higher education in the English language. While most of the Christian institutions for higher education were built up by the Western missionaries, there were some, such as the Union Christian College, Aluva which were run by Indians.[16] The Christian concern in liberal education was not so much in the overt preaching of the gospel or on conversion to Christianity, but on building up the character of the individual to be open to the values of the gospel. In this sense, it can be stated that while these institutions served all sections of the society, they were seen by the missionaries as *praeparation evangelica*, as creating a fertile ground among the non-Christian intelligentsia of the country for Christianization.

While the leaders of the Serampore Mission and the other Protestant missionaries of an earlier period emphasized the renewal of the vernacular languages with its potential for cultural interaction between the Western culture, Christian religion, and India, it is important to note that the focus of the Indian church in more recent times has been on the promotion of English medium education, often at the cost of the regional

---

16. Gerald Studdert-Kennedy, *British Christians, Indian Nationalists and the Raj* (New Delhi: Oxford University Press, 1991), 117.

languages and cultures. The question can legitimately be asked if at least a part of the religious fundamentalism and communal violence that bedevil public life in India today can be seen as the people's revolt against the neglect of their traditional cultures. In a highly pluralistic context such as India, the commitment of the church to take seriously the diverse cultural–linguistic concerns of the people needs to be seen as key to building India as a nation of diverse cultures.

How far the missionaries, the new converts, and the indigenous people were agents of resistance against the Western colonial forces in India is an important question. While there were exceptions, by and large, historians—both Christian and secular scholars—have argued that the missionaries more often created mission compounds for the security of the new converts. This was, perhaps, understandable because the overwhelming majority of the Christian converts were Dalits and their outcaste status made it virtually impossible for them to successfully lead a protest movement against the might of the Western colonizers. In general, however, it can safely be said that Protestant Christianity worked primarily among the lower sections of the society and played a catalyst role in the liberation and empowerment of the people.

While the Western Protestant missionaries defined, to a large extend, the theological direction of the Indian church till the nineteenth century or so, as the nationalist movement gained momentum in the country, strong indigenous Christian voices too began to emerge. The International Missionary Conference that met in Tambaram in 1938 was a watershed event that brought to the limelight strong indigenous Christian theological voices. In particular, it needs to be noted that the Madras Rethinking Group, of which P. Chenchiah,

Vengal Chakkarai, and others were leaders, provided the framework for a lay and indigenous Christian response to the quest for nationalism and ecumenical unity in the country. The message that emerged from the Tambaram conference—that mission and unity were inseparable—was criticized by several Indian lay leaders who feared that the emphasis on the church might reduce mission to be the business of the ecclesiastical bodies, in the process, leading to the marginalization of the struggles of ordinary people.

Perhaps no other social topic has concerned the Indian Christian theologians as much as the Christian relation to people of other religions, particularly Hinduism, and a few Indian Protestant leaders who led this process may be mentioned here. V. S. Azariah, the Indian churchman and a pioneering voice in the modern ecumenical movement, dialogued with Mahatma Gandhi (his contemporary) on the meaning and relevance of Christian conversion in India. A fundamental religious and philosophical disagreement lay at the heart of their debate as Gandhi called for a reform of Hinduism and Azariah proposed conversion to Jesus Christ.[17] Another scholar who systematically engaged with Hinduism in independent India was P. D. Devanandan, the ecumenical leader, historian of religion, and noted pioneer in interfaith dialogue. By engaging Christianity in dialogue with Hinduism and the other religions, he sought to make a detailed and sympathetic study of humanity and society in modern India.[18]

---

17. Susan Billington Harper, *In the Shadow of the Mahatma: Bishop V. S. Azariah and the Travails of Christianity in British India* (Grand Rapids, MI and Cambridge, UK: Eerdmans Publishing Co.; London: RoutledgeCurzon, 2000), 295.
18. See the writings of P. D. Devanandan: *The Concept of Maya: An Essay in Historical Survey of the Hindu Theory of the World With Special Reference to the Vedanta* (London: Lutterworth Press, 1950); *Resurgent Hinduism: Review of Modern Movements* (Madras: CLS/CISRS, 1958); *Christian Concern in Hinduism*, with a foreword by S. Radhakrishnan (Bangalore: CISRS, 1961); *Preparation for Dialogue: Essays on Hinduism and Christianity in New India*, Nalini Devanandan and M. M. Thomas, eds. (Bangalore: CISRS, 1964).

Yet another Indian Christian scholar who contributed richly to the process of dialogue with people of other faiths and represented these concerns at the international level was Stanley J. Samartha. At a crucial stage in the programmatic history of the World Council of Churches, Samartha played a central role by defining Christian relationship to people of other religious traditions. His expertise in Hinduism, and especially his attraction to the Advaitic thought, was evident in his approach to the dialogue of religion.[19] It must also be added that the focus of Indian Protestant theologians was not so much to grapple with traditional or textual Hinduism, but with the renascent religion and the fervor created by this process in modern India.[20]

Along with interfaith relations, dialogue with secular ideologies was a major concern for Indian Christian theologians. Undoubtedly, M. M. Thomas played a pioneering role in acknowledging secularism as an area that the church needed to take seriously in independent India. His book, *Salvation and Humanization*, was a valuable guide for interreligious dialogue as well as dialogue with secular movements and represented his most mature thinking on the issue. As he put it,

> It is my conviction that the relation between salvation and humanization i.e. between the ultimate destiny of man and his historical destiny which we saw as fundamental in Christian re-thinking is also the fundamental issue debated within all religions and secular movements of India. Only the language of discourse varies from one movement to another. My thesis

---

19. See the writings of Samartha: *The Hindu view of History: Classical and Modern* (Bangalore: CISRS, 1959); *Living Faiths and the Ecumenical Movement* (ed.) (Geneva: WCC, 1971); *The Hindu Response to the Unbound Christ* (Madras: CLS, 1974); *Courage for Dialogue: Ecumenical issues in inter-religious relationships* (Geneva: WCC, 1982).
20. In particular, see M. M. Thomas, *The Acknowledged Christ of the Indian Renaissance* (3rd Edition, I. T. L. series N. 4) (Madras, C. L. S. 1991).

therefore is the theme of humanization which provides the most relevant point of entry for any Christian dialogue with these movements—at spiritual and theological depth.[21]

Thomas believed that the salvific presence of Christ was not limited to the church, but extended to the liberation movements in the wider society as well. In this context, he affirmed that the impact of Jesus's lingering presence in history can also take a secular character and that all who are committed to building up a just society can be part of a secular *Koinonia*, along with all religious believers who are open to the potential of the love of Jesus that was revealed on the Cross.[22]

During the last three centuries, as India moved from being a colony of the Western countries to be an independent nation and as Indian Christianity outgrew its "missionary" phase and became self-supporting and self-governing, the character of Protestantism in the country too assumed newer forms. The denominational divisions of Europe and America that the mission bodies faithfully carried on in India gave way, under a visionary indigenous Christian leadership, to a united Church of South India (CSI), formed in 1947 on the eve of the nation's independence, with four churches merging together their differences. In 1970, this process was repeated in North India, when the united Church of North India (CNI) was formed, and later three churches—CSI, CNI, and the Mar Thoma Church—came together to form the Communion of Churches in India. True, in spite of such historic ecumenical steps, the journey forward was not without setbacks. Yet, in and through all these different stages, the deep commitment of the Indian Protestant churches to be faithful witnesses to the Gospel of

21. M. M. Thomas, *Salvation and Humanization: Some Crucial Issues in Contemporary India* (Madras, CISRS, 1971), 20.
22. See also M. M. Thomas, *Secular Ideologies of India and Secular Meaning of Christianity* (Bangalore: CISRS, 1976).

Christ in an independent and increasingly self-confident India lingered on. From the translation of Christian literature and vernacular renewal, the building up of excellent institutions for educational and health care work, the eradication of social evils to seeking relevant forms of Christian witness, through the years and centuries, Protestant Christianity in India was less interested in doctrinal differences and denominational divide, and more in a meaningful process of Christian participation in the life of the nation.

Roman Catholic Mission: Indigenization and Liberation

While de Nobili disassociated himself from the outcaste people and considered himself to be a Christian Brahmin, by the twentieth century, the large majority of Indian Catholics, like the Protestants, hailed from the Dalit and other lower-caste sections. The Indian Catholic theologians of the nineteenth and twentieth centuries too, like de Nobili, took seriously the path of indigenization, but they adopted a course of adapting not so much to the Brahminical way, but to the rich plurality of Indian religions, cultures, and traditions. By the latter half of the twentieth century, the reforms of the Second Vatican Council and Liberation theology too had reached India and resonated well with the two realities so immediate to the Indian people—religiosity and poverty. This section of the chapter will argue that indigenization and liberation theology were, perhaps, the major trends in Indian Catholicism, especially in the twentieth century. In this context, special references will be made here to some of the leading Catholic theologians in these areas.

One of the earliest Indian Christian theologians who grappled with interfaith issues was Brahmabandhab Upadhyay

(1861-1907), who developed a Christology in the light of the Advaitic framework. Born as a Bengali Hindu, as a young man he was converted to Christianity and was drawn to the Advaitic teaching of Sri Sankara. Soon after conversion, he attempted to find a foundation for Indian Christianity in the Vedas, and subsequently sought to build an Indian Christian theology on Vedanta philosophy.[23] Upadhyay was inspired by de Nobili and believed that Christianity, to be authentic in India, needed to be rooted in the cultural and religious milieu of the country. "Brahmabandhav understood Christianity not as destroyer of Hinduism but as its fulfilment."[24] He went along with de Nobili's position on embracing an orthodox view of the caste system in India, and, unlike the Renaissance leaders of that period, advocated the integration of the caste system into the Christian church.[25]

Following de Nobili and Upadhyaya, there was a long line of Catholic scholars who contributed richly to Hindu–Christian dialogue and indigenization. Like Upadhyaya, Swami Abhishiktananda (1929-73) too grappled with the relationship between Advaita and Christianity, but the latter expressed a desire to go beyond all things, even thoughts of God, to God himself. "Hence, throughout his life Abhishiktananda pursued a contemplative surrender to the Godhead, but did so in his last twenty years in a ways he had never envisaged as a monk in Europe."[26] Raimon Panikkar (1918-2010), on the contrary, took history seriously and affirmed that believers of all religions

23. M. M. Thomas and P. T. Thomas, *Towards an Indian Christian Theology: Life and Thought of Some Pioneers* (Tiruvalla: The New Day Publications of India. 1992), 72.
24. Ibid., 73.
25. See also K. P. Aleaz, "The Theological Writings of Brahmabandhav Upadhyaya Re-Examined," *Indian Journal of Theology*, April–June 1979, 55–77 and, Raimon Panikkar, *Unknown Christ of Hinduism* (London: Darton, Longman, and Todd, 1964).
26. Edward T. Ulrich, "Convergences and Divergences: The Lives of Swami Abhishiktananda and Raimundo Panikkar," *Journal of Hindu-Christian Studies* 24, article 9 (2011): 36–45.

meet "here in this World where we are fellow-pilgrims, where we commune in our humanness, in the samsāric adventure, in our historical situation."[27]

In the period following the Second Vatican Council, several Indian Catholic scholars sought to reinterpret the meaning of indigenization and inculturation. The work of D. S. Amalorpavadass (1932–90) in this regard is particularly noteworthy. He believed that the worship and witness of the church should be rooted in the ethos and worship forms of the local land, rather than on any foreign forms of worship. He affirmed that the salvific plan of Christ was not confined to the church alone, but included other religions as well. Inculturation should not only be in theological discussions, but should translate into the liturgy of the church. With this concern, he founded the National Biblical, Catechetical, and Liturgical Centre in Bangalore as an ecumenical space for experiments in evolving indigenous forms of liturgy.

Bede Griffiths (1906–93), the British-born Benedictine monk who lived for long in the Indian Ashrams and was one of the leaders of the Christian Ashram movement, was another scholar who attempted to blend the Christian monastery movement with the Hindu tradition of renunciation and ascetic life. He articulated his vision of Cosmic Revelation, wherein there existed "marriage between east and west, man and woman, matter and mind, time and eternity."[28] Griffiths challenged the primacy given by the modern society to science and rationality and affirmed the need to seek commonality between those and develop a transcendental dimension. He believed that the spiritual realm "has a logic that requires

---

27. Raimon Panikkar, *The Unknown Christ of Hinduism: Towards an Ecumenical Christophany* (Maryknoll, NY: Orbis Books, 1981), 26.
28. Bede Griffiths, *Marriage of East and West* (Springfield, IL: Templegate Publishers, 1992), 204.

a special kind of [perception] that is more than mere rationality."[29] The efforts of some key Catholic scholars to incorporate elements from the Indian religious traditions in the life and ministry of the Christian church can, perhaps, be seen as a key factor in the acceptance by the Indian general public of Christianity as a truly *Indian* religion.

The second major trend in Indian Catholicism, especially in recent decades, has been liberation theology. While liberation theology has been closely associated with Latin America, Asia has developed its own distinct form. By not putting the primacy on economic issues alone, but on the role of religion in the composition of a healthy society, the Asian cultures take a much more organic view of the challenges facing our world.[30] Indian Catholic scholars advocated a unique form of liberation theology and ecumenical social ethics that was adapted to suit the socio-religious and cultural context of the country. In the 1960s and 1970s, several seminarians and young people were challenged to plunge into the struggles of the poor and the marginalized people. While Indian Christians of several denominational backgrounds associated themselves with liberation theology, there is little doubt that the Catholic priests, nuns, and social activists were foremost among them. They understood social action inspired by Christ as their vocation and fanned out among the urban and rural poor and among the industrial workers.

Along with direct action, Christian liberation theologians provided the theoretical and theological framework, which became the conceptual basis for the movement. Sebastian Kappen (1924–93), who believed the relevance of the liberating

---

29. Alejandro Garcia-Rivera, "Aesthetics," in *The Blackwell Companion to Christian Spirituality*, ed. Arthur Holder (Malden, MA: Wiley-Blackwell, 2011), 346.
30. See Michael Amaladoss, *Life in Freedom: Liberation Theologies from Asia* (Maryknoll, NY: Orbis Books, 1997).

and humanizing potential of Jesus to be an important vehicle in India's journey toward a transformed society, was one among them. In recognition of the powerful influence of two forces—communism and Christianity—in his home state of Kerala, he believed that Marxism had the tools to analyze social structures. Samuel Rayan (1920–), on the contrary, blended the theme of liberation with the Asian realities. For him, the central concern of the Christian faith is its immersion in the lived experiences and concrete everyday realities of the people. At a time when India was poised on a path of economic development and industrialization, people like Rayan rejected the developmental option, and instead advocated the need for structural changes to eradicate poverty and inequality and to ensure justice for all. He summed up his case in a poem:

> rice is for sharing,
> bread must be broken and given.
> Every bowl, every belly shall have its fill,
> to leave a single bowl unfilled is
> to rob history of its meaning;
> to grab many a bowl for myself is
> to empty history of god.[31]

George Soares-Prabhu (1929–95) was yet another Catholic scholar who understood the theme of liberation through the eyes of both the Christian scriptures and the Indian realities. He was aware of the limitations of the traditional historical critical method in the study of the Bible and he maintained that the Indian situation called for both a *religious* reading and a *social* reading. "He held that the point of departure for Christological reflection in India should neither be the 'Jesus of history' nor the 'Christ of faith,' but the 'Jesus of faith.'"[32]

---

31. Samuel Rayan, "Meditation. Worship Him With Bread and Rice," in *VJTR* 50:6 (July, 1986): 312–16.
32. "George M. Soares-Prabhu SJ (1929–1995)," in *Asian Christian Theologies: A Research Guide*

In his concept of "Jesus of faith," Soares-Prabhu combined the Jesus of history with the unique way the Lord becomes a reality to his faithful followers. He was convinced that the liberative message of the Gospels can be the basis for the church's social mission in India.

Two noted Indian Catholic scholars who contribute richly to concerns related to liberation theology in the twenty-first century are Michael Amaladoss (1936–) and Felix Wilfred (1948–). Amaladoss is interested in exploring the acknowledgment of Christ in the various Indian and Asian traditions. His book, *The Asian Jesus*, discusses how the various images of Jesus are perceived by Asian Christians and opens "up new and dynamic questions for theological discourse. Indeed, these images cannot be excluded when entering into Christological and theological reflection in Asia."[33] Amaladoss' focus, however, is on the *liberative* stance in religions such as Buddhism, Hinduism, and Islam. As he put it, the liberation movement led by Mahatma Gandhi and others, especially at the level of social and political reform rooted in the Gospel and rooted in the values of the Hindu and Christian scriptures, points the way toward interreligious dialogue.[34] Felix Wilfred, however, asks the pertinent question—where are the sources for the liberation of India, which is a land of intense poverty as well as spirituality? In his book, *Leave the Temple,* he explores the question whether the challenge of social transformation and freedom involve a situation where the people will have

to *Authors, Movements, Sources*, vol. 1, eds. John C. England, Jose Kuttianimattathil SDB, John M. Prior SVD, Lilly A. Quintos RC, David Suh Kwang-sun, and Janice Wickeri (Maryknoll, NY: Orbis Books, 2002), 278.

33. Adrian Bird, "*The Asian Jesus* (Review)," *Studies in World Christianity* 14:2 (2008): 182–83.

34. See Michael Amaladoss, *Life in Freedom. Liberation Theologies from Asia* (Maryknoll: Orbis, 1997) and, "Together Towards the Kingdom: An Emerging Asian Theology" by Michael Amaladoss, https://insecttheology.files.wordpress.com/2013/11/worldwide_asia-amaladoss.pdf (Accessed August 31, 2015).

to "leave the temple" in order to embrace the freedom of secularization? Or, can realizing God in the midst of the suffering humanity provide us with a richness and empowerment that the secular models cannot offer?[35]

The impact the Catholic theological thinking had in India, especially during the last one hundred years, is truly unparalleled. At the level of educational institutions of a high academic caliber that benefitted generations of Indians, in terms of indigenization and inculturation that sought to blend the Christian principles with the sociocultural and religious traditions of India, in addressing the causes of inequality and marginalization experienced by the poor masses and finally, as dedicated teams of priests, nuns, and the laity fanned out among the urban and rural poor of the land in order to precipitate prolonged struggles so as to liberate the people from their exploitative conditions and sources of injustice, the Catholics did unparalleled work. At the center of most of their work stood the shift in paradigm initiated by the Second Vatican Council. If today, the Indian Catholics have an impact in India that is disproportionate to their numerical strength, that is largely because of the legacy that has been left behind by the pioneers in these areas.

Orthodox Perspective

While the Indian Orthodox churches have, down the centuries, remained faithful to the apostolic tradition of St. Thomas, it was primarily in the twentieth century, and especially as a part of the fellowship of the WCC, that they began relating their theological insights in relation to the wider Christian world. It is, perhaps, a matter of great pride for the Indian Orthodox

---

35. See Felix Wilfred, *Leave the Temple: Indian Paths to Human Liberation* (Wipf & Stock, 2010).

churches that their first representative on the international ecumenical scene was neither a bishop, nor a priest, nor even a male, but a lay woman named Sarah Chakko.[36] Even before the Orthodox communion became a formal part of WCC, Chakko played an important role in the ecumenical movement. She was particularly concerned about the lack of women's leadership in the life and work of the church and she criticized the church's neglect of women, their needs, and their aspirations. For her, hope lay in women becoming "more fully ourselves. She saw clearly that this meant giving up a certain kind of power and recognition."[37] She believed that the reward for service should never be expressed in gratitude or appreciation by others; the reward is in "what service does to you yourself—the richness, the sympathy, the humanness it brings you."[38]

There is little doubt that it was partially in recognition of the growing importance of the Indian Christian community, including the Orthodox churches, that the WCC decided to hold the third assembly in New Delhi in 1961, the first assembly to be held outside the Western world. It is also important to note that the New Delhi Assembly set in motion a long-term study on the theological questions involved in the full integration of the Orthodox communion in the WCC. Even before the assembly, in response to the demand of the Eastern Orthodox churches, discussions had begun about the need to revise the christocentric affirmation in the theological basis of WCC to a

---

36. Sarah Chakko was an educationalist, the principal (president) of Isabella Thoburn College, Lucknow (India), an ecumenical youth and student movement leader, first chair of the WCC Commission on the Life and World of Women in the Church, and the first woman on the WCC Presidium (1951–54). In 1954, as she sat down to rest during a basketball game with some students, she died of a heart attack, at the age of 49 years.

37. Susannah Harris-Wilson, "Sarah Chakko 1905–1954," in *Ecumenical Pilgrims: Profiles of Pioneers in Christian Reconciliation*, eds. Ioan Bria and Dagmar Heller (Geneva: WCC Publications, 1995), 58.

38. Ibid.

more Trinitarian setting. "Recognizing the central importance given in the Orthodox tradition to the conciliar process in the church of the early centuries, the assembly recommended that a study be undertaken of the councils of the early church and their significance for the ecumenical movement."[39]

In the decades that followed, several leaders of the Orthodox churches of India contributed significantly to the life and witness of the ecumenical movement. Foremost among them was Metropolitan Paulos Mar Gregorios, who was not only one of the first Orthodox theologians to hold key positions in WCC, but because of his deep theological insights, left an indelible mark on the ecumenical movement. His main contribution in the ecumenical movement, and particularly in the meetings of the WCC, was the clarity and depth of the Bible studies he conducted. His interpretation of the Scripture reflected a patristic-liturgical flavor, along with his innate intelligence and grasp of the current social and political realities.[40] He has acknowledged with gratitude that his passion for the study of the Scriptures can be traced back to his study, as a young boy, of the Orthodox spiritual and liturgical resources at his home parish in Kerala.

There were other Indian Orthodox leaders who influenced the life and work of the ecumenical movement in fresh and constructive ways. For Metropolitan Geevarghese Mar Osthathios, the focus was on a paradigm shift in the WCC's commitment to mission.[41] His area of particular concern was

---

39. "Orthodox contribution to the WCC," Public lecture by Rev. Dr. Konrad Raiser at an international symposium on "Orthodox theology and the future of ecumenical dialogue: perspectives and problems," June 3, 2003, at Thessaloniki, Greece, http://www.oikoumene.org/en/resources/documents/wcc-programmes/ ecumenical-movement-in-the-21st-century/member-churches/special-commission-on-participation-of-orthodox-churches/orthodox-contribution-to-the-wcc (Accessed August 31, 2015).

40. See Paulos Mar Gregorios, *Love's Freedom—The Grand Mystery: A Spiritual Autobiography* (Kottayam: MGF, 1997).

the WCC Commission on World Mission and Evangelism (CWME), where he attempted to impart an Orthodox perspective.[42] V. C. Samuel, an Indian Orthodox priest, focused his attention on the Faith and Order Commission. As Lukas Vischer, the former director of the Faith and Order Commission, put it, Samuel combined in himself high scholarship, deep humility, and quiet spiritual strength.[43] C. I. Itty, K. M. George, M. Kurien, and scores of other Orthodox clergy and lay women and men have, over the years and decades, contributed richly to building up the ecumenical movement, at the national, Asian, and global levels.

Before the WCC Uppsala Assembly, the Indian bishop John Sadiq predicted that the Orthodox churches, and the newly independent churches from Africa will, for the first time, be able to play a significant role in the global church. He added: "One could prolong this list considerably. God does not stand still, even though we are tempted to do so. We are convinced that the Holy Spirit has guided this movement towards unity."[44] There is little doubt that this prediction turned out to be true as the presence of the Indian Orthodox churches as an active participant at the global level has been essential in shaping the understanding of our common calling for unity and witness. This was not an easy road and there have been a

41. Metropolitan Geevarghese Mar Osthathios was one of the clearest voices of the Indian Church on social justice. He grounded his passion for justice, equality, sharing, and love on the Christian doctrine of the Holy Trinity. He was a member of the Faith and Order Commission and a faculty member of the Orthodox Seminary in Kottayam, Kerala.

42. See Osthathios's writings: *Sharing God and a Sharing World* (Delhi: ISPCK, 1995); *Theology of a Classless Society* (Maryknoll: Orbis, 1984); *The Sin of Being Rich in a Poor Society* (Madras: CLS, 1983).

43. M. K. Kuriakose, ed., *Orthodox Identity in India: Essays in Honour of V. C. Samuel* (Bangalore: V. C. Samuel 75th Birthday Celebration Committee, 1988), 26.

44. "Episcopal Press and News 1962–2006," The Archives of the Episcopal Church, http://www.episcopalarchives.org/cgi-bin/ENS/ENSpress_release.pl?pr_number=61-8 (Accessed September 1, 2015).

number of stumbling blocks on the way. According to Russell Chandran, despite all the hesitation and questions for both the Orthodox churches and the rest of the Christian world, the former "have shown sufficient evidence of willingness to understand and interpret themselves as a Church in via needing the fellowship of other Churches."[45]

A line must be added here on women's participation in the life and witness of the Indian Orthodox churches. Despite pioneers such as Sarah Chakko, it should be noted that the Indian Orthodox churches have, in general, been reluctant to embrace the full potential of women in the church. While the question of women's participation in all realms of the church may be a settled matter in most Protestant churches, this continues to be debated vigorously in the Orthodox churches. The Catholic and Orthodox churches at the global level do not ordain women as priests, but they often follow a less rigid approach with regard to the presence of women at several leadership positions in the church. Several Orthodox churches around the world had even the practice of female deacons though, for a number of reasons, it fell into disuse. Such a practice has, however, not been abolished by canon or a council nor has it completely disappeared. The Inter-Orthodox Theological Consultation that met in Rhodes, Greece, in 1988 noted that deaconess were ordained within the sanctuary during the Divine Liturgy with two prayers: she received the orarion (the deacon's stole) and received Holy Communion at the altar. The consultation affirmed the need to revive the practice of women deacons.[46] It is heartening to note that the Indian Orthodox churches too have initiated several steps in

---

45. Kuriakose, *Orthodox Identity in India*, 83.
46. "Orthodox Deacons: Frequently Asked Questions," http://orthodoxdeacons.org/node/15 (Accessed September 1, 2015).

recent years to bring women to the forefront of the leadership in the church. This is a process that needs to be continued.

Pentecostal, Neo-Pentecostal, and Independent Movements

While the birth of Pentecostalism in the West is often traced back to certain historic incidents—such as the ones in Topeka, Kansas, in 1901 and Azusa street, Los Angeles, in 1906—the Pentecostal movement originated in India within the context of the traditional churches, and often as movements rather than as separate denominational entities. Any discussion of Pentecostalism in India, therefore, will have to consider the evangelistic revival movements in the country which were often of an indigenous nature. Several of the early indigenous evangelical leaders of India whose heritage several mainline Protestant churches claim—such as Sadhu Sundar Singh, Pandita Ramabai, Sadhu Kochukunju Upadesi, and others—demonstrated certain characteristics that can be described as Pentecostal even as the major part of their work was prior to the establishment of the official Pentecostal churches in the country. The difficulty to draw a sharp distinction between Pentecostal and non-Pentecostalism in the Indian context is not only a characteristic of the last century, but, as we will note further down in this section, has assumed newer forms, especially with the waves of neo-Pentecostalism and the charismatic movement that is sweeping many mainline Protestant and Catholic churches in the twenty-first century.

A concern for indigenization was a key characteristic of the early Indian Pentecostal leaders. John Arulappan (1810–1867), who lived in Tamil Nadu and was a pioneer whose work led to the emergence of the Pentecostal movement in south India and beyond, "stands tall in Christian history both for his leadership in the development of the indigenous church as well as for the Christian revival that swept south India during the latter half of the nineteenth century."[47] While the mainline Protestant churches were often Western in their format, liturgy, and financial resources, during the nineteenth century, there developed among Indian Christians a concern for self-reliance and independence. According to Sudharakar Reddy, "There was a leaning among early converts in South India (from 1820s to 1910s) to seek Indian ways of expressing their Christian devotion because they realized that the Western forms of worship were inappropriate to the Indian cultural norms and practices."[48] K. E. Abraham (1899–1974), the pioneer of the Indian Pentecostal Church, whose work had a direct impact on the growth of Indian Pentecostalism, was convinced that the evangelistic work in India must be done primarily by indigenous Christians, not overseas missionaries. While Western Pentecostal missionaries were active in India during that period, Abraham dissociated himself with the foreigners and started the South India Pentecostal Church of God, becoming a well-known preacher and evangelist. Because of his work, many joined the Pentecostal Church.[49]

Pentecostalism, by its very nature, defies any classical theological definition. Yet, as a Christian movement that is increasingly gaining momentum in India, it is difficult not to

---

47. Paul Joshua Bhakiaraj, "Aroolappan (Arulappan), John Christian," in *Oxford Encyclopedia of South Asian Christianity*, vol. 1, ed. Roger Hedlund et al. (New Delhi: OUP, 2012), 37–38.
48. Y. A. Sudharakar Reddy, "Nurturing Globalized Faith Seekers: Mega Churches in Andhra Pradesh, India," in *A Moving Faith: Mega Churches Go South*, ed. Jonathan D. James (New Delhi: Sage Publications, 2015), 146.
49. See H. E. Varghese, *Abraham K. E.: An Apostle of Modern India* (Kadambanad: Christian Literature Service of India, 1974) and, Stanley Burgess, "Pentecostalism in India: an overview," *Asian Journal of Pentecostal Studies* 4:1 (2001): 85–98.

consider the theological characteristics of Pentecostalism. This discussion does not seek to enter into a semantic discourse on the theology of Pentecostalism; rather, the attempt here is to have a general discussion on some of the broad aspects of the movement in the Indian context. While Indian Pentecostalism exhibits several characteristics of the evangelical movement, V. V. Thomas argues that because of the "divine factor," the Pentecostals are often known as "Evangelicals with a plus."[50] The Pentecostals are in agreement with the major ingredients of the theological basis of the evangelicals, but "they go one step further and give a lot of emphasis to the role of the Holy Spirit in the lives of every Christian."[51]

The *Dalit* component is an important factor of Indian Pentecostalism. While the Dalits constitute the majority in most Indian churches, a sizable section of their vanguard emerged from the supposedly upper-caste sections. The emergence of Pentecostalism in India in the beginning of the twentieth century, with its simple message of universal salvation devoid of any elaborate liturgical or hierarchical framework, appealed greatly to the lower sections of the society—in particular, the Dalits. Michael Bergunder noted thus about the situation in Kerala: "(i)n the beginning of the 1920s the majority of Pentecostals in Kerala were mostly from a 'low caste' or 'untouchable' background, people who would call themselves Dalits today."[52] Elsewhere in India too, it was largely the Dalits who flocked to Pentecostalism in the twentieth century. It must, however, be noted that in recent years, there has been a radical shift in the social appeal of

50. V. V. Thomas, *Dalit and Tribal Christians of India: Issues and Challenges* (Nilumbur Post, Malapuram: Focus India Trust, 2014), 308.
51. Ibid., 309.
52. Michael Bergunder, *The South Indian Pentecostal Movement in the Twentieth Century* (Grand Rapids, Michigan/Cambridge, UK: Eerdmans Publishing Company, 2008), 29.

Indian Pentecostalism. According to V. V. Thomas, unlike the last century when Pentecostalism was embraced primarily by the Dalits and the other lower sections of the society, "it is now making inroads among the middle class notwithstanding the fact that its base is still among the poor, the down trodden, the lower middle caste people."[53] Thomas goes on to analyze the theological basis of such a shift and for the lingering appeal of Pentecostalism to the lowly of the land:

> In such situations the down trodden people develop their moral and spiritual life potential to survive, resist, and build new alternatives like forming their own spirituality which answers their life questions and empower them to be dignified human beings. The Pentecostal movement of our time should be seen against this kind of background of people's quest for empowerment.[54]

Probably because there was a strong Dalit component in both the leadership and the followers of Indian Pentecostalism, the movement could pose an effective challenge to the upper-caste hegemony of the other Indian churches and the wider social structures, especially in the early days of Indian Pentecostalism. P. L. Paramjyoti, who hailed from Andhra Pradesh, but was, for twelve years, the president of the Indian Pentecostal Church of God, which is based in Kerala and has a strong concentration of Malayalees, employed passages from the Acts of the Apostles to prove that, "Churches birthed by Holy Spirit do not have any caste, color or language barriers. The Church started on the day of Pentecost was united."[55] He further maintained that he could prove with his own life-story

---

53. Thomas, *Dalit and Tribal Christians*, 307.
54. Ibid., 306.
55. Rachel Jyoti Komanapalli, *A Man Sent from God: Life Story and Messages of Apostle P. L. Paramjyoti* (Bangalore: Manna Ministries, 2012), 152.

that it was possible for a Christian to rise above considerations of caste:

> When I admitted my children into school we needed to write caste name. I wrote, God's caste and I taught my children to answer the same as God's caste when others asked . . . Pentecostal churches of God in India, it is God's will that we don't have caste or color or language barriers and become one family of God, and we live like brothers and sisters of the same family.[56]

It must also, however, be noted that V. V. Thomas and other scholars have argued that in more recent years, the Indian Pentecostals too have been plagued by caste factors.[57] It is never possible to fully overcome caste or race considerations in the church, and the vigilance against any corruption in the core message needs to be an ongoing concern.

Since the 1970s or so, there has been a drastic change in classical Pentecostalism that focused on a church structure and a certain level of hierarchy. Pentecostalism in recent decades has often assumed characteristics that defy conventional analysis. The charismatic movement within the Catholic and other churches exhibited certain characteristics of Pentecostalism, such as an evangelistic revival and personal salvation. The charismatic movement, however, often became mere renewal movements within mainline churches, thus blending the traditional with the Pentecostal. In India, there were other manifestations of neo-Pentecostalism as well. House churches, where believers and seekers gathered together for worship and fellowship, was an important one, especially in South India. Jonathan James' recent study points toward mega churches, usually understood as big independent

56. Ibid., 153.
57. See V. V. Thomas, *Dalit Pentecostalism: Spirituality of the Empowered Poor* (Bangalore: Asian Trading Company, 2008).

congregations in Europe and America—now becoming a phenomenon in the Southern hemisphere as well.[58]

The phenomenal rise of Pentecostalism in India was often seen as a response to a certain "crisis" in the spirituality of the traditional mainline churches. This crisis has variously been described as emerging from a stagnation in pastoral care, over-ritualism in worship service, and the inability to offer spiritual and emotional support to the young and the old. The Pentecostal churches of the twentieth century were viewed as holding a viable and holistic alternative to the ritualism and traditional patterns of the mainline churches. We have, however, seen that the classical Pentecostal churches too have become, to a certain extent, institutionalized—in the process, demonstrating certain characteristics of the "crisis" that had earlier gripped the traditional churches. The wide range of charismatic, neo-Pentecostal, non-denominational, and mega churches becoming popular today emerged as alternatives to both the traditional Protestant/Catholic churches as well as the classical Pentecostal churches. The whole situation, however, throws up significant theological and sociological questions. The spiritual alternatives that people seek range from the "supplementary role" played by the charismatic movement in relation to the churches to the "alternative spiritual communities" represented by the house churches. At a dialogue between theologians from the Pentecostal and traditional churches held in the 1990s, K. C. Abraham noted that what is needed by both the mainline and the Pentecostal churches is a "prophetic spirituality" that stands in opposition to the dominant, elite spirituality.

---

58. Jonathan D. James, ed., *A Moving Faith: Mega Churches Go South* (New Delhi: Sage Publications, 2015).

I recommend prophetic spirituality as a paradigm for the spirituality of the community. The ultimate value of this spirituality is freedom realized in people's concrete struggles against forces of bondage against . . . their own rulers (elite domination), against golden calves (false security, consumerism etc.).[59]

Marginalized People Theologize

Liberative ecclesiology and hermeneutics have been the themes for Indian Christians who have been involved in theologizing from the perspective of the marginalized people. While a large section of the Indian Christians are Dalits (the outcastes or the untouchables in the Hindu tradition) and the tribals or the Adivasis (indigenous people), the tradition, history, and liturgy of the church have generally been alien to them and the leadership of the churches have often come from upper class-caste sections. The waves of change that swept India from the middle of the twentieth century—including the country's freedom from colonialism and the departure of the Western Christian missionaries, the social reform movements in different parts of the country, and the impact of global developments such as the ecumenical movement, the Second Vatican Council, and liberation theology—however, all had their impact on the Indian church too. In general, the Dalit and tribal Christians felt that Indian Christian theology had, by and large, been serving the interests of the elite sections of the society—in the process, sidelining the faith of the ordinary people; consequently, they set about the task of initiating a counter-theology movement. They affirm that the marginalized people should be the foci for theologizing and

---

59. K. C. Abraham, "The Crisis of Pastoral Ministry and the Search For Holistic Spirituality," in *The Community We Seek: Perspectives on Mission*, ed. Jesudas M. Athyal (Tiruvalla: CSS, 2003), 112.

that the Indian Church should journey with the oppressed Dalits and Adivasis. They understand the missionary objective of the churches as the recognition and affirmation of this prophetic task in our times.

Since the caste system is a self-contained and immutable social order ordained by religious traditions, Dalit theologians have found in the scriptures the resources to analyze and counter the forces of oppression. According to V. Devasahayam, we "need to make it known that in the Indian context, caste system is Satan and the original sin that stands in contradiction to the kingdom Jesus proclaimed and the cross needs to be reinterpreted as the revelation of counter-consciousness to the oppressive caste consciousness."[60] They are convinced of the need to enable Dalit sensibility to enter into dialogue with the biblical word/text, making the Scripture more meaningful to their lives.

For the marginalized people, the Christian mission is not just what has been traditionally called evangelism or the proclamation of the Gospel to the unbeliever. As James Cone, the prominent American theologian, noted: "Neither is mission simply dialogue with people of other faiths in the hope of bringing them to Jesus. Mission is making solidarity with poor people in their fight for justice. To proclaim Jesus Christ without bearing witness to the justice he brings is to distort the emancipatory power of the gospel."[61] Christian commitment is to discern ever anew the liberative and "multicolored" wisdom of God in all her rich diversity through imaginative dialogue

---

60. V. Devasahayam, *Doing Dalit Theology in Biblical Key* (Chennai: ISPCK/Gurukul, 1997), 55. See also V. Devasahayam, *Outside the Camp: Biblical Studies in Dalit Perspective* (Madras: Chennai, 1994).
61. Foreword to the book, *Liberative Solidarity: Contemporary Perspectives on Mission* by K. C. Abraham (Tiruvalla: CSS, 1996).

with diverse cultural expressions of Christian and other religious traditions.

During the last few decades, programs that focus on Dalit concerns have been a regular component in ecumenical institutions, but it is debatable if these had any significant impact on the work of the churches. Deenabandhu Manchala reflects thus on both the parallels and the challenges for Dalit theology as it is in dialogue with the theological reflections of the ecumenical movement:

> To some extent, one can say that ecumenical theology too, like Dalit theology, has been a counter-theological discourse, an alternative to the dominant ways of theological reflection that is often grounded in western denominational/confessional ecclesial settings. Likewise, it is also faced with the need to make itself relevant to the changed realities of the twenty-first century as it is cast in and remains in the methodological mould of the twentieth century western ecclesial reality.[62]

The twenty-first century has witnessed new perspectives on theologizing from the perspective of the marginalized people. The new generation of Dalit scholars believe that treating Dalits, tribals, or women as a collective/essentialist/unitary category and creating solidarity programs while keeping the paternalist consciousness is untenable. According to Y. T. Vinayaraj, in "the changed theoretical-theological-epistemological context, 'solidarity' means a re-imagination of ourselves; not merely a sense of 'standing along with' or 'speaking for' or 'representing somebody.'"[63] Rather, it should

---

62. Deenabandhu Manchala, "Expanding the Ambit: Dalit Theological Contribution to Ecumenical Social Thought," in Sathianathan Clarke, Deenabandhu Manchala & Philip Vinod Peacock, eds., *Dalit Theology in the Twenty-first Century: Discordant Voices, Discerning Pathways* (New Delhi: OUP, 2011), 41.
63. Quoted by Mani Chacko in "Decoding Edinburgh-1910: Subaltern Perspective," in *Decoding Mission Beyond Edinburgh: Revisiting Mission and Ecumenism Today*, ed. M. C. Thomas (Tiruvalla: Commission on Ecumenical Relations of the Mar Thoma Syrian Church, 2011), 90.

be a new journey that looks at our own faith, tradition, theology, and ontology. In short, the impact of Dalit theology during the last few decades in re-formulating Christian theology in India has been significant, and there has been a growing sensitivity elsewhere too on understanding theology from the people's perspective.

Earlier in this chapter, we discussed "permeation" as a pattern of mission in India, especially during the early centuries, when Christianity was understood as a lived experience and diffused presence in relation to the wider society rather than as a proselytizing one. There is no doubt that permeation was, and will continue to be, a pattern that has a certain place in the history and praxis of Christian mission in India. However, we will also need to take seriously the criticisms to this approach, especially from a Dalit perspective. Over a century before B. R. Ambedkar employed religious conversion as an effective weapon for the liberation of the oppressed and the marginalized people, the Dalits and the Adivasis, by converting to Christianity, had found "a place under the sun." The Christian mass movements led to a large number of Dalits joining the Christian church, and thus escaping, to a certain extent, the dehumanizing elements of the Brahminical tradition and culture.[64] However, while the "mainline" Christian tradition of India accepted at the theological level the invitation of the gospel that was open for all, the rigid caste structures continued to have their sway, even within the church. This is the context in which the Dalit theologians differed with the position of the ecumenical and

---

64. For a discussion of the Christian mass movements in India, see J. Waskom Pickett, *Christian Mass Movements in India: A Study with Recommendations* (New York: Abingdon Press, 1933) and Susan Billington Harper, *In the Shadow of the Mahatma: Bishop V. S. Azariah and the Travails of Christianity in British India* (Grand Rapids, MI and Cambridge, UK: Eerdmans; London: RoutledgeCurzon, 2000).

interreligious theologians of India, who argued for "permeation" as a viable pattern of Christian witness. V. Devasahayam maintained that the traditional and mainline society in India is, in effect, a casteist society with which Christianity can never associate. As he put it,

> After all, what is a church? To me the church is a place where we celebrate our identities in Christ as the primary identity. If we still want to hold on to our social and cultural identities, I do not know how it will become a church of the Christ where the primary identities need be withdrawn in terms of our relations, in terms of our faith to Jesus Christ. So to me the sin of the church is not that it has isolated itself from the social and cultural community but precisely it has failed to isolate itself to come out of this cultural and social community and it has failed to evolve a new social order.[65]

It is the affirmation of "protest over permeation" as a pattern of Christian witness that distinguishes Dalit theology from the more established Christian theologies of India. The protest of Dalit theology is against both a caste-ridden social structure as well as a theology and ecclesiology that legitimized the situation of the downtrodden people. Protest, in fact, is not confined to the Dalits alone, but is a common characteristic of all subaltern theologies. The tribals and the Adivasis, in their re-reading of the history of mission and colonialism and its impact on the indigenous people too, have developed a theological framework distinct from the dominant theological trend. The tribals, who in large numbers responded to the Christian faith, too stayed in the periphery of the Indian church in the early days, but have recently begun playing a more prominent role. For Nirmal Minz, the primary area of concern was the tribals (indigenous people) who constitute

---

65. J. John and Jesudas Athyal, eds., *Religion, State and Communalism: A Post-Ayodhya Reflection* (Hong Kong: Christian Conference of Asia, 1995), 112.

around 8 percent of the Indian population, and who, in large numbers, responded to the Christian gospel in the nineteenth and twentieth centuries. He argued that "what Christian missions gave the tribals was a shift in the centre of their life from the ageless rhythm of nature to the dynamism of salvation history in Christ."[66] However, "the crisis it brought had both possibilities of cultural disintegration and potentialities of cultural growth and reintegration."[67] Minz further affirmed that the tribal Christian communities need the experience of Pentecost so that they would be bold enough to bear witness to Jesus Christ among Adivasis and Dalits, and even before the dominant society, and fulfill the mission and evangelism in this region.[68]

One of the crucial contributions of Indian Christianity during the postcolonial period was the assertion that Christian unity needs to be a totalizing experience that embraces men and women of all social, ethnic, and racial categories. Inherent in such a recognition is the fact that certain sections of the church and society have historically been marginalized, and therefore the just and equal participation of all would be a prerequisite for unity. It is the recognition that the ecumenical movement is not only a theological entity, but also a sociological one, and therefore unity in Christ will become a reality only when we are able to negotiate not only our ecclesiologies and orders, but also our social identities and distinctions in terms of the identity of Christ.

Where do we go from here? While the Dalit and tribal theologies during the last few decades have provided a virtual

66. M. M. Thomas, *My Ecumenical Journey* (Trivandrum: Ecumenical Publishing Centre, 1990), 226.
67. Ibid.
68. Nirmal Minz, "Mission & Evangelism in Jharkhand Context," in *Mission Today: Subaltern Perspectives*, ed. Jesudas M. Athyal (Tiruvalla: CSS, 2001), 54.

paradigm shift in theologizing in India, today, we can go ahead only by grappling meaningfully with the rapid changes taking place around us and struggling with the need to provide a theological articulation of the challenges they throw to the oppressed communities everywhere—more specifically, to the Dalits. What are the challenges around us in the twenty-first century? The devastating effects of modernization have left crucial questions for the oppressed and marginalized communities the world over. In India, the forces of sectarianism and religious fundamentalism have made serious inroads into the Dalit movement as well. The situation calls for an urgent and radical review of our paradigms of theologizing today.

Hindu Christians and Non-Baptized Believers

While Christianity is generally considered to be identical with the organized church, in India, there is a long history of Christ-centered fellowships outside the formal Christian communities. The missionaries often presented the gospel as a package that included Christ, the organized church, and the Western culture, but this was perceived as alien to the Hindu ethos of the land, which generally shunned any hierarchical religious structures, and instead, provided the space for the people to maintain allegiance to multiple deities and diverse practices. While Christ-centered fellowships outside Christian community was never a mass movement in the country, both theologians and sociologists of religion have taken this phenomenon seriously and it needs to be seen as an essential part of the history of Christian witness in India.

What is unique about the Indian situation that gave rise to several cases of non-baptized believers and Christ-centered fellowships outside the framework of the church? One was, of course, the highly pluralistic context steeped in a rather diffused Hindu ethos, which permeated into all the other religious groups as well. In his study of the ancient Christian community of Kerala, John England noted:

> In the Christian community, Hindu culture in particular was accepted within Christian observance, in the shaping of offerings, pilgrimages and processions, in symbolic acts in weddings or funerals, and as at Cranganore, in many customs followed by groups accorded high social status. The context for Christian Indians was a symbiotic one where they were able to be "Hindu in culture, Christian in religion and Oriental in Worship"![69]

Secondly, baptism, in the Indian context, is much more than a mere sacrament that confirms one's allegiance to Christ as Lord and Savior and membership in the church. In a society such as India, where communal and family ties are central to one's identity, baptism, in effect, amounts to one's self-removal from his/her own society and family. Herbert Hoefer, a Lutheran missionary who had done empirical research on "Churchless Christianity"[70] in India argued: "the average convert in India must find a new family, a new community, a new social and economic life along with the new spiritual life he has adopted. His own people force him to this by completely ostracizing him."[71] Baptism in the Indian context, in short, is far more than a mere religious act; it amounts to a person's rejection of his/her identity, family, and community, and the embrace of a new identity, habits, and history—even a new name, alien to his/her culture.

---

69. John C. England, *The Hidden History of Christianity in Asia: The Churches of the East before 1500* (Delhi & Hong Kong: ISPCK & CCA, 2002), 66.
70. Herbert E. Hoefer, *Churchless Christianity* (California: William Carey Library, 2001).
71. Ibid., 153.

Earlier in this chapter, we discussed "permeation" as the pattern of mission, followed by the St. Thomas Christians of Malabar in the ancient days. During the period of Hindu renaissance in the nineteenth and twentieth centuries too, there was a tradition in India of permeation at the deeply spiritual level of relating faith in Christ to the pluralistic context. M. M. Thomas, while tracing the Christian understanding of the Indian renaissance,[72] says that in the history of the modern neo-Hindu movements, the person of Jesus was a strong component. There were many Hindus who kept themselves in spiritual fellowship with other Christians without joining the church after baptism. Kandasamy Chetty of the Madras Christian College, who was one such, stated:

> There is nothing essentially sinful in Hindu society any more than there is anything essentially pure in the Christian society—for that is what the Christian church amounts to—so that one should hasten from the one to the other. So long as the believer's testimony for Christ is open and as long as his attitude towards the Hindu society in general is critical, and his attitude towards social and religious practices inconsistent with the spirit of Christ is protestant and practically protestant, I would allow him to struggle his way to the light with some failure here and some failure there perhaps, but with progress and success on the whole.[73]

There were several other forms of Christian witness, represented by individuals and local worshipping and witnessing communities, outside the established churches. A. N. Sattampillai, founded the Hindu-Christian Church of Lord Jesus at Prakasapuram near Tirunelveli in 1857 by rejecting Western missionary domination. He not only rejected the Western hegemony, but also interpreted the Christian faith

72. M. M. Thomas, *The Acknowledged Christ of the Indian Renaissance* (Madras: CLS, 1970).
73. Kaj Baago, *Pioneers of Indigenous Christianity* (Madras: CISRS-CLS), 207–14.

and scriptures in Indian context, thus representing a rudimental form of indigenization. Roger Hedlund, in his study,[74] identifies and describes several such indigenous "little traditions" of Indian Christianity, movements largely unstudied and unknown.

There were also others who were personally committed to the Crucified Christ as savior and healer, but refused to go along with the rituals and practices of the organized church. Manilal C. Parekh (1885–1967) accepted baptism, but because he felt that the church was too Westernized, kept only in loose contact with it. "He did not consider Hinduism and Christianity as opposed to each other, but as integrated in Jesus Christ."[75] Parekh tried to form a Hindu Church of Christ, which would be a fellowship of followers of Jesus who remained within Hinduism. Subba Rao (1912–81) was another such seeker who "became widely known as a Hindu follower of Christ who was opposed to religion and religious ritual and particularly to Christianity and Baptism."[76]

The presence of Christ-centered fellowships that transcend the present communal identity of the church is essentially a part of the history of Christianity in India. In a survey done by the Gurukul Lutheran Theological College some years ago, it came to light that a large number of people in Madras—far higher than the official number of Christians in the city—accepted Jesus Christ as their personal savior, but had chosen to continue in their own religious, cultural, and caste

---

74. Roger E. Hedlund, ed., *Christianity is Indian: The Emergence of an Indigenous Community* (Chennai & Delhi: MIIS & ISPCK, 2000).

75. "Manilal C. Parkeh," in *Asian Christian Theologies: A Research Guide to Authors, Movements, Sources*, vol. 1, eds. John C. England, Jose Kuttianimattathil SDB, John M. Prior SVD, Lilly A. Quintos RC, David Suh Kwang-sun, and Janice Wickeri (Maryknoll, NY: Orbis Books, 2002), 226.

76. H. L. Richard, "Subba Rao, K.," in *Oxford Encyclopedia of South Asian Christianity*, vol. 2 (New Delhi: Oxford University Press, 2012), 666.

communities without conversion to the Christian community. Among them, there are those who maintain close spiritual fellowships with other Christians and others who pursue their devotion to Christ without such support.[77]

In more recent times, there is also the increasing popularity of house churches and para churches where formal church members, "seekers," and others have fellowship together and where most of them find their deepest spiritual experience and Christian fellowship. In a missiological study of the non-baptized Christians in India, Sam Thompson affirmed that one of the best ways to bring the ministry of Word and Sacraments to the non-baptized believers could be to take the model of house churches:

> House churches do not carry any institutional structures or official form in public eyes. The outsiders view it as a small prayer gathering or fellowship of a few like-minded people who meet in a particular house or in different houses each week. This safety and security could well provide a non-threatening atmosphere and space for the non-baptized believers to interact with one another, receive further catechizing, support, prayers, encouragement from the mature believers. This place could well become a place where the non-baptized journey themselves to the waters of Baptism and receive God's Word and the Lord's Supper regularly. Reaching people where they are is nothing but emulating the great mission model of our Master, who came to us to save us and who keeps coming to us through His Word and Sacraments to nourish and strengthen our lives.[78]

The central point in a discussion of the non-baptized believers is that theological issues and sociological realities are seldom present in clear-cut terms, especially in intensely

---

77. For details of the survey, see Herbert E. Hoefer, *Churchless Christianity* (California: William Carey Library, 2001).
78. Sam Thompson, "Reaching Out to the Non-Baptized Believers: Missiological Implications from a Lutheran Perspective," *Lutheran Society for Missiology*, http://www.lsfm.global/MA-11-14-A6.html (Accessed August 29, 2015).

pluralistic societies such as those in India. There is the need for intimate contact between institutional churches and the fellowships outside, and between baptized and unbaptized believers. The challenge for us is to be open to discern the mission of God in such contexts.

Indian Presence in the Ecumenical Movement

In terms of key Indian Christian leaders who played significant roles in international ecumenical organizations, path-breaking steps in church unity such as the founding of the Church of South India and the Church of North India, and developments such as Dalit theology and Urban–Rural Mission that triggered off a process that resulted in re-defining the core of ecumenism in our times, it can, perhaps, be argued that India played a most significant role in the modern ecumenical movement. One of the pioneers in this movement was V. S. Azariah, whose address at the Edinburgh Mission Conference in 1910 to an overwhelmingly Western audience—"You have given your bodies to be burned. We ask for love, give us Friends"—is often cited as a turning point in the history of the ecumenical movement.[79] The inauguration of the CSI in 1947 and V. S. Azariah's key role in it was, undoubtedly, a significant ecumenical event of that period. It was "unique in that for the first time in history a church that had maintained the historic succession of the episcopate succeeded in entering into full corporate communion with non-Episcopal churches."[80] Azariah's distinctive contribution might well have been his focus on the necessity of an Indian Christian identity, of

---

79. Brian Stanley, *The World Missionary Conference, Edinburgh 1910* (Cambridge, UK: Eerdmans Publishing Co., 2009), 129.

80. Ninan Koshy, *A History of the Ecumenical Movement in Asia*, vol. 1 (Hong Kong: WSCF AP, YMCA & CCA, 2004), 90.

"church unification as part of a larger program of church indigenization," a Church of India.[81] In that sense, he can be considered as a forerunner of the reality of "world Christianity" as it now is seen, its leadership increasingly from India. Another pioneer in the modern ecumenical movement was M. M. Thomas who, as the first lay person and non-Westerner elected to be the moderator of the Central Committee of the WCC was, undoubtedly, one of the key architects of the modern ecumenical movement. Convinced that the gospel offers the dynamics for Christian engagement in politics, Thomas wrote extensively about the political responsibility of Christians with a clarity and commitment that is rarely matched.

While Indian Christians played key roles in several areas of the ecumenical movement, for our brief discussion here, we will consider only four of them: (1) Interfaith relations, (2) Unity and Justice, (3) Lay Leadership, and (4) Ecumenical theological education.

Interfaith Relations

In a country as multireligious and pluralist as India, it was, perhaps, not surprising that interfaith relations was an area of utmost importance for many Indian Christians. The work of Indians in this area is widely acknowledged as having a decisive impact on the programs and priorities of the ecumenical movement, especially during the last century. As a pioneer in this area, P. D. Devanandan made a significant contribution by arguing that the theology of religious pluralism should be an ecumenical issue of immense

---

81. Susan Billington Harper, *In the Shadow of the Mahatma: Bishop V. S. Azariah and the Travails of Christianity in British India* (Grand Rapids, MI and Cambridge, UK: Eerdmans; London: RoutledgeCurzon, 2000), 240.

importance and consequence. His fundamental concern was to assist the Indian Church understand Jesus, the Christ as the key to and fulfillment of God's work in and for the world of Indian religion, culture, and society, and to restate and communicate that truth.[82] Stanley Samartha, a fellow Indian, was a stalwart at the global level, who contributed a great deal in removing some of the initial hesitations that people of other religions had about Christians wanting suddenly to engage in dialogue with them. He did much to remove the notion among many Hindus and Buddhists that dialogue is yet another tool in Christian zeal for evangelism, and instead, argued that we "cannot limit the extent or the mode of God's redeeming work, because it is as universal as His love which embraces all humankind at all times." We as Christians, therefore, need to recognize God's saving work in "areas outside the hedges of the Church."[83]

Apart from the work of such key individuals, the emergence of ecumenical study centers was a significant step toward interfaith relations in India. Of particular relevance in this context is the Christian Institute for the Study of Religion and Society (CISRS) in Bangalore, the Henry Martyn Institute of Islamic Studies (HMI) in Hyderabad, and the Christian Institute of Sikh Studies in Batala, Punjab. By influencing the course of the global ecumenical movement and by undertaking grassroots-level work at interfaith dialogue in India, Indian Christians in dialogue have left a deep impact in a better understanding of interfaith relations.

---

82. See P. D. Devanandan, *The Gospel and Renascent Hinduism* (London: SCM Press, 1959).
83. S. J. Samartha, "The Quest for Salvation and the Dialogue between Religions," in *International Review of Mission* 57:228 (October 1968): 432.

Unity and Justice

It has often been pointed out that Indian Christian leaders pioneered the connection between unity and justice at the international ecumenical level. There were both people and movements from India that raised relevant questions about whether there can be real unity as long as the church is divided on racial, class, and gender lines. While the church was often content with acts of charity, the situation of poverty, inequality, and injustice in the country prompted the ecumenical leaders to go beyond these into affirming the need to build up a just and sustainable social order and the struggles needed for these. As the Indian church leader Subir Biswas put it,

> Some people in India would be quite happy to see the church just keeping to itself, maintaining the beautiful grounds in the midst of violence and tension. Yet we ourselves who are within this feel we can't do it. We have to expose ourselves, to put our property and our church in jeopardy. It is a way of asking repeatedly, what does the incarnation mean in our lives?[84]

As the independent India embraced industrialization, the situation presented the nation's Christians with the great responsibility of discerning and declaring God's hand in the social change wrought by science and technology. "It has to work with Him in response to the needs of the time, and the need in India to-day is for a definition of new social goals and a new direction; to give people, especially those coming under the shadow of industry, a new set of values and to help them to become fellow workers with God."[85]

---

84. "Voices of Hope: Call to Action and Incarnation," The Anglican Church of Canada. See also, *Lord, Let Me Share: Life and Writings of Canon Subir Biswas*. Compiled by, E. C. John (Tiruvalla: Jointly published by the Ecumenical Christian Academy, National Council of Churches in India and Christava Sahitya Samithy, 2012).

The Indian Christian participation in the ecumenical movement contributed richly to theological reflections on a "spirituality for combat"[86] with participation, transcendence, and transformation as the three determinants of spirituality.[87] The political Emergency declared on June 25, 1975, when Indira Gandhi was the prime minister provided the Indian Church with an immediate situation where the civil liberties and democratic rights of ordinary citizens stood suspended. Many ecumenical leaders found in the situation an occasion to affirm "what it means to be the Church in face of the fundamental ethical challenges of our time or, to put it differently, how church fellowship can be maintained in face of ethical conflicts."[88]

The challenges before the ecumenical movement with regard to unity and justice has continued well into the twenty-first century. As the forces of fundamentalism and religious nationalism have renewed their presence in India, thus threatening the secular fabric of the nation, as large-scale developmental projects pose a grave threat to the environment, as the solidarity of the movements led by the urban and rural poor, women, Dalits, and the other indigenous people gain momentum, the ecumenical movement will constantly be challenged to be partners in the process of building a just and sustainable social order.

85. M. A. Z. Rolston, "A New Frontier For the Church in India," *International Review of Missions* 54:214 (April 1965): 184. Also see M. A. Z. Rolston, *Christian Concern in Urban Industrial Situation* (Christian Industrial Service) and *Violence and Peace* (Nagpur: ISPCK, 1987).
86. See M. M. Thomas, "A Spirituality for Combat," in *The Princeton Seminary Bulletin* (Princeton, NJ: Princeton Theological Seminary, 1984), 144.
87. Hielke T. Wolters, *Theology of Prophetic Participation: M. M. Thomas' Concept of Salvation and the Collective Struggle for Fuller Humanity in India* (Delhi: ISPCK/UTC, 1996), 129.
88. Konrad Raiser, "Ecumenical Discussion of Ecclesiology and Ethics," in *The Ecumenical Review* 48:1 (January 1996): 7.

Lay Leadership

Virtually every ecumenical institution in India in the early twentieth century—the National Christian Council (later the National Council of Churches), the National Missionary Society, the Student Christian Movement (SCM), YMCA, YWCA, and many of the missionary organizations that ignited the Christian Mass Movements in India—were lay initiatives. Throughout the century, as India had an active presence in the ecumenical movement, it was widely appreciated that a strong laity perspective was an integral component of unity and Christian witness, especially in a pluralistic context such as Asia. The primary mission of the laity was understood as "being Christian in the world." In the words of Rajah D. Paul, "The effective evangelistic method for the future in this part of the world is the promulgation of the Gospel by consecrated Christian laymen in their secular occupation."[89]

According to C. I. Itty, who had worked for several years in both SCM and the WCC Laity Department, the mission of the ecumenical movement should involve a

> new conversion to the world, a new engagement with social problems and their demand for social change; A conversion to mission; to present the gospel message to those who are not Christians; A new rhythm of life, worship and work, contemplation and action, distance and commitment, social service and social action, suffering and rejoicing, doubt and hope, repentance and pardon; New understanding of the cosmic vision of redemption, the worldwide nature of Christianity, the sacramental character of the church, and the sacramental vision of life and work.[90]

Unlike for the professional leaders of the church, for the

---

89. Cecil Hargraves, *Asian Christian Thinking* (Delhi: ISPCK, 1979), 138.
90. Patricia Lloyd-Sidle, *Celebrating Our Call: Ordination Stories of Presbyterian Women* (Louisville, Kentucky: Geneva Press, 2006), 117.

Christian laity, "protest" is an inherent part of the "new engagement with social problems." As injustice, violence, and caste polarization sharpened in the second half of the twentieth century, and as the forces of liberalization and globalization threatened the social and economic fabric of the society, the Christian youth and SCM activists went out and lived with the poor and the oppressed and participated in the struggles of the subaltern, anti-dam, and ecological movements. They focused their attention on understanding the ethics of the subaltern life—their politics, theology, and knowledge mediated through social movements.

Ecumenical Theological Education

India's role in promoting ecumenical theological education is particularly noteworthy. The role of the United Theological College, Bangalore, Tamilnadu Theological Seminary, Madurai, the Union Biblical Seminary, Pune and other such institutions have been pioneers in providing an ecumenical basis for theological education. While the indigenization and localization of theological education was an ecumenical response to the spirit of independence and nationalism in the non-Western world, it can be argued that Christian ministry in our churches has not effectively addressed the existential challenges and rapidly evolving context of the people. There is the need for ecumenical theological education to evolve patterns of Christian ministry that are flexible enough to provide a faith-response to the changes in the world around.

Conclusion

This chapter discussed some major Christian theological trends in India. However, many people and trends remain unmentioned. As the twentieth century spilled over into the twenty-first, even several names and issues discussed in this volume have gained fresher perspectives and moved on into new challenges. In the ultimate analysis, Christian theology is an ongoing movement, the complete story of which will forever remain incomplete. Yet, every milestone counts. And the people and issues discussed here contributed richly, in diverse ways. Often, the discussion overlapped with other issues, but all complement toward creating a theological base for Indian Christianity.

Index